IMAGES
of America

ONTARIO COUNTY TRANSPORTATION

IMAGES
of America

ONTARIO COUNTY TRANSPORTATION

Timothy D. Munn and Zachary M. Buttaccio

ARCADIA
PUBLISHING

ISBN 978-0-7385-0918-1

Published by Arcadia Publishing
Charleston, South Carolina

Printed in the United States of America

Library of Congress Catalog Card Number: 2001091061

For all general information contact Arcadia Publishing at:
Telephone 843-853-2070
Fax 843-853-0044
E-mail sales@arcadiapublishing.com
For customer service and orders:
Toll-Free 1-888-313-2665

Visit us on the Internet at www.arcadiapublishing.com

Contents

ACKNOWLEDGMENTS

As another journey in historical research has come to its completion, we wish to thank those who contributed to the compilation of this book: Ed Varno, Wilma Townsend, Sheila German, Mike Blonairz, Chuck Callari, Bruce Stewart, Dr. Preston Pierce, and Bonnie Yonker of the Ontario County Historical Society; Charles Bauder, John Marks, and Barbara Lamb of the Geneva Historical Society; Don Tiffany, Bob Spink, and Doris Spink of the Phelps Historical Society; Ann Walker and Stuart Gwilt of the Shortsville Historical Society; Mary Angeline, Florence Angeline, Pauline Angeline, Dorothy Liberati, Rita Gurewitch, Phil D'Arduini, Margaret Vienna, and Ike Moses of the Manchester Historical Society; Babette Huber of the Victor Historical Society; Roger and Emma Halderman of the Lehigh Valley Railroad Historical Society; Bill Vierhile; Jim Duffy; George Grube; Charles Goodberlet; Kerry Adams; Paul Millhausen; Don Green; Richard Combs; Fred Gifford; Rand Darrow; Esther Williams; Budd Farnsworth; Randy Farnsworth; Steve Mumby; Norma Purdy; Larry Bowerman; Bill Shannon; Mr. and Mrs. John S. Blazey; Harlan and Linda Munn; Stuart and Molly Rainey; and Richard Hamilton of the National Museum of Racing in Saratoga Springs. We would like to extend our thanks and appreciation to the Buttaccio family and Nancy and Daniel Munn for their patience and support.

INTRODUCTION

Ontario County Transportation encompasses two centuries of vestigial means of travel from such communities as Canandaigua, Geneva, Phelps, Naples, Victor, Clifton Springs, Manchester, and Shortsville. Beginning with the primitive horse and buggy and ending with the state-of-the-art automobile, this volume explores the history of transportation in a realistic and fascinating way. Also featured in this diverse volume are never-before-seen pictures of locomotives and railroads, early aviation and the Flying Farmers, delivery vehicles, water vessels, fire trucks, and more.

During the 1900s, Ontario County was regarded as a favorable area to make an influence upon others. For this very reason, it has had visitors such as Franklin D. Roosevelt, who is shown addressing the town of Phelps, and Andrew Johnson, who is seen in the city of Geneva. Also among the eminent men from the region are Canandaigua native and automobile pioneer John North Willys; Geneva native and Secretary of the Treasury Charles J. Folger; and Phelps innovator Charles Lane, whose chief achievement was building one of the first fire trucks in Ontario County.

To maximize the enjoyment for both the families of those pictured and for all readers, names have been given whenever possible. The Ontario County Historical Society feels this facet, along with the ones already mentioned, will provide the necessary components for a nostalgic and pleasurable experience that will be felt each time the book is opened.

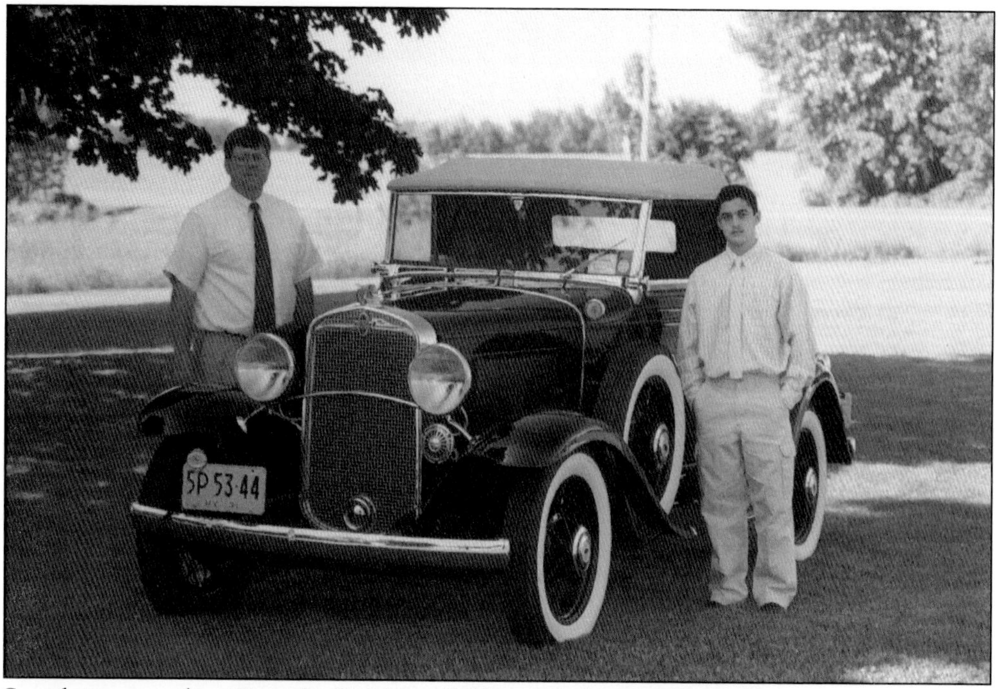

Seen here are authors Timothy D. Munn (left) and Zachary M. Buttaccio.

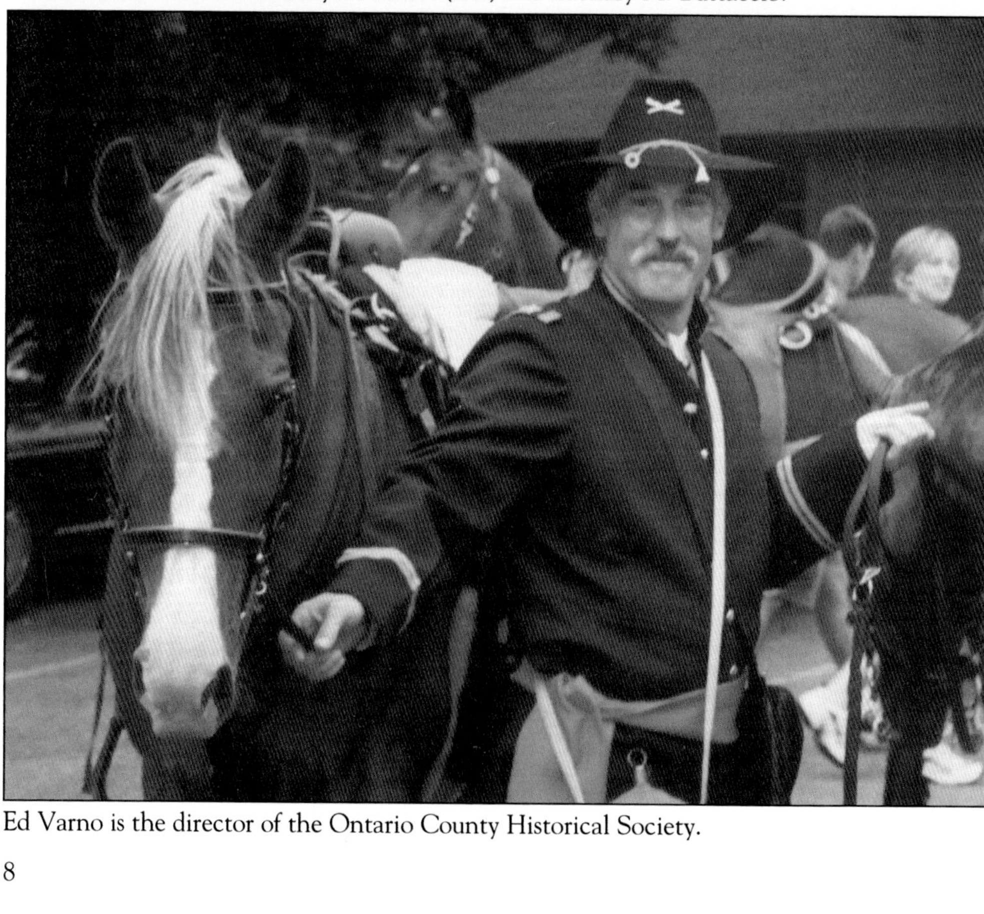
Ed Varno is the director of the Ontario County Historical Society.

One

Horse and Buggy

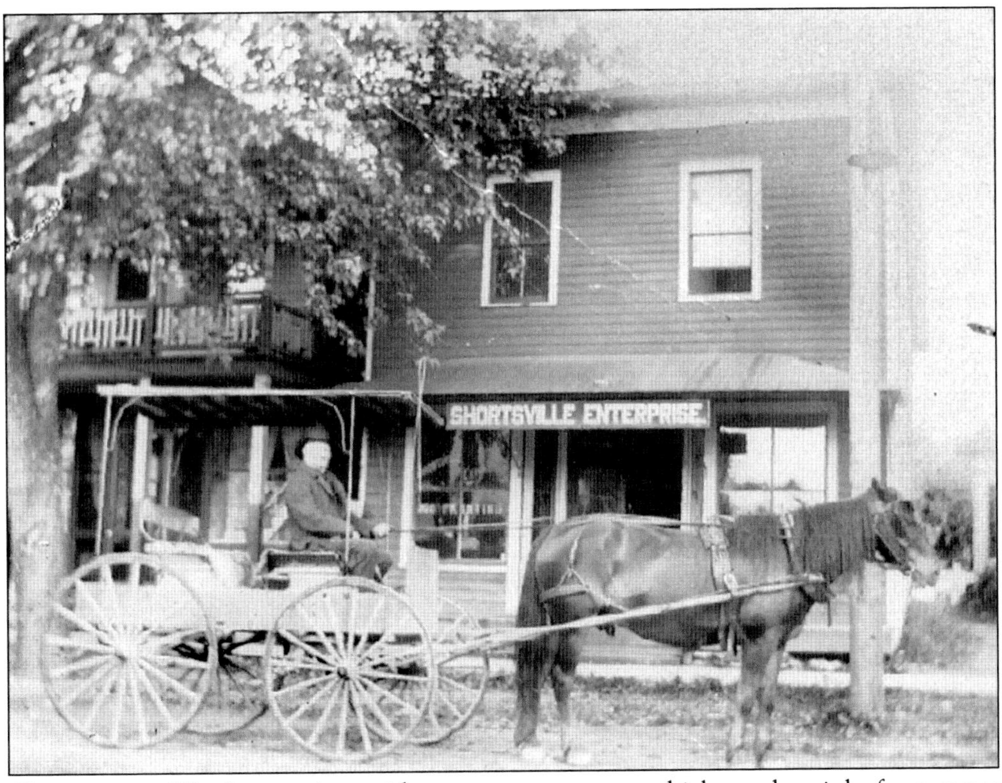

This two-seat Windsor carriage with canopy top was a vehicle used mainly for summer transportation. Beside the carriage is the Shortsville Enterprise. Managed by Earl F. Perry of Shortsville, a 3¢ issue was published every Thursday. The Shortsville Enterprise was established in 1882.

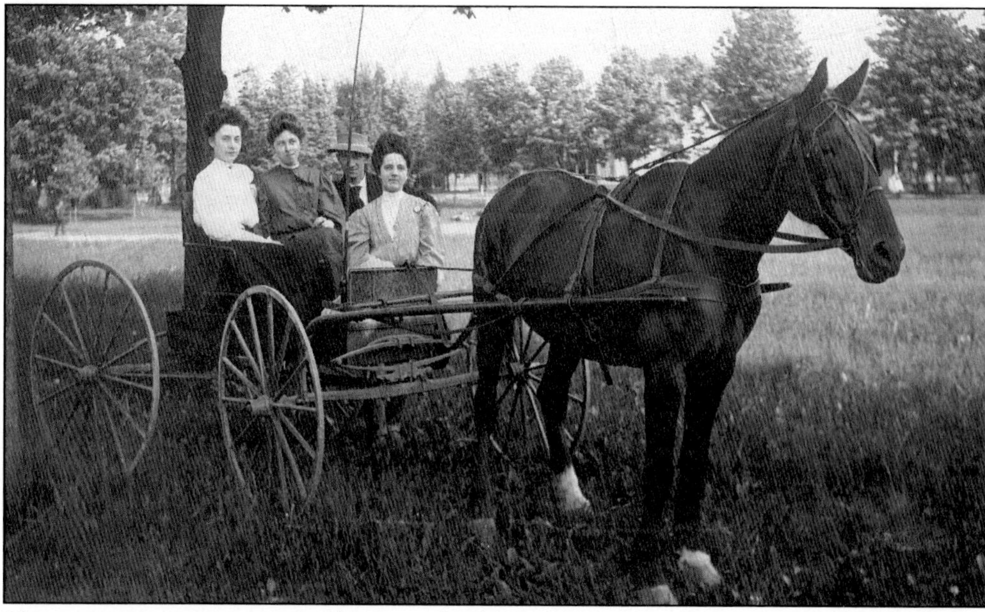

This open-air surrey—a carriage known to be driven by unwed people—is occupied by Leidinger Clark, the great-grandfather of noted artist Rand Darrow, as well as female residents of Lyons. The photograph was taken in 1909 at Redfield Park in Phelps.

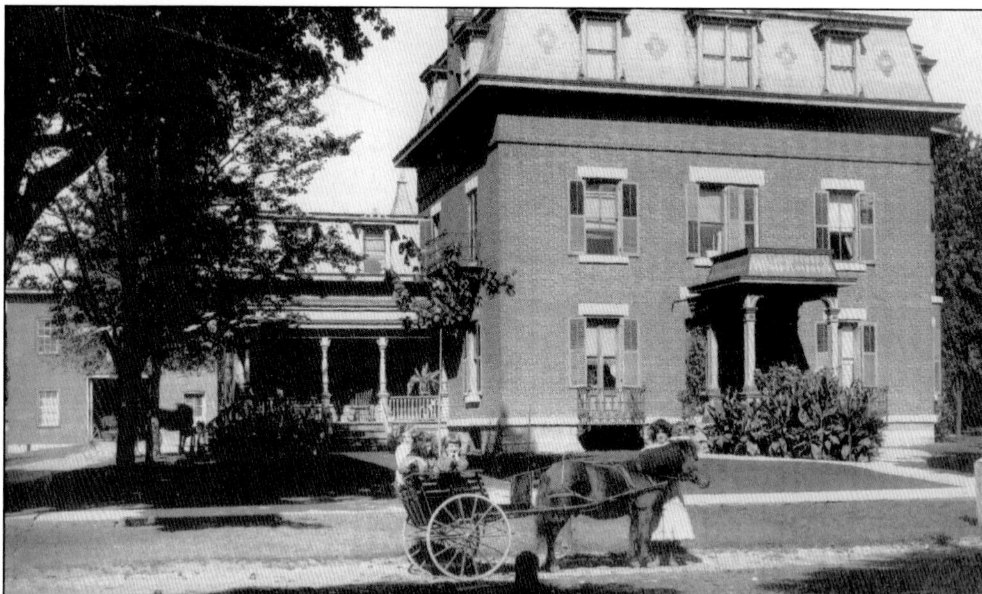

The Howe house, which was built in 1869 by Moses Barlow for Dr. John Q. Howe, stands in this 1906 photograph as a big contrast to the small carriage before it. Inside the governor carriage (a two-wheeled pony cart with a capacity to hold two adults and one dog) are the Howe children: Elizabeth, Francis, John Jr., and Margaret. Today, the Howe house is the location of the Phelps Historical Society and Museum, whose auspicious faculty includes Donald Tiffany, historian; Robert Spink, president; James Caves; Marian Donnelly; Lisa Murphy; Margaret Facer; Floyd Ridley; Gerald Gibbs; F. Lee Walters; Kenneth Overslaugh; and Doris Spink, curator and director.

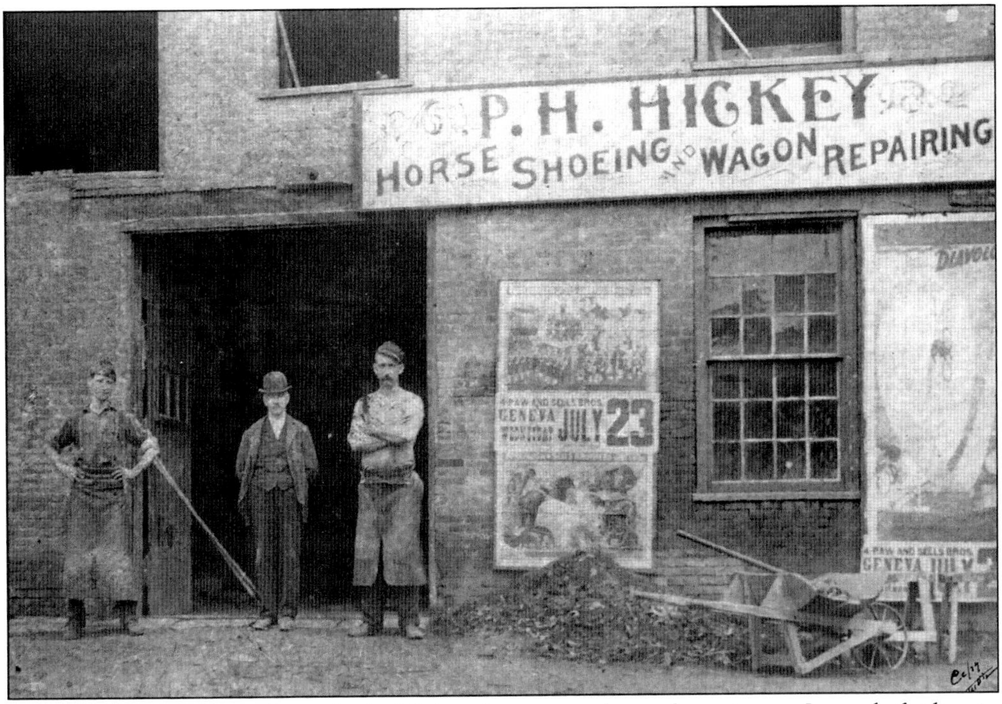

These Geneva men stand outside the Hickey doorway and pose for a picture. Instead of riding in the enjoyable horse-drawn carriages, these men were hard at work ensuring that others would.

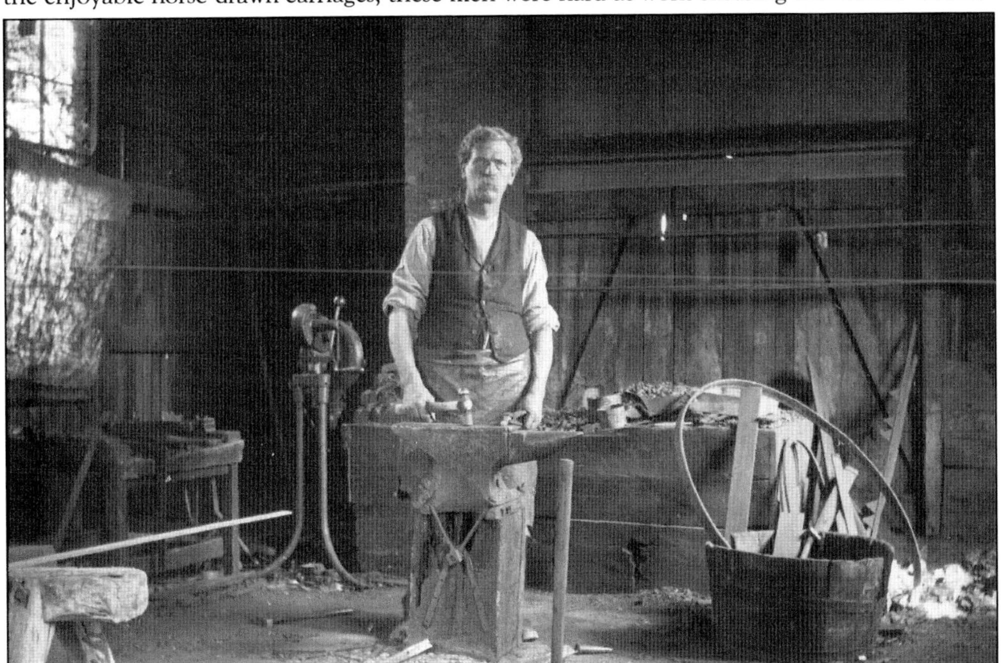

Blacksmith Henry H. Burgess's countenance conveys the pain and labor that was invested in everyday tasks. The Wagon & Carriage Shop, for which Burgess and his brother worked, was founded by their father in 1845. The brothers retained the shop until they retired in 1918. This picture was taken in 1909 in Flint.

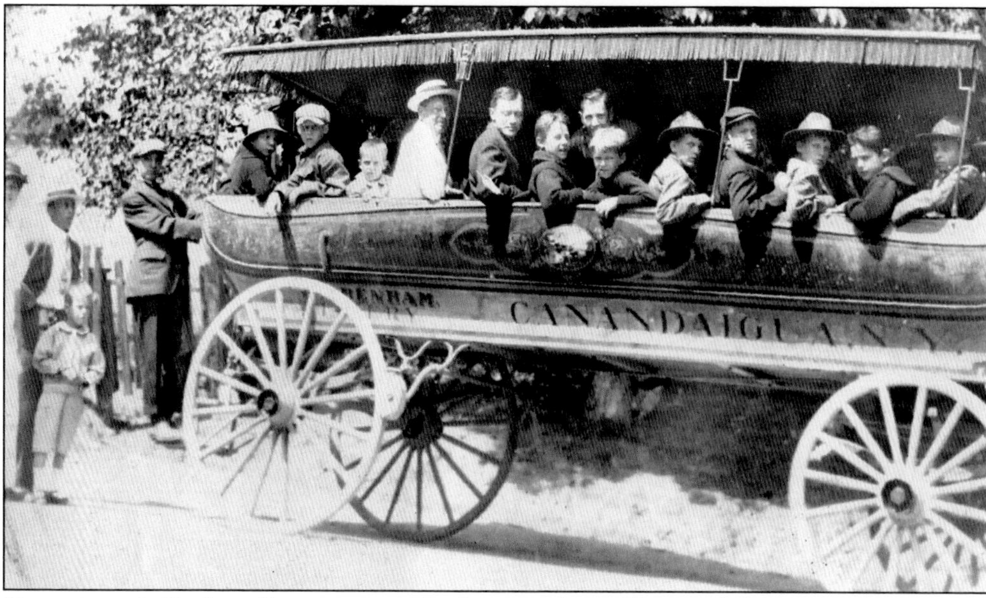

Canandaigua's Benham Livery, owned by Benham himself, provided horse-drawn buses for local residents. This bus had a capacity of 30 people. It is shown here transporting boy scouts from the lake.

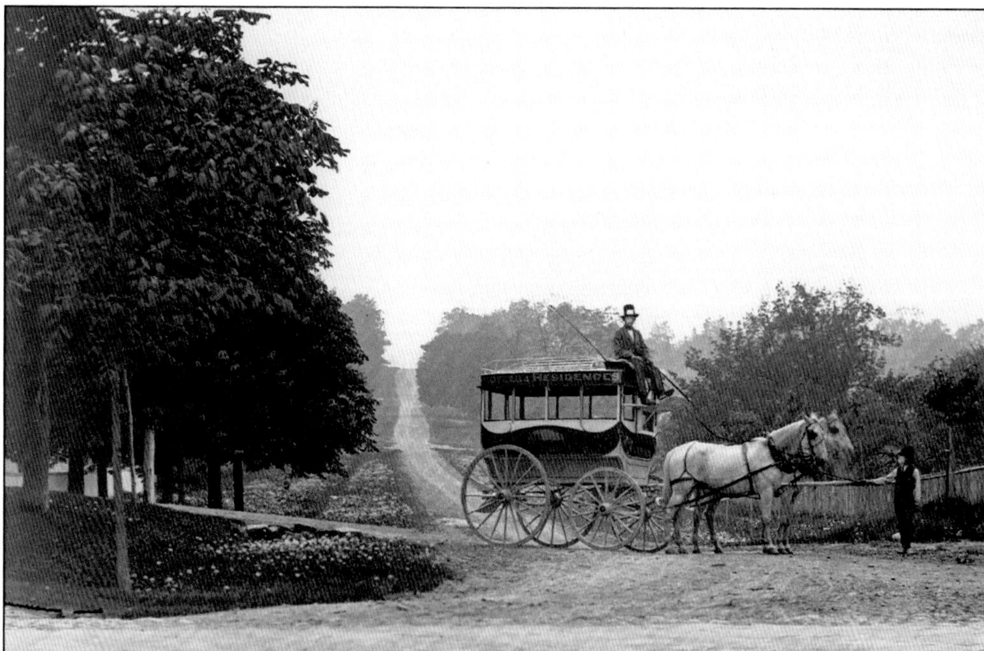

The omnibus, which first appeared in the 1820s, had a typical capacity of 13 to 14 people. Passengers would often hail the drivers, much like today's taxi frequenters. Although it offered a new and different means of transportation, it was said that the ride itself was quite uncomfortable. This omnibus is shown at the juncture of Jay and South Main Streets in Geneva. Michael Keleher and John Malone were listed as the owners of an omnibus line in the Geneva city directories from 1892 to 1906.

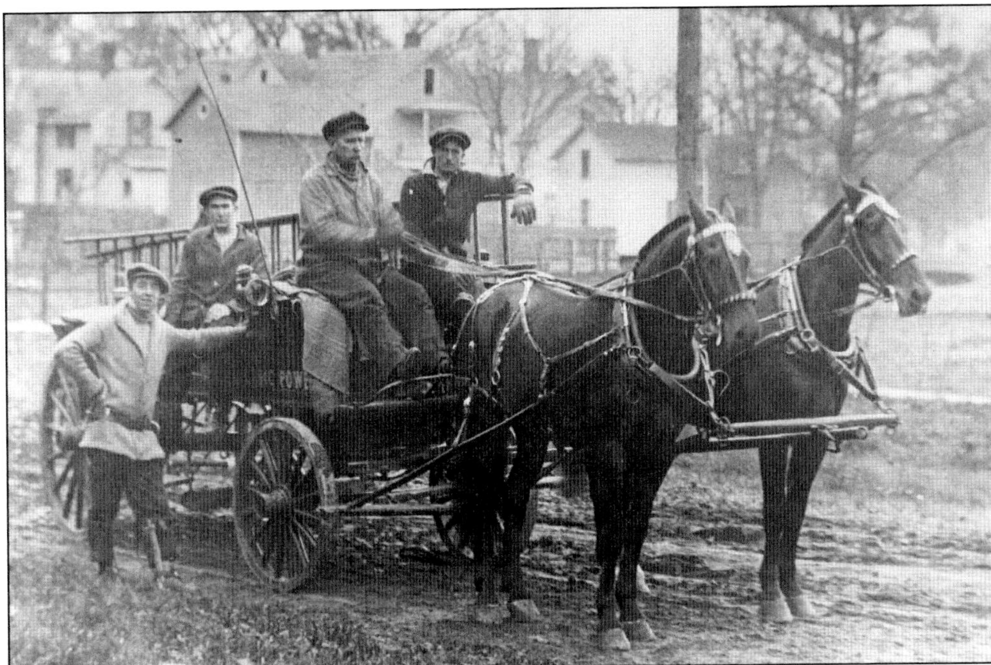

Venturing out into a foggy morning in 1914, a group of electric power employees heads to work. The employees, from left to right, are James Carey, teamster; Stewart Gade, lineman; Howard Squire, lineman; and Bill Green, lineman. By 1910, Canandaigua offered full electric service to the city.

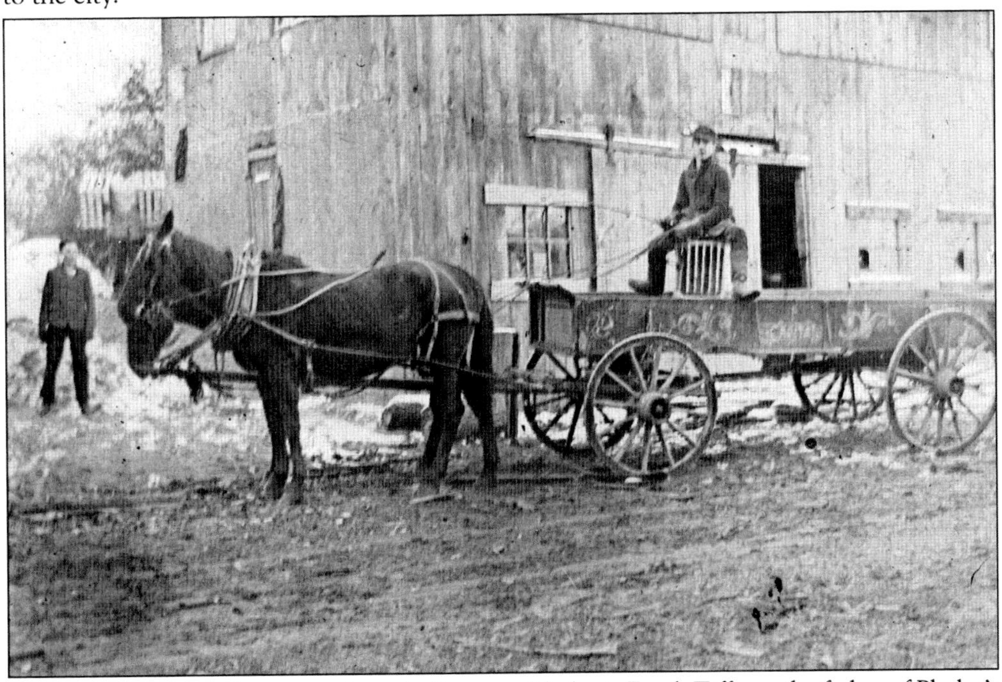

Riding before a crate factory on Ontario Street in Phelps is Frank Tiffany, the father of Phelps's current historian Donald Tiffany. The wagon was referred to as a "democrat wagon," which was used mainly for business in the 1900s.

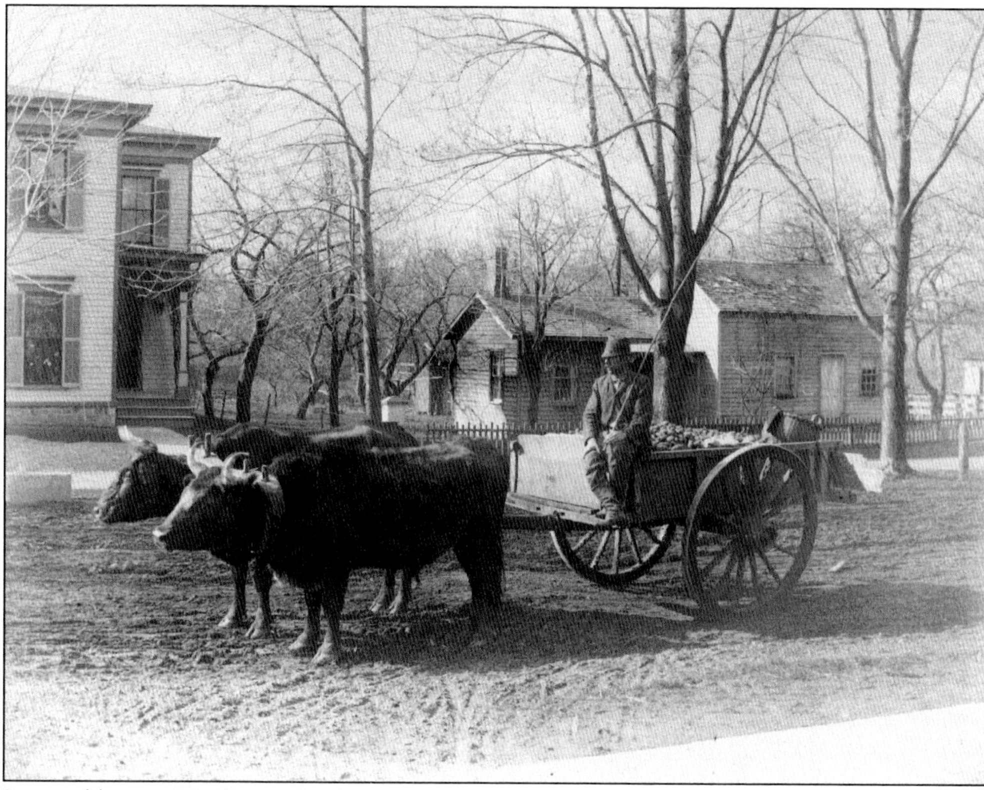

Pictured here is Mr. Brown hauling a carriage full of potatoes on Booth Street in Shortsville. During the winter, Brown would deliver cut ice taken from the Canandaigua outlet. The house behind the carriage was a teahouse.

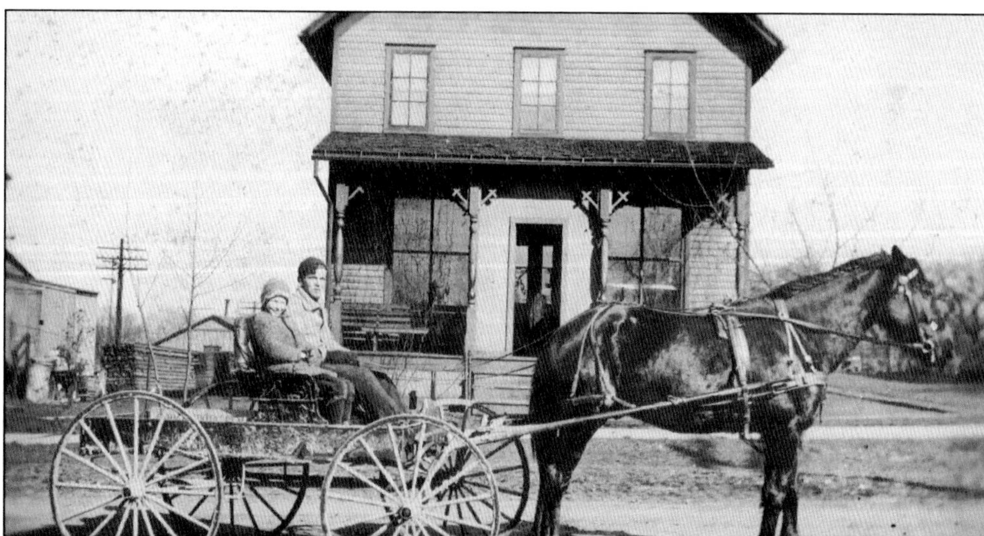

Seated inside this buckboard wagon—pulled by a horse named Old Charlie—are Myrle Record and Eve Carney. The building directly behind them is the Lehigh Valley bunkhouse. The house on the left is the Old Crandall restaurant, once owned by Harry Bennett.

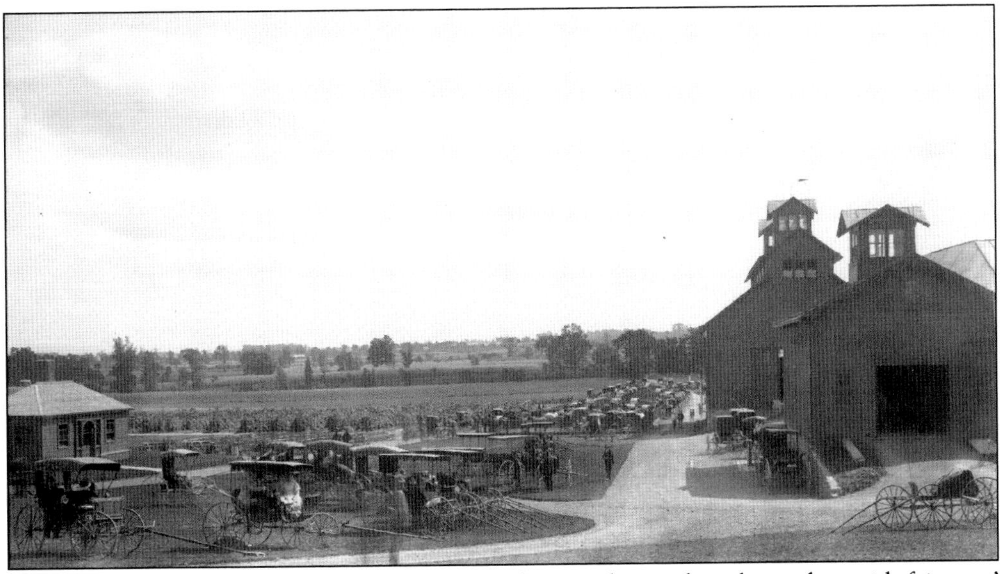

What may look like a late-19th-century junkyard is merely a parking lot replete with fairgoers' carriages. The building next to the many carriages is the New York State Agricultural Experiment Station, a division of Cornell University, which is located on West North Street in Geneva.

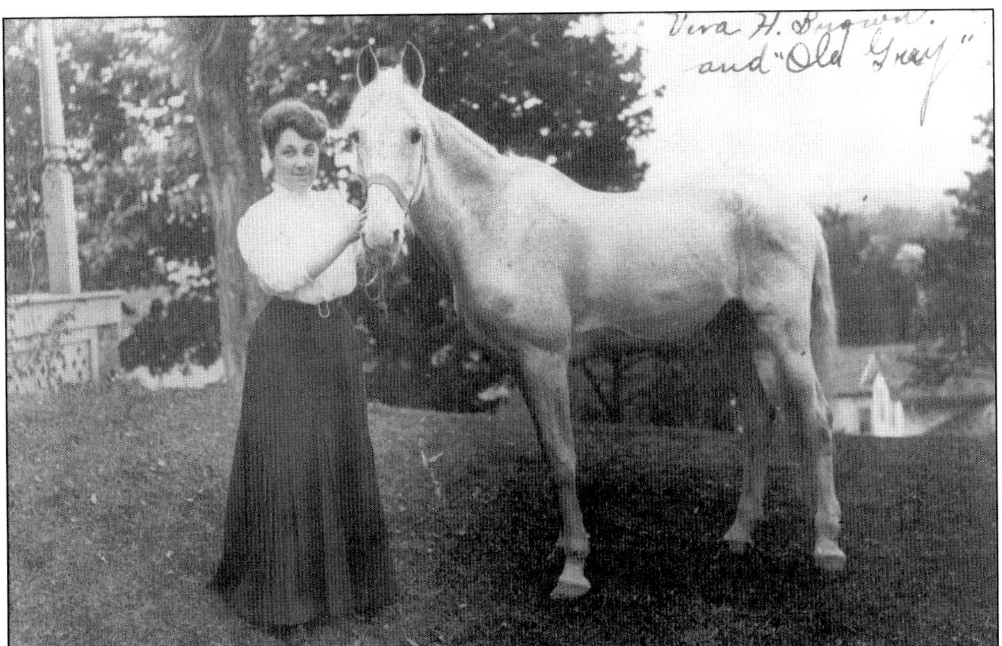

Standing by Old Grey in 1909 is Vera Brown. Brown was a teacher for Victor Central School from 1906 to 1959—one of the longest teaching careers in Ontario County. A scholarship in her honor has benefited Victor students in the past.

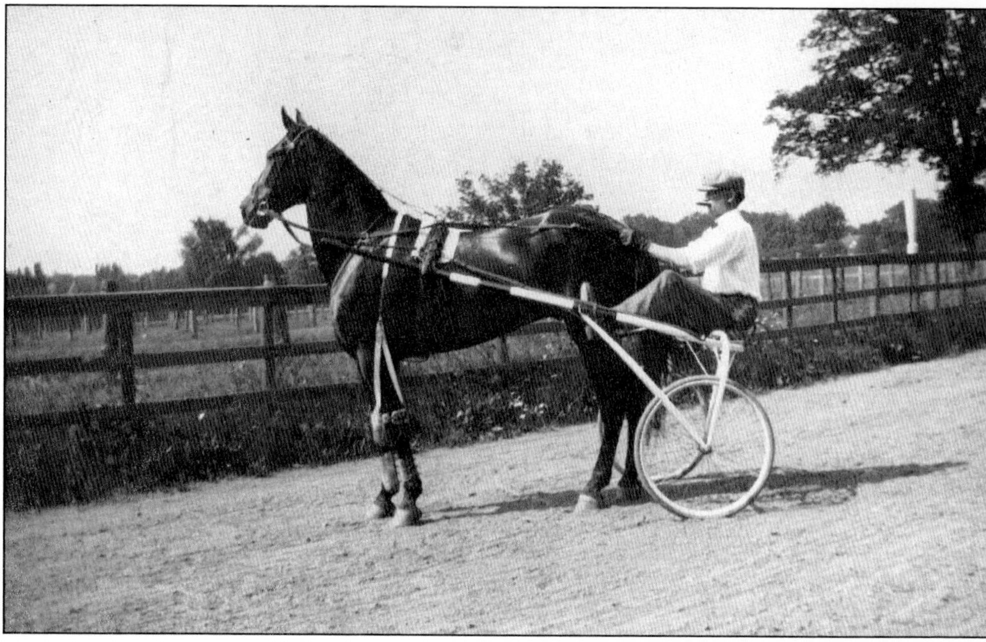

Reclining in what was called a "trotter" at the Ontario County Fairgrounds is Manchester's justice of the peace, Jake Malter, in this 1911 photograph. The fairgrounds—17 acres of land located on Fort Hill Avenue and North Pleasant Street—were purchased in 1873. Fairground admission fees were 25¢, races often started at 2:00 p.m., and an individual purse would sometimes reach $200.

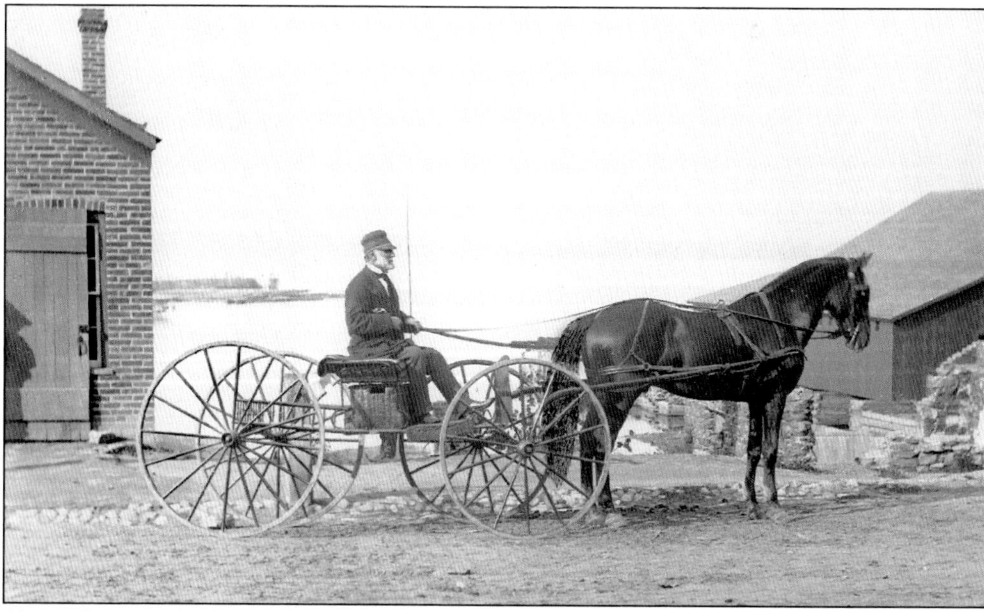

Shown here is Charles Dudley Miller, whose name would later be adjusted to "Colonel" due to his success in serving the National Guard Militia Company. He was born on December 3, 1818, in Utica and died on February 2, 1896, in Geneva. This Corning wagon's intricate mechanisms, running from the horse to the wagon, suggest not only that it was employed for speed but also that it cost a pretty penny.

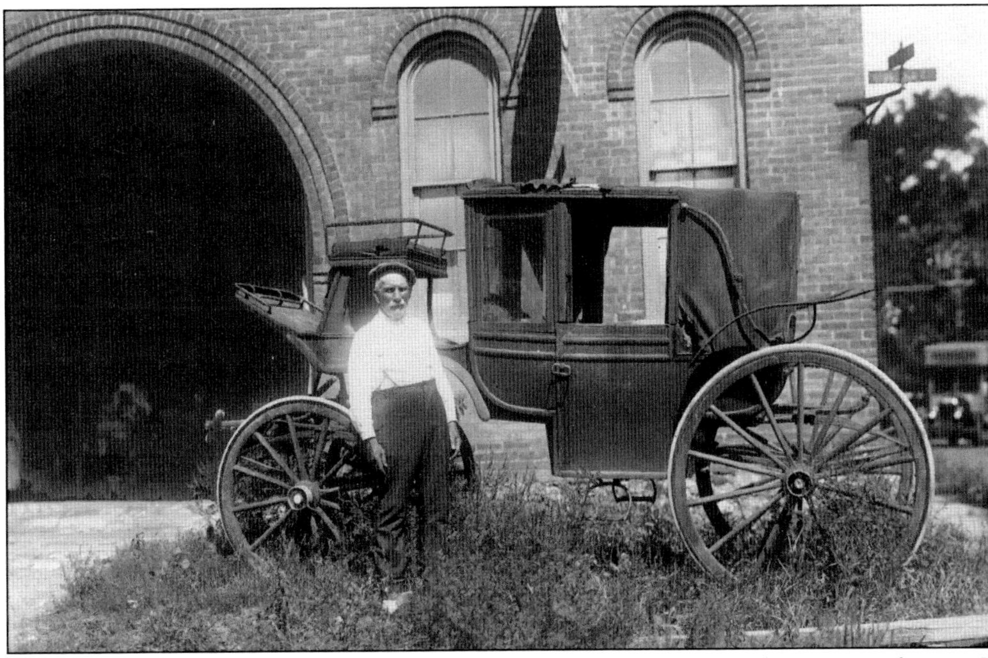

This sovereign carriage, sometimes called the Clarence, is shown as merely a vestige of its era. It stands motionless amid the consuming weeds while the truck to the right signifies the changing times. In its heyday, the carriage was suited for small families, accommodating two to six people, and was sometimes seen being pulled by two to four horses.

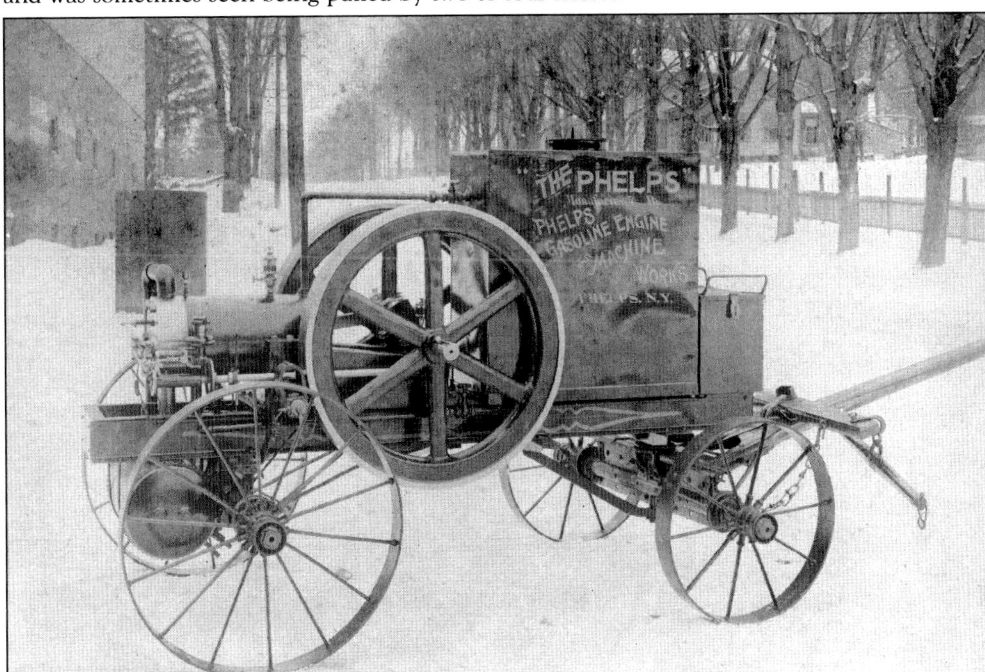

Although transported by horse, this 1890 gas engine, called "Old Hit & Miss," provided not only a portable supply of power but also a precedence of such technology. It was built at the Old Stone Shop in Phelps, the location at which the Old Mill Liquor Store stands today.

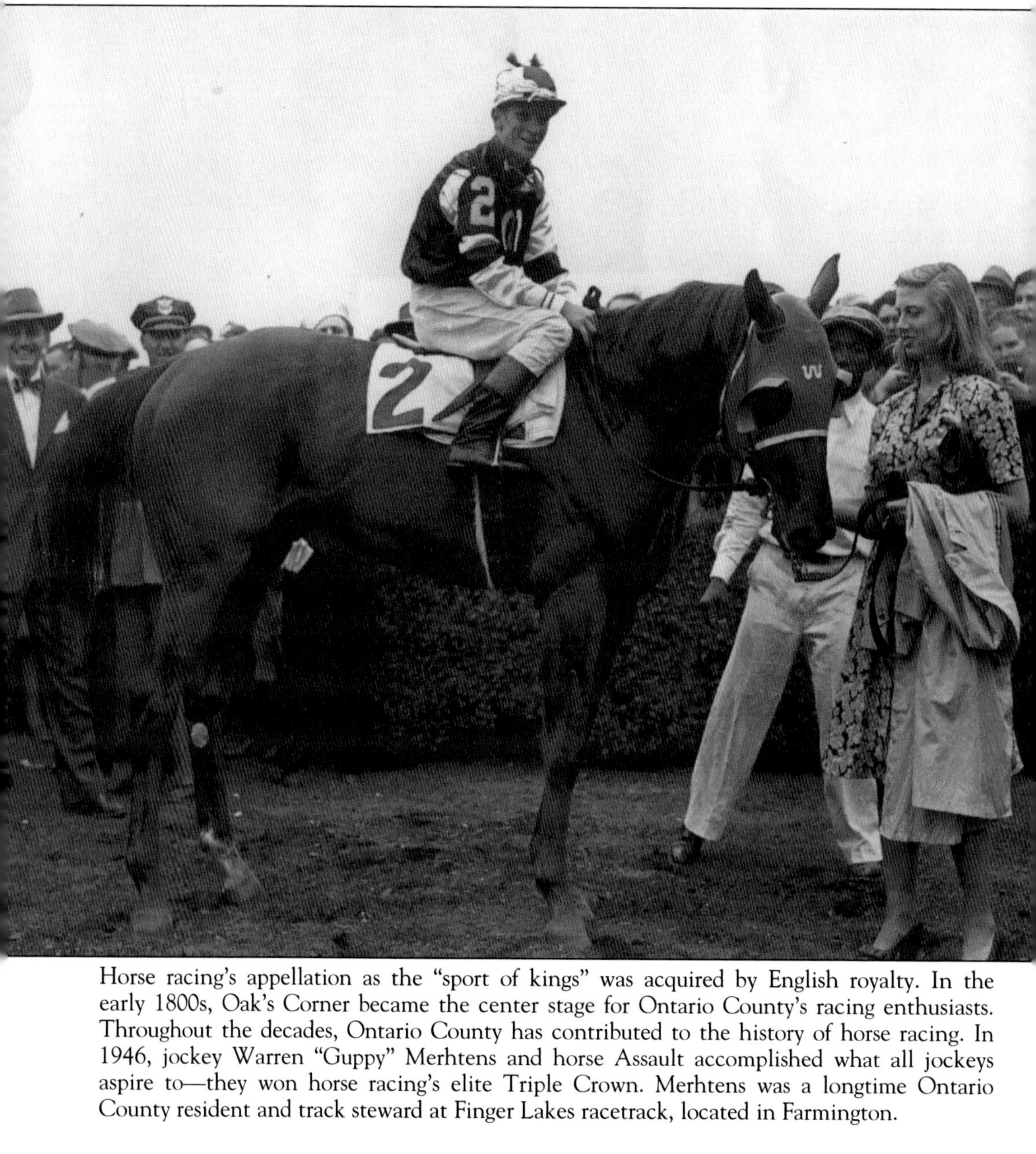

Horse racing's appellation as the "sport of kings" was acquired by English royalty. In the early 1800s, Oak's Corner became the center stage for Ontario County's racing enthusiasts. Throughout the decades, Ontario County has contributed to the history of horse racing. In 1946, jockey Warren "Guppy" Merhtens and horse Assault accomplished what all jockeys aspire to—they won horse racing's elite Triple Crown. Merhtens was a longtime Ontario County resident and track steward at Finger Lakes racetrack, located in Farmington.

Two

Railway Classics

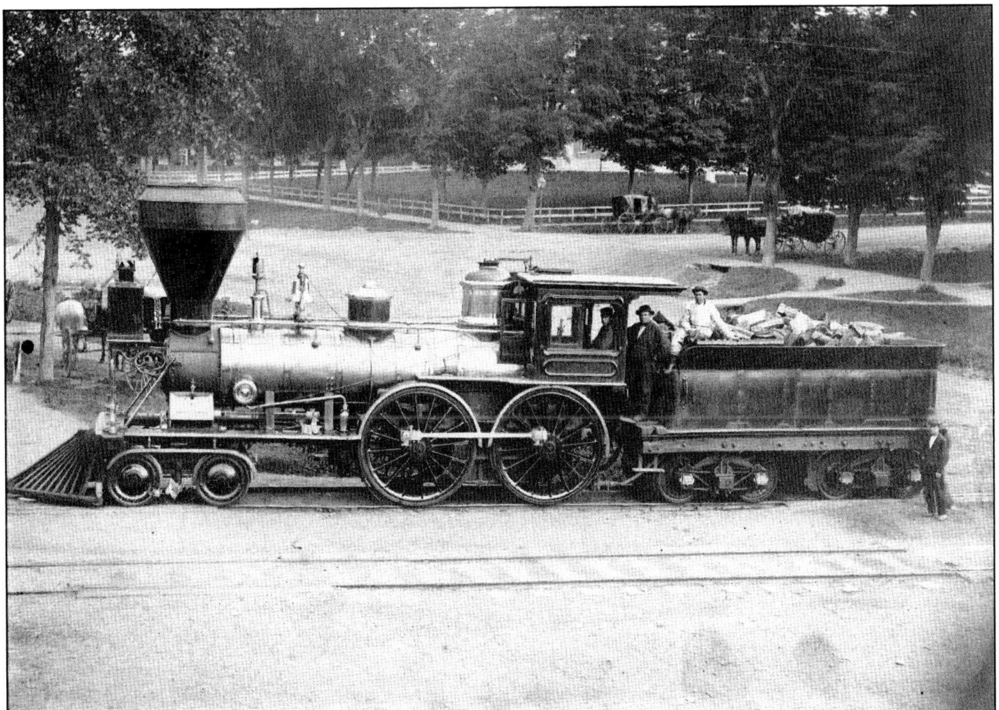

Although they often competed with other means of freight travel (especially boats traveling through the Erie Canal), trains emerged in the 1830s as state-of-the-art transportation. No sooner did such technology make its debut than 3,000 miles of track were laid down by 1840. On this date in Ontario County, the iron for the distance between Rochester and Canandaigua was obtained, and the cost per mile for the 29-mile track was estimated to be $7,000. This 4-4-0 wood burner was typically seen running on the freshly laid tracks of Canandaigua. Seen by the train are engineer John Barker, his son John Barker Jr., and two unidentified people.

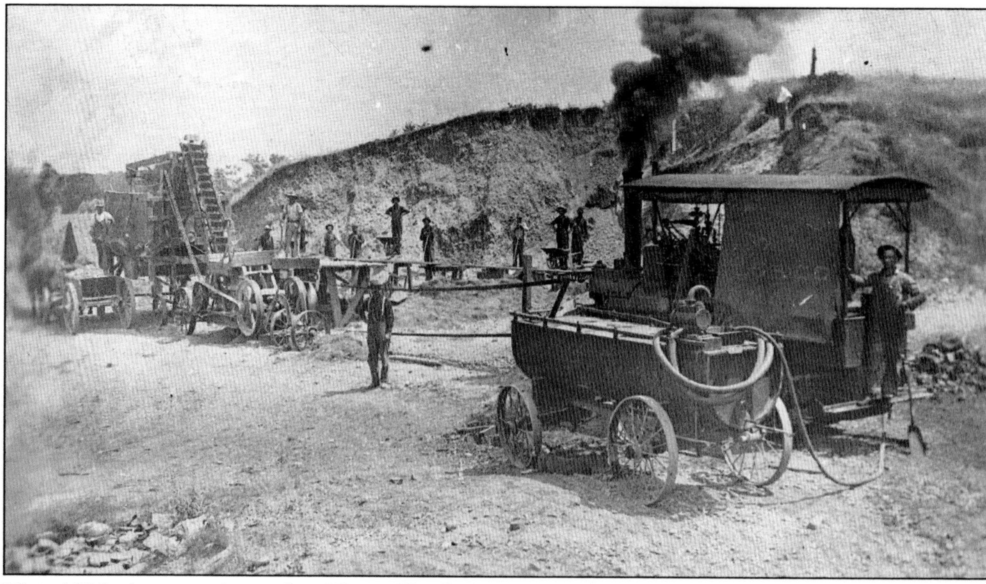

This 1890 photograph catches Harry Huxley's crew working in the gravel pit that was located between State Street and Pratt Road in Manchester. It is no surprise that these laborers regulated a tedious six-step process that included blasting with dynamite, working the steam engine and water pump, and maneuvering the transport wagon.

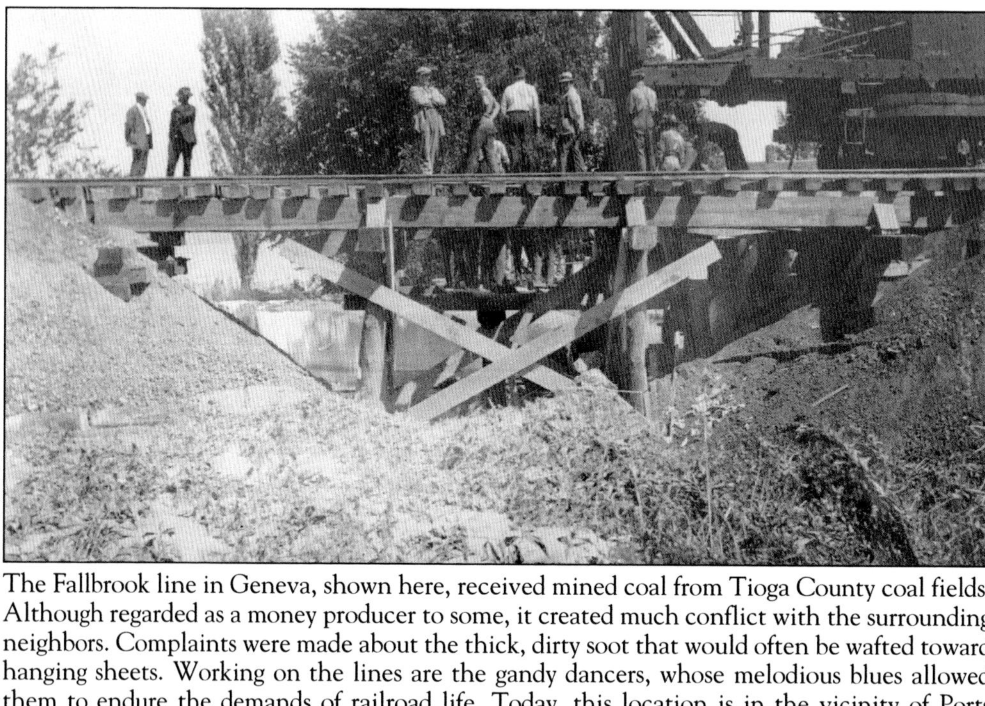

The Fallbrook line in Geneva, shown here, received mined coal from Tioga County coal fields. Although regarded as a money producer to some, it created much conflict with the surrounding neighbors. Complaints were made about the thick, dirty soot that would often be wafted toward hanging sheets. Working on the lines are the gandy dancers, whose melodious blues allowed them to endure the demands of railroad life. Today, this location is in the vicinity of Ports Market & Café, a popular wine tour stop along Route 14.

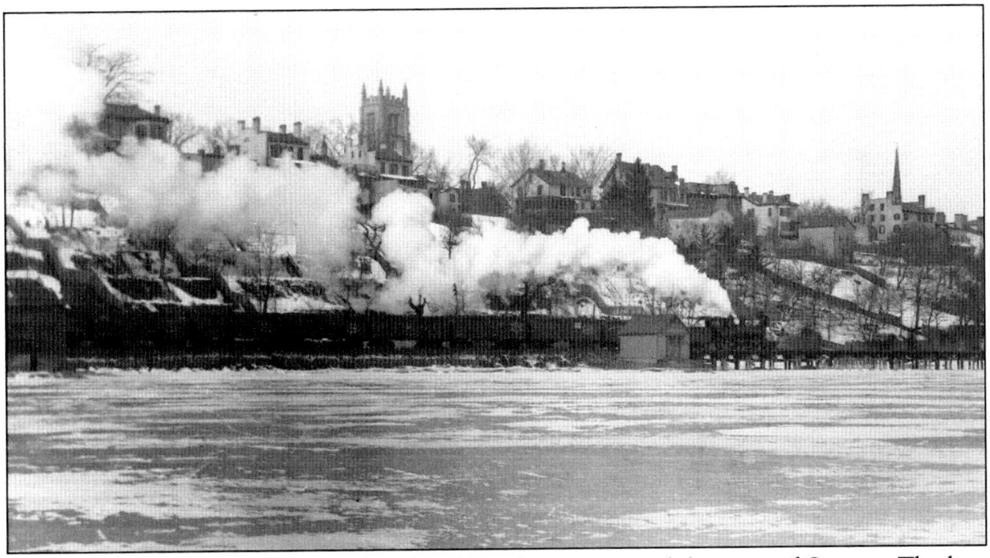

On December 10, 1887, the first official Fall Brook train entered the town of Geneva. The line was also referred to as the Syracuse & Geneva & Corning Railway. Despite the wintry weather, the train shown here makes its way through the Geneva lines. The photograph, taken from the frozen Seneca Lake, shows the distinctive terraced yards and the square tower of Trinity Episcopal Church.

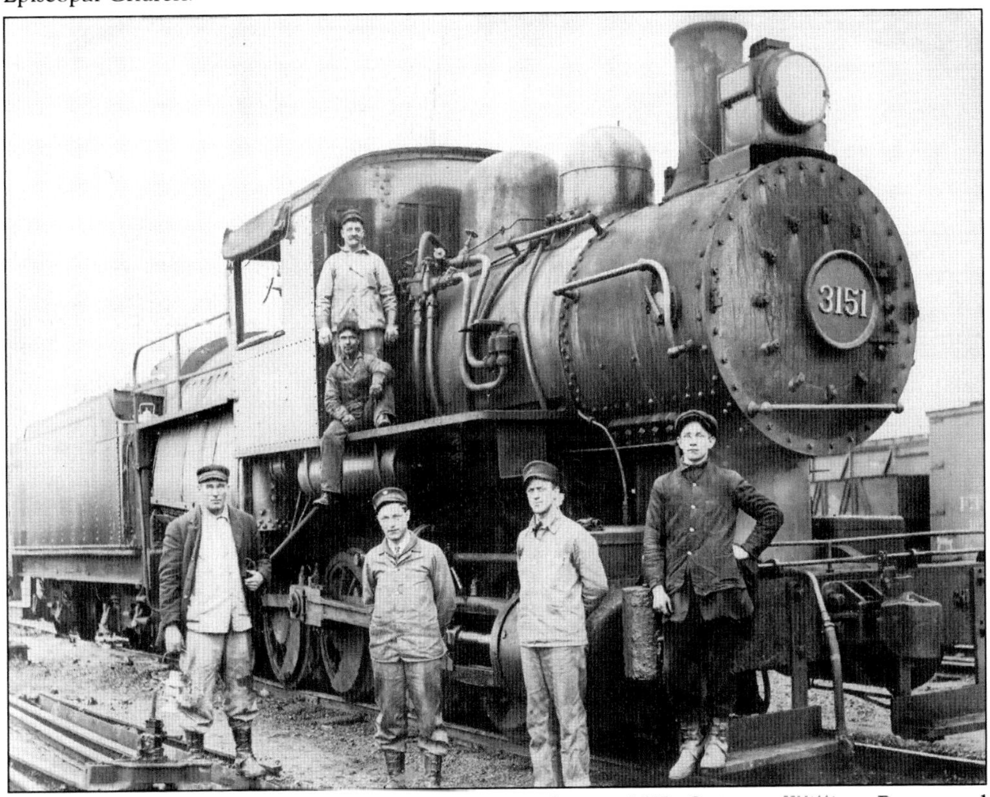

Standing before this switcher are R.B. Young, conductor; H.E. Quinter; William Ryan; and H. Sweinfurt. Atop the train are engineer L.J. Smith and fireman Neil Smith.

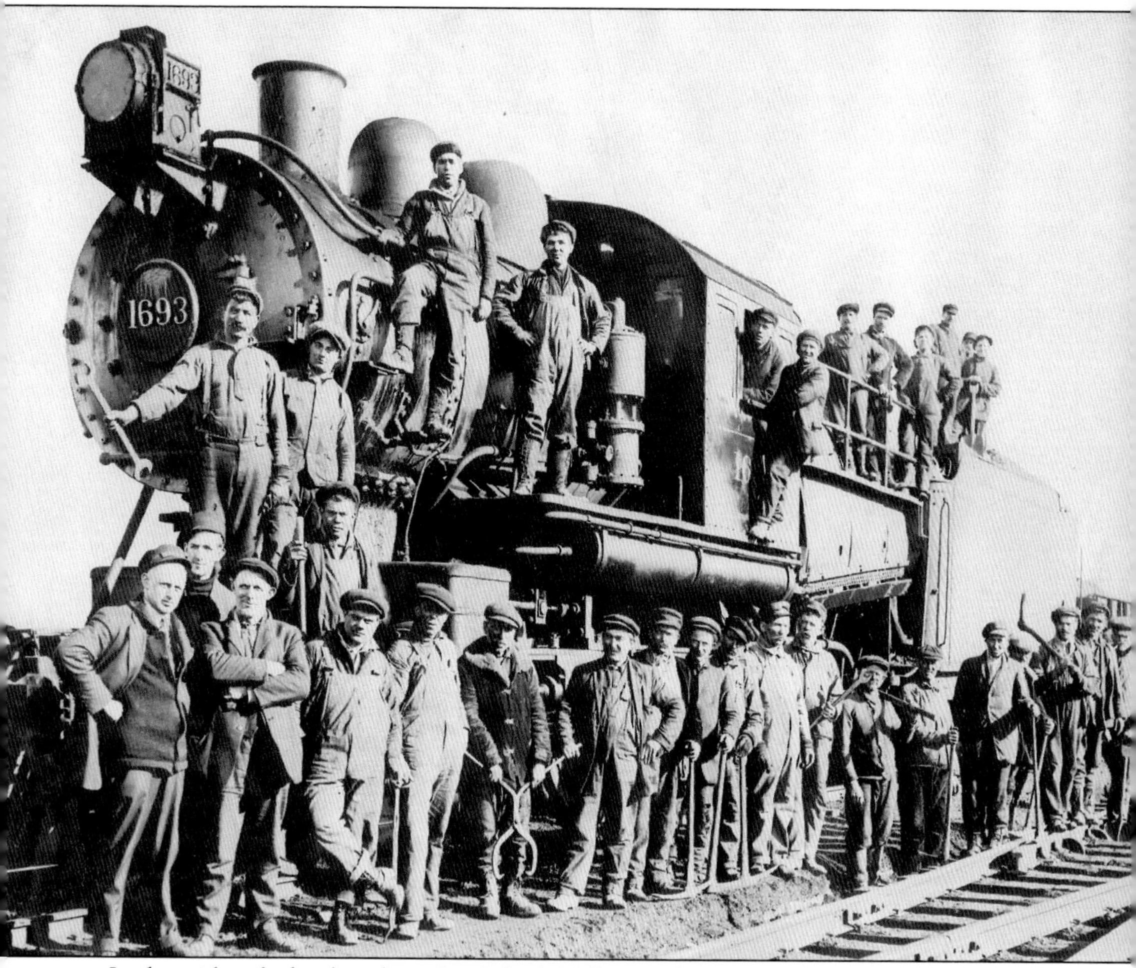

In the midst of a hard working day, Lehigh Valley employees take a respite to pose for a formal picture. Because Lehigh Valley was one of the largest freight transfers in 1914, it demanded an abundance of employees. Lehigh Valley workers during this time included the following: F.J. Howard, C.E. Moyer, J. Downey, William Edinger, J. Anderson, S.J. Hurlburt, A. Quinter, T.C. Craig, M.F. Bolan, A.B. Moore, H.C. Quinter, R.B. Loring, W.P. Brown, William Ryan, H.Y. Chambers, E. Quinter, R. Stonebridge, R.S. Chambers, C. Hillyer, O.M. Walters, J.B. Lester, F. Chadwick, J.E. Barrows, S.J. Turner, L. Van Orman, H. Gross, S. Beachy, F. Chappell, J. Fogarty, P. Conlon, H. Barrows, N. Shepard, O.L. Herman, J. Kerins, H. Herman, M. Bennett, H. Sweinfurt, J. Sloppey, J. Robinson, D. Robinson, T.E. Stage, H. Vienna, G. Leakey, G. Stroud, E. Lowry, F. McIntyre, J. Manion, J. Meehan, C.H. Williams, W. Segbers, G.E. McLean, D.W. Wolcott, William J. Rhoader, C. Cumming, F. Ellis, N. Hurlburt, W.J. King, E. Maloney, F. Dumond, C. Hackett, C. Boyer, M.F. Carney, R. Knowles, L.D. Covel, J. Doley, J.E. Mulligan, C. Smead, B. Magary, G.L. Redfield, L. Romeiser, J.S. Walters, R.H. Wood, F. McCloud, C. Ruggles, C. Peck, M. Record, K.R. Moyer, H.W. Turner, C.F. Cunningham, F. Carey, K. Herman, C.A. Quinter, H.C. Chambers, T. Henry, F. West, L. Smith, Caulkins, F. Hildreth, T. Kerins, G. Hesney, J. Repsher, T. Repsher, J. Meehan, C. Williams, G. Deyo, C.E. Corser, J. VanNorman, M. St. John, E.D. Salem, E. Quigley, H. Howe, F. Groves, T. Parker, R.D. Wood, R.P. Broomfield, J. Mottelo, J. E. Kreidler, G. Rotundo, P. Hardman, William Stambach, N.D. Lyon, G.H. Skeyner, W.C. Callister, L. Pasquale, J. Weaver, J. Minute, F. Angeline, L. McNally, B. Knauss, and J. Boardman.

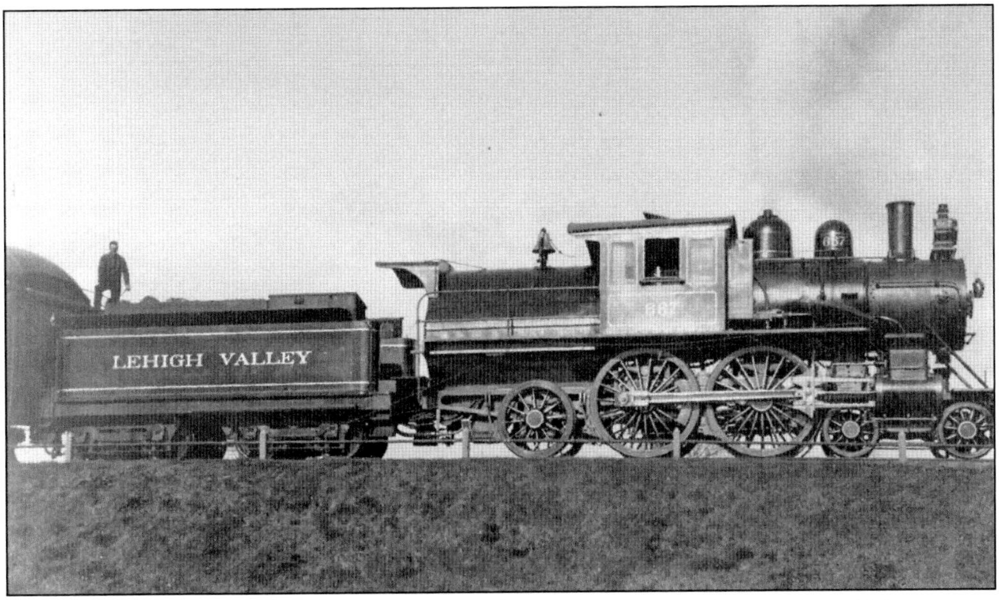

By the early 1940s, the Lehigh Valley Railroad owned 400 steam locomotives, 300 passenger cars, and 16,000 freight cars. Its track from Buffalo to New York City was 448 miles long, and its 800-mile branch line tracks extended to portions of Pennsylvania. On September 1, 1892, the first passenger train used the Lehigh Valley Railroad in Manchester.

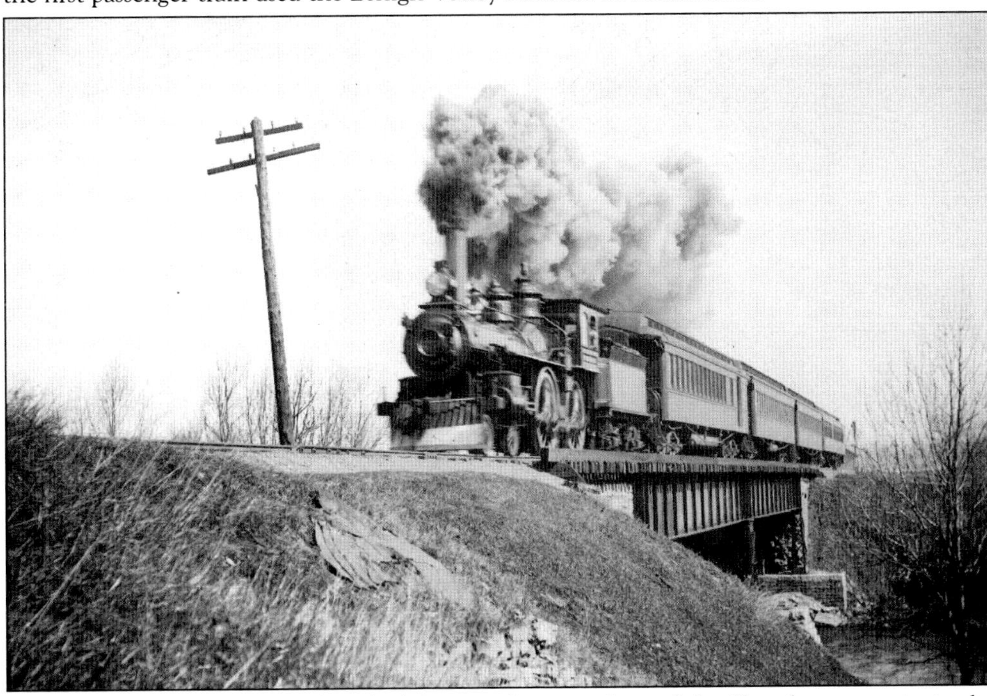

Immediately after its debut, the Black Diamond was acclaimed the "handsomest train in the world." Its luxurious interior and such accommodations as kitchen and dining facilities were undoubtedly the reasons for which it was given the impressive name. In 1896, the Black Diamond flaunted its sophistication to Manchester bystanders, and soon after it stopped in Clifton Springs.

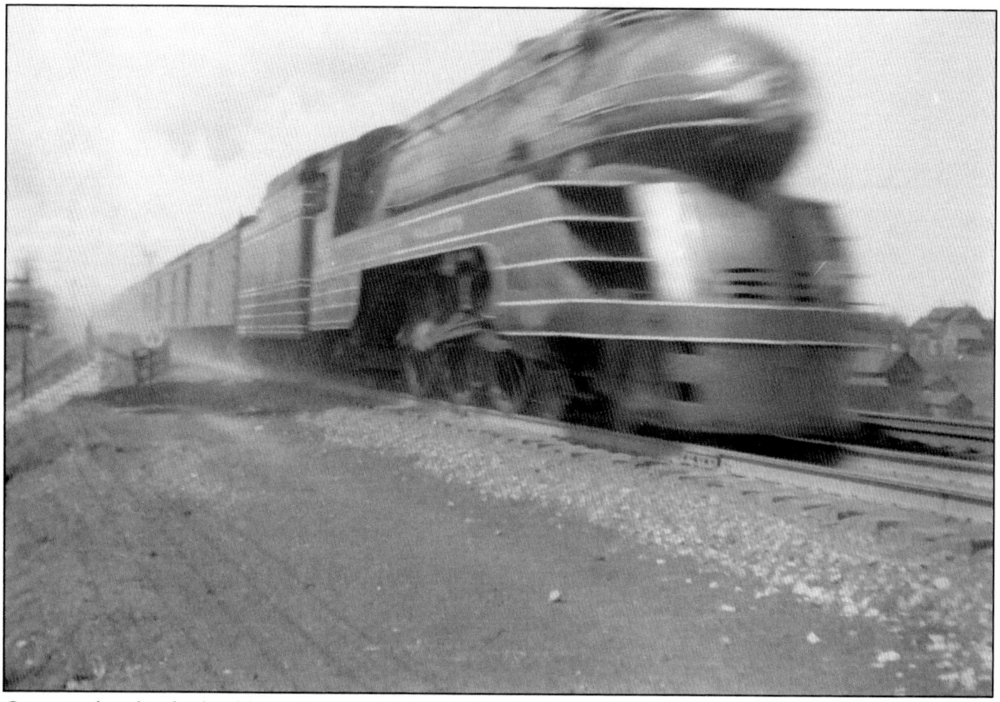

One might think the blur in this picture is the result of poor film developing. However, it is merely the result of a Black Diamond Express topping out at speed of 80 mph on Manchester's overpass. This 1940 picture was taken by Mike Bolonda.

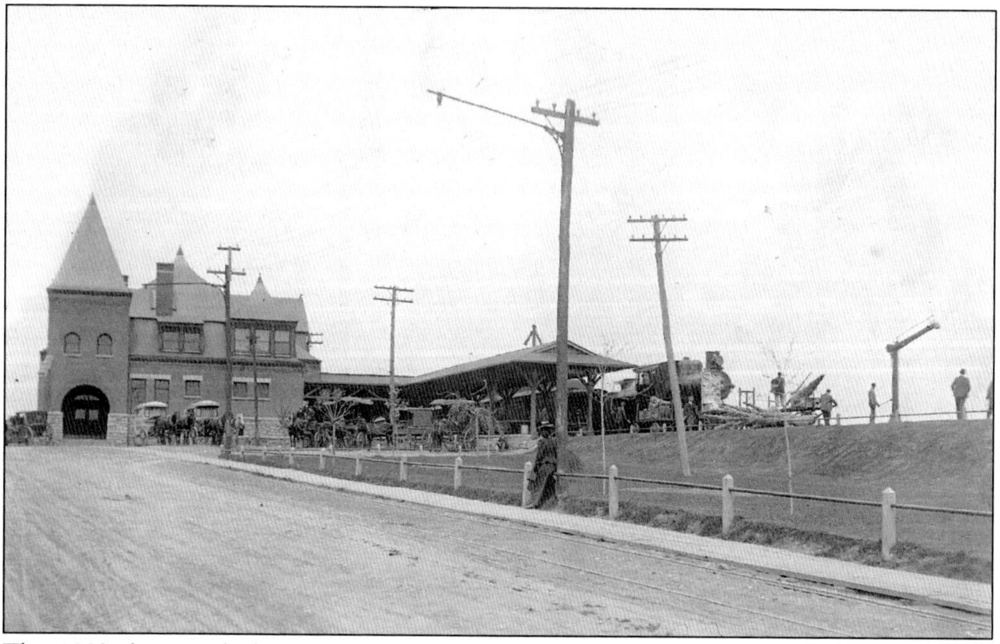

This 1903 photograph shows the Lehigh Valley depot, which is located at the end of Sherrill Street in Geneva. Because of its charming features, the station was a favorite destination of Finger Lakes summer tourists. Today, the depot overlooks Uncle Joe's restaurant, which is owned by the Cosentino family and is located on Genesee Street.

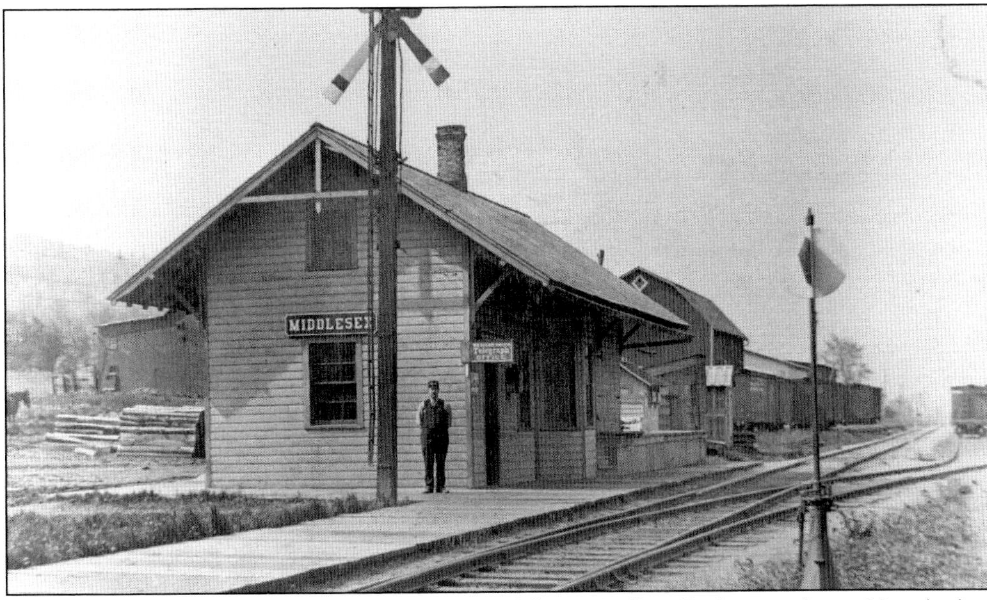

In 1895, the Lehigh Valley acquired the Middlesex Valley Railway, whose 29-mile line extended from Geneva to Naples. The solitary man awaiting the arrival of a train is the telegraph operator.

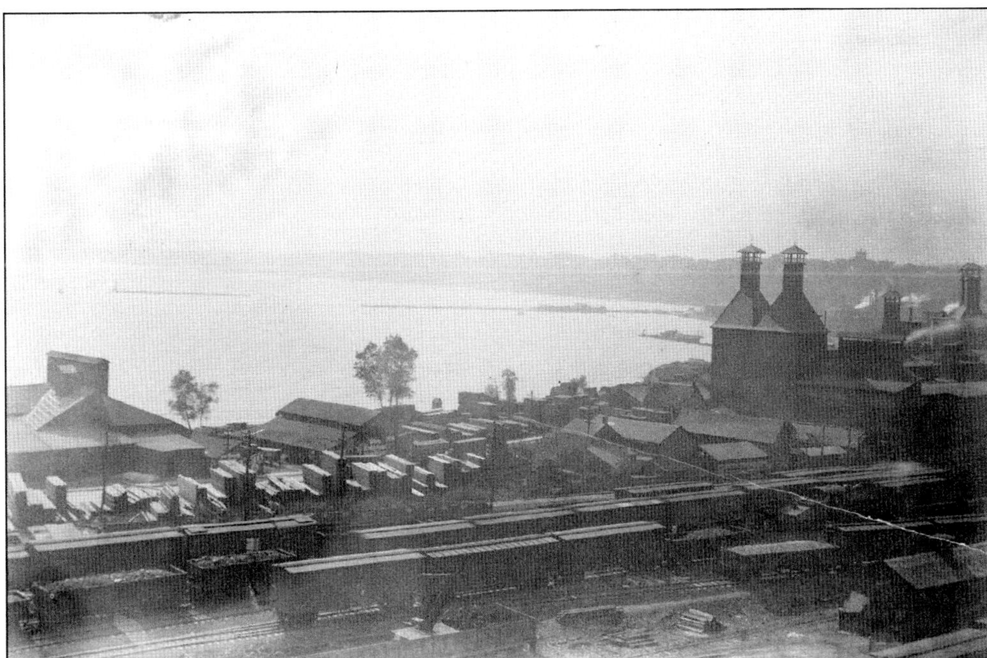

Prior to the 1850s, steamboats and canal boats were the top shippers to local mills and factories in Geneva. However, once the New York Central Railroad became mainstream, it supplied such companies as the Nester Malt House (shown as the identical towers in the photograph), Patent Cereals Company, and New York Central Iron Works.

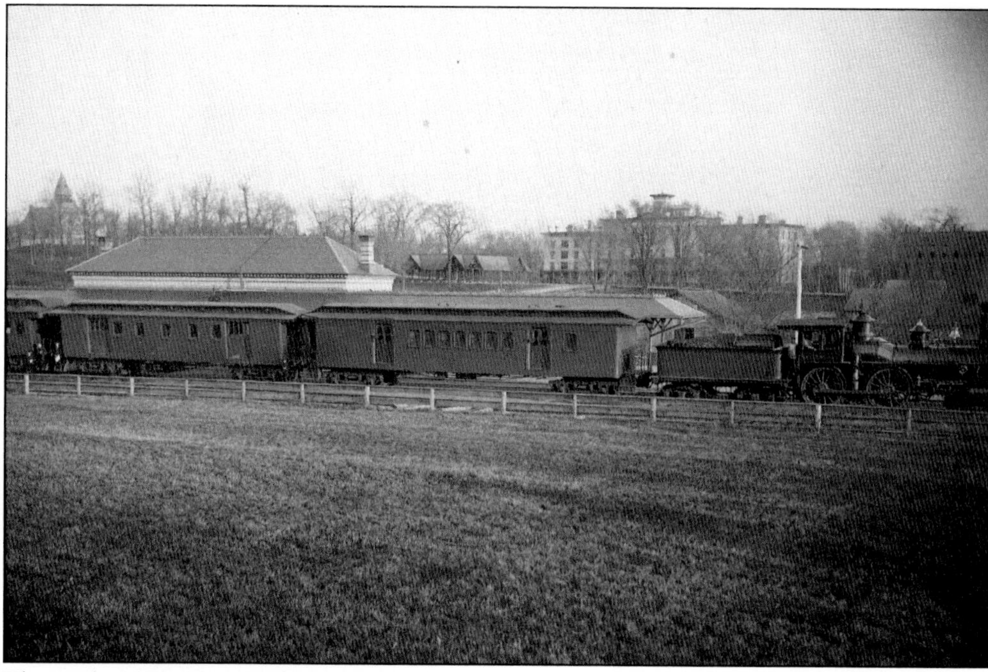

This early-1870s New York Central passenger train is making its way to the Clifton Springs sanitarium, pictured here above the coal tender. Among the passengers were celebrities seeking the sanitarium's known healing power.

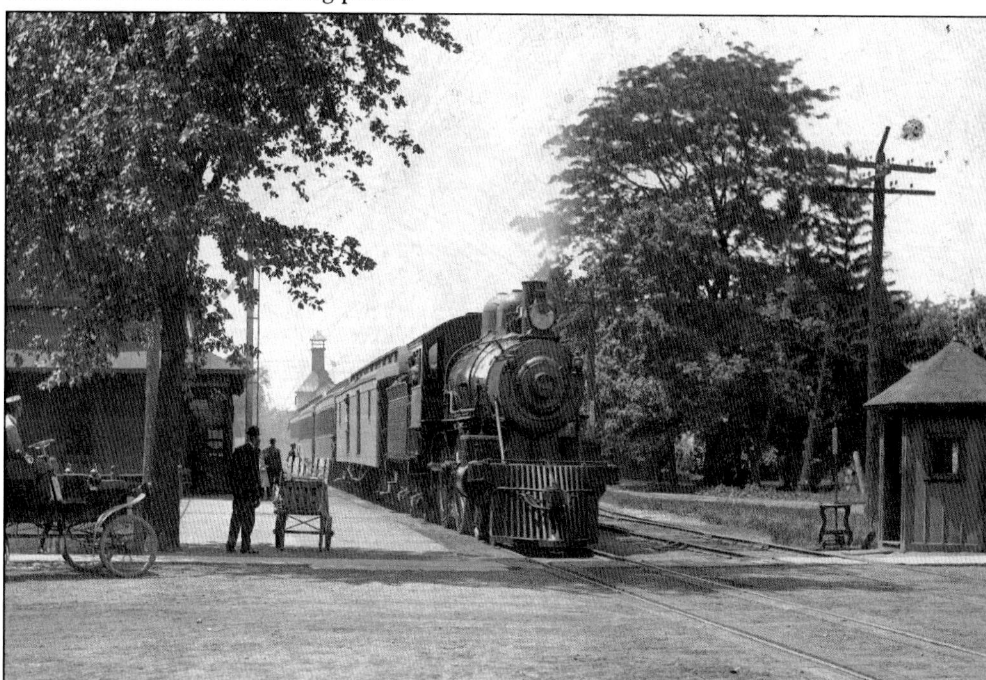

This is a 1906 photograph of a train leaving the New York Central depot, passing by the corner of Pleasant Church Street in Phelps. On the left is automobile pioneer Charley Lane, and on the right is a type of building best known as a "flag shanty."

During the 1850s, the Middlesex Valley served the Naples wine industry. Here, a locomotive and its crew stop to pose for picture before heading to a Naples vineyard.

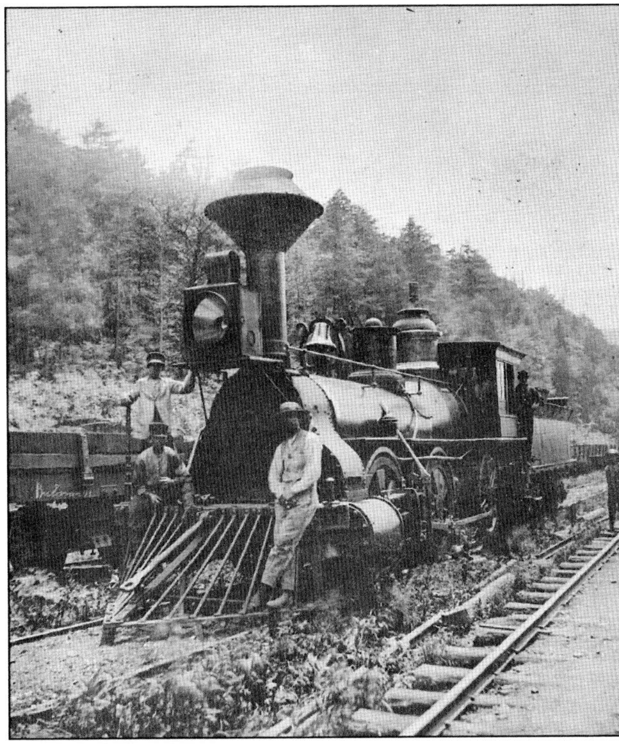

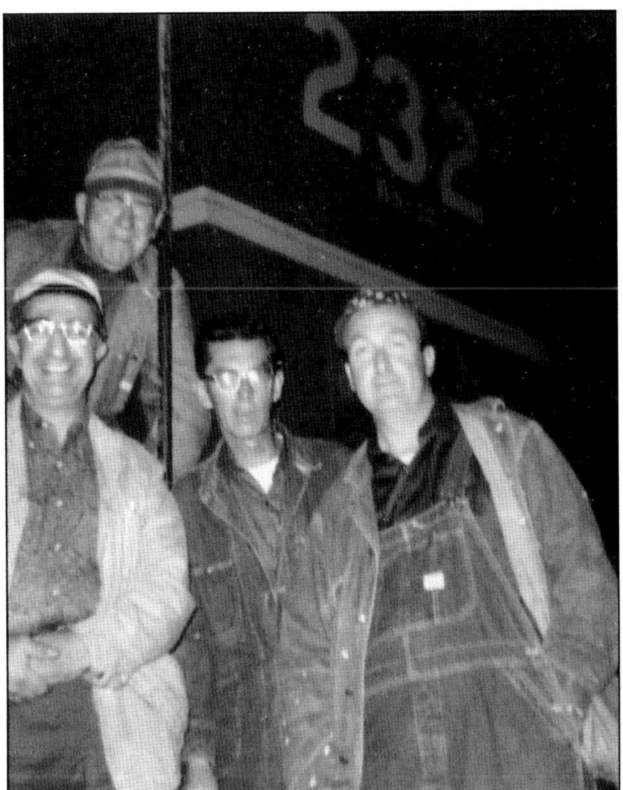

This July 1, 1970 photograph shows the last switching crew of the Lehigh Valley Railroad of Manchester. From left to right in the front row are Jake Hessney, Joe Barry, and Earl Robinson. Ed Schier is in the back.

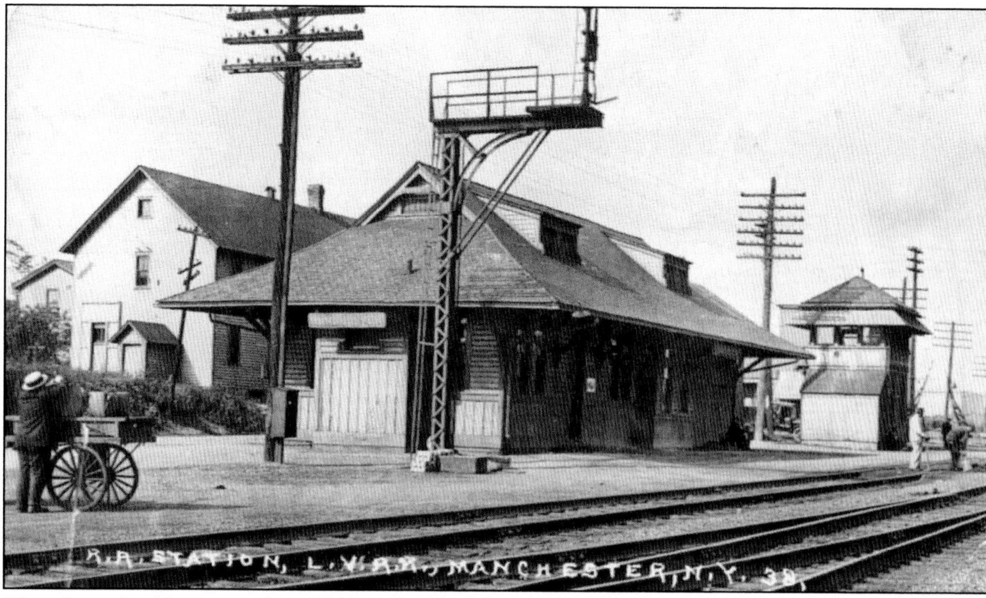

The three buildings in this 1920s photograph of Manchester's depot are the control tower (right), the depot (center), and the bunkhouse (left). Within 24 hours, baseball enthusiasts would embark at Manchester's depot, travel to New York City to watch the New York Yankees compete, and return home.

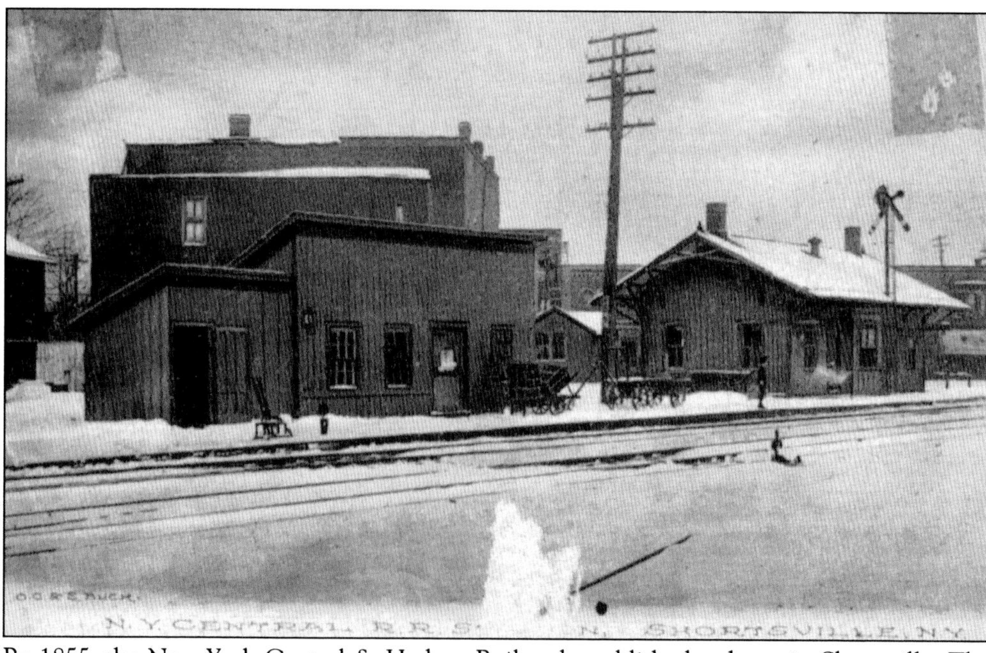

By 1855, the New York Central & Hudson Railroad established a depot in Shortsville. The depot (right) and the jailhouse (left) are shown in this picture. Today, the depot is Butch 25's restaurant, whose nostalgic atmosphere and delicious food attract many. The restaurant is owned by Bob Santella and David Liberty.

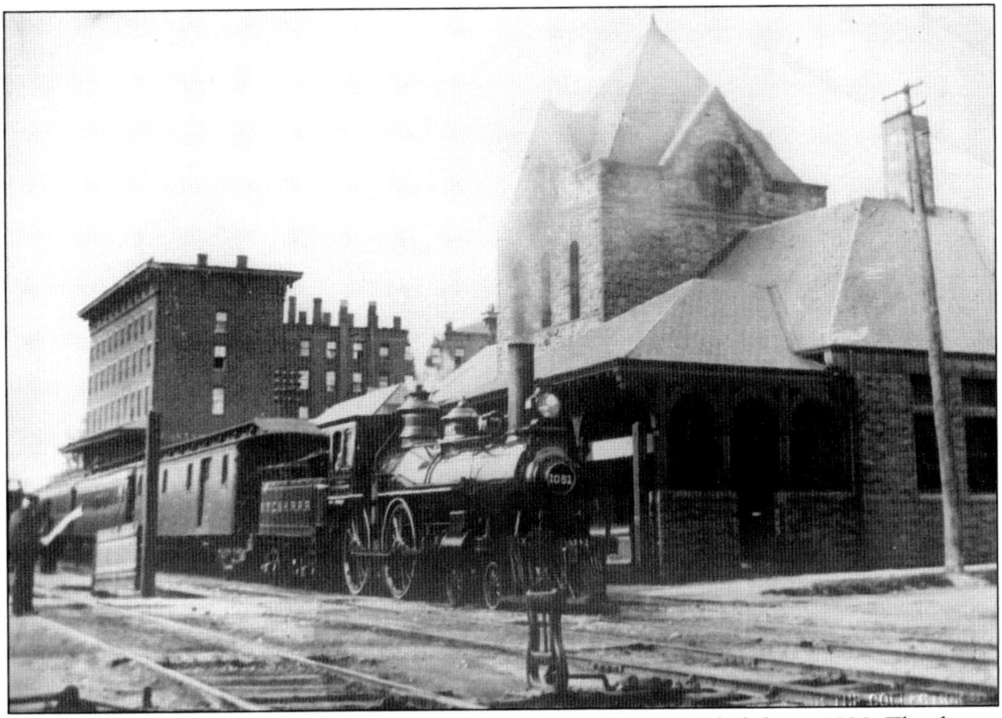

The New York Central depot in Canandaigua was built by the Vanderbilts in 1890. The depot, whose service lasted until 1958, had initially been opposed by Mrs. F.F. Thompson. She argued that it would be environmentally detrimental. However, for unknown reasons, she later urged her friends, the affluent Vanderbilts, to construct the depot.

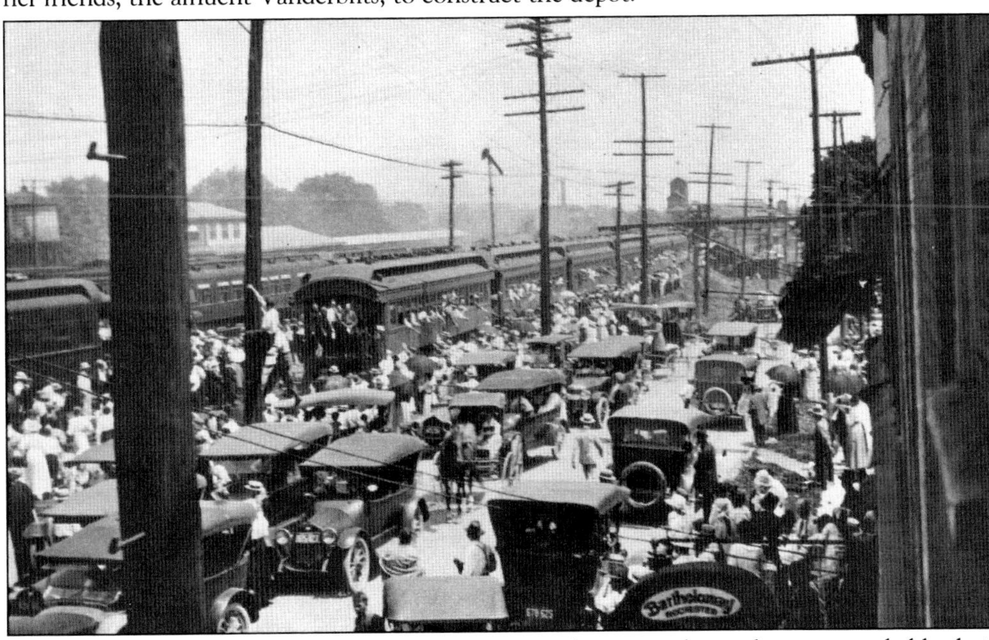

On the emotional day of July 27, 1918, relatives are shown speaking what were probably their last words to the departing World War I soldiers at the New York Central depot, across from Dwyer's Café and Billiard Hall, at 49 Niagara Street in Canandaigua.

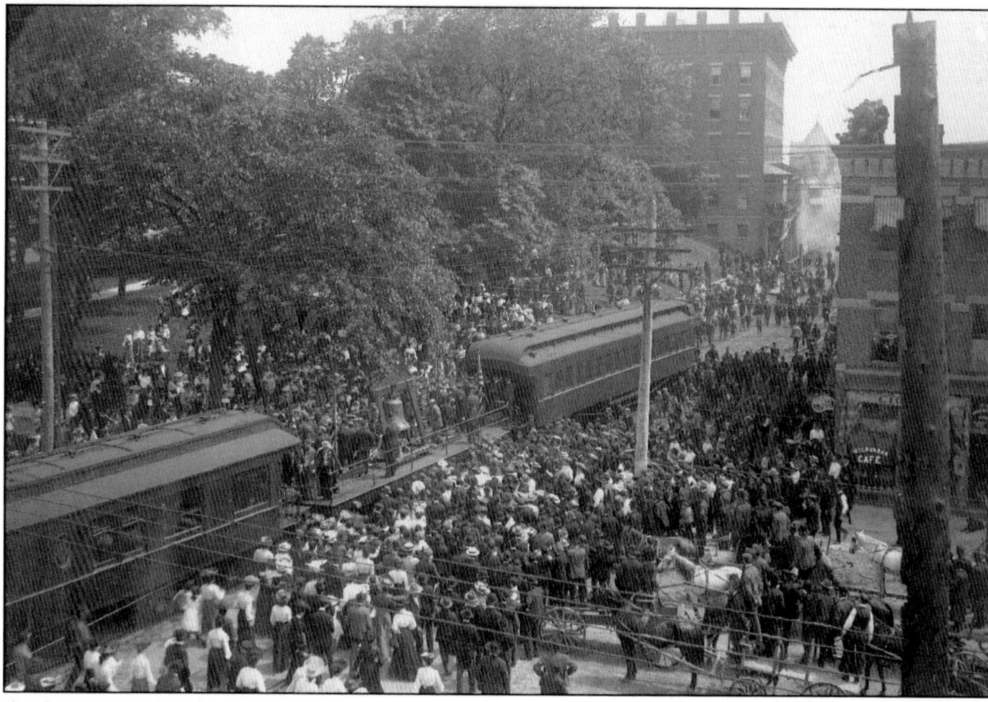

On June 4, 1904, the Liberty Bell passed through Canandaigua on its way to the world's fair in St. Louis. Note the security surrounding the bell.

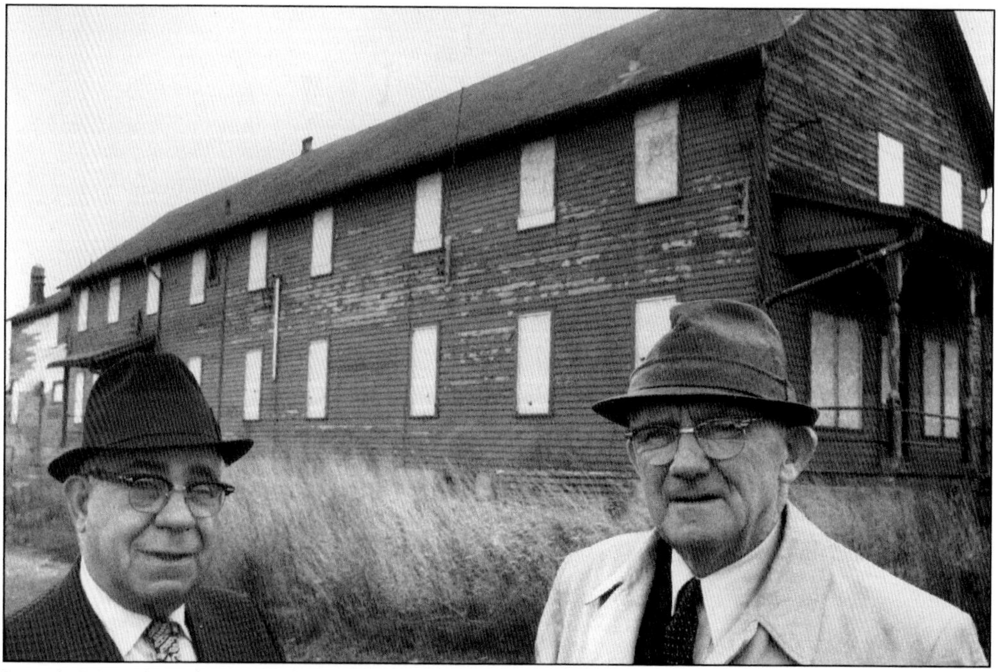

Joseph Mottelo, who served for 53 years as an oil house clerk for Lehigh Valley, and Johnny Boardman, a fireman for the railroad, stand before an obsolete bunkhouse, which was located on South Main Street. In the early 1920s, the bunkhouse served beyond its initial purpose, as it had an adjunct restaurant that was managed by Harry Bennett.

This 1918 photograph shows Franklin Delano Roosevelt making an appearance in Phelps in his earlier political days. In 1928, Roosevelt was elected governor of New York.

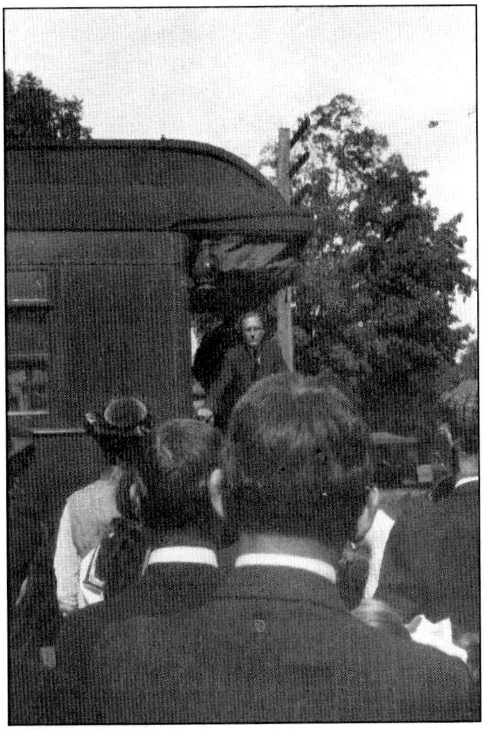

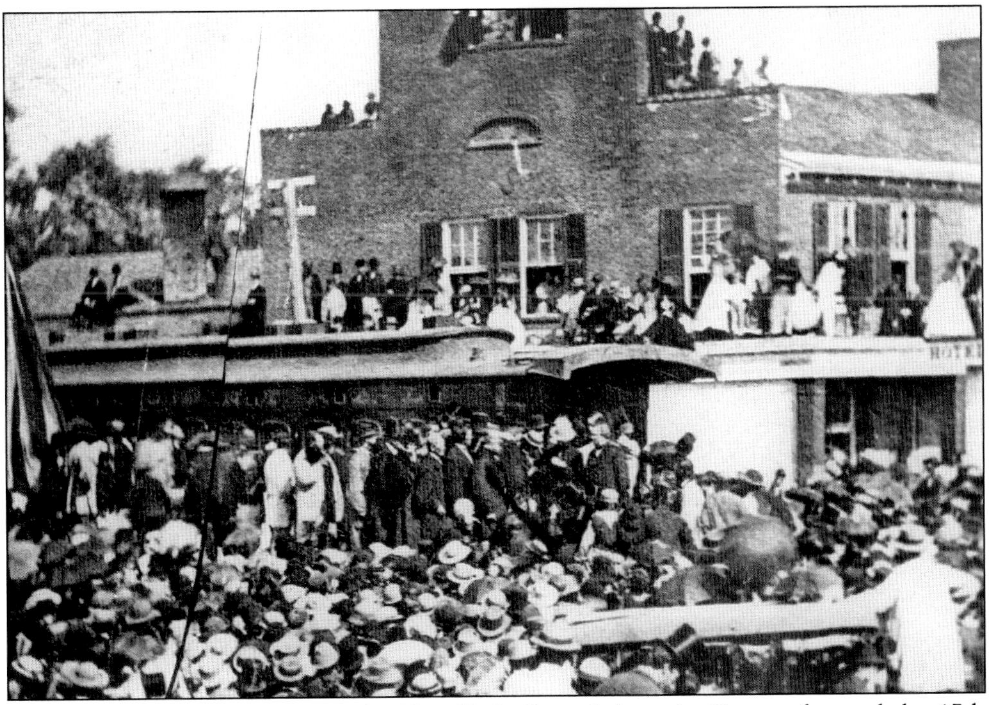

This 1865 political reception at the New York Central depot in Geneva featured the 17th president, Andrew Johnson. Johnson was considered the "stump speaker" for his charismatic speeches. Gen. Ulysses S. Grant, Secretary of State Seward, and Admiral Farragut also attended the reception.

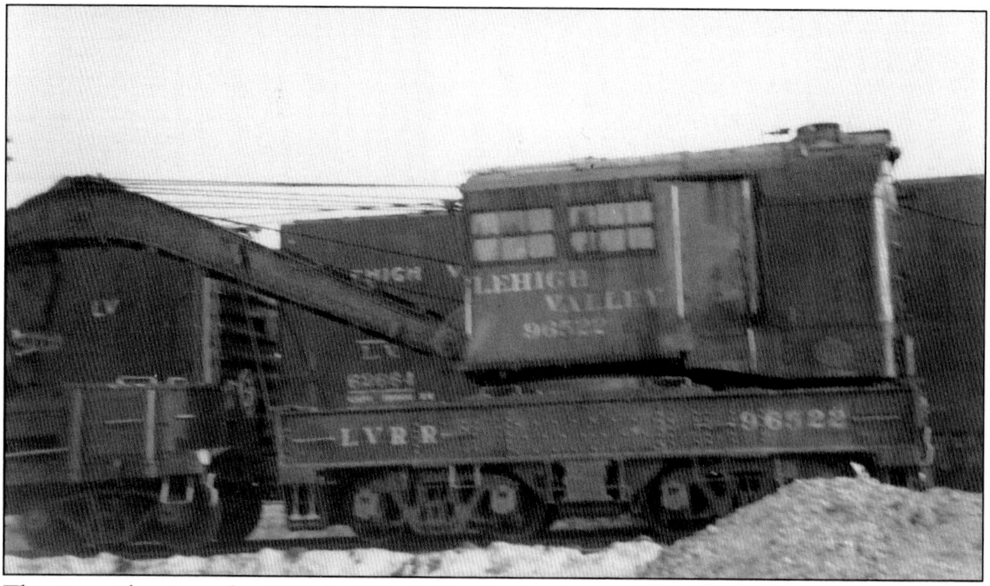

This is a side view of a 1918 Lehigh Valley Railroad crane, also known as the "Big Hook." Because of the many derailments, the crane was constantly fed by the firemen, ensuring it would be prepared to do its work when needed.

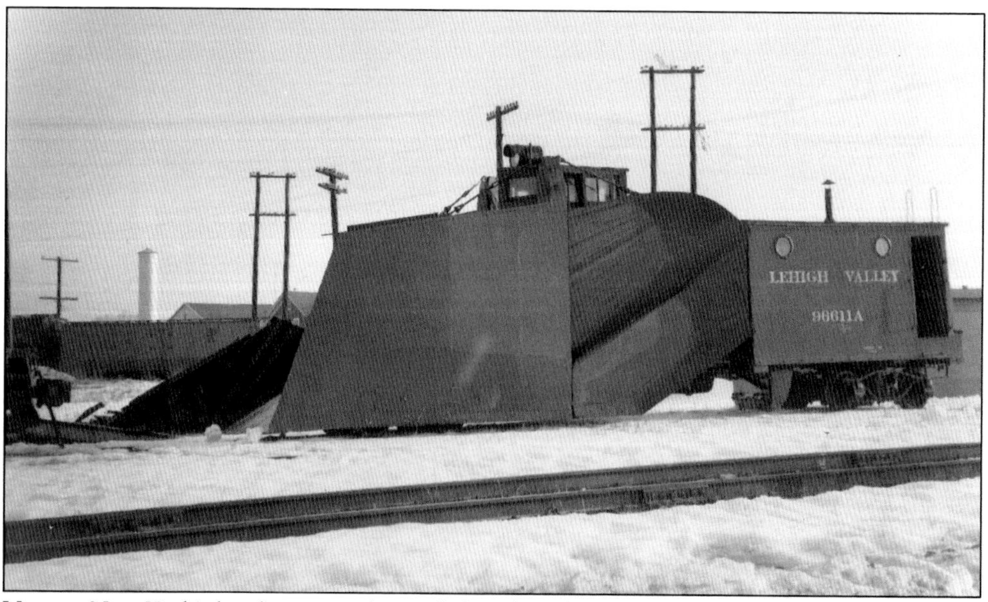

Upstate New York's harsh winters demanded nothing less to blow the snow off the tracks than this V-plow, which was pushed by a locomotive. Its 15-foot height and large dimensions overall caused the plow to derail frequently.

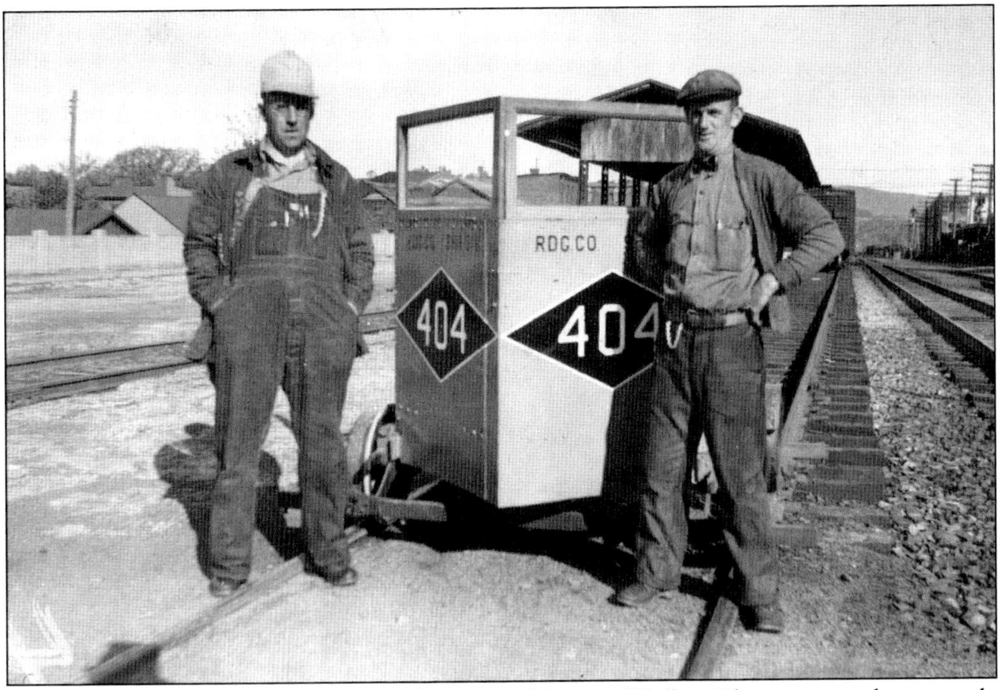

Standing before this 404 cart are Ray Quinter and Francis Welker. The cart served as a supply carrier to gandy dancers and the section crew, who were responsible for fixing damaged rails.

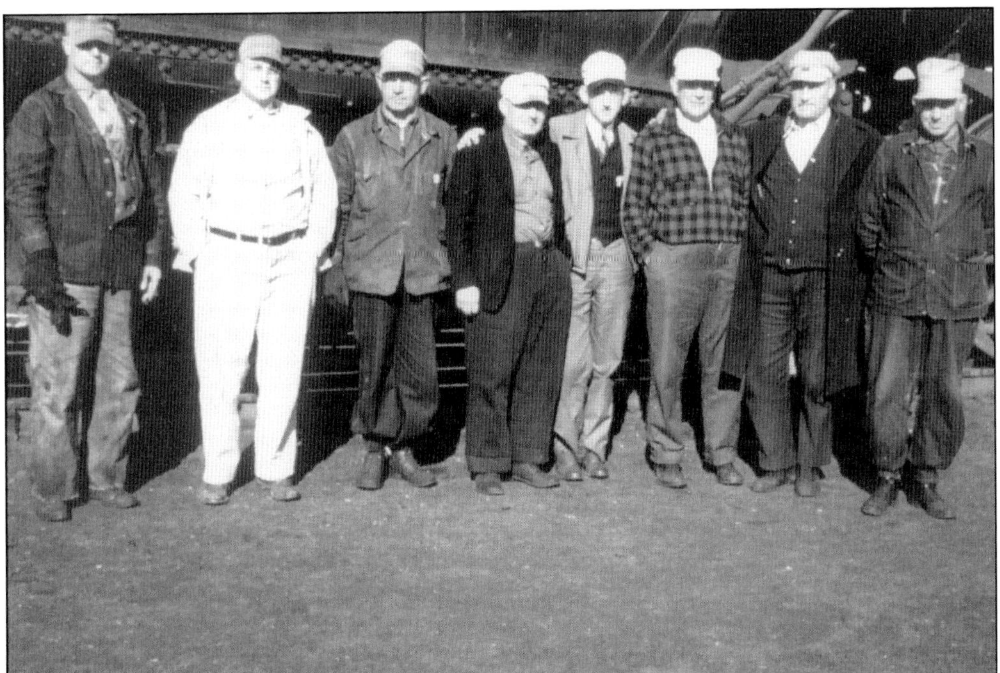

This 1942 image shows a group of Lehigh Valley workers. They are, from left to right, Ken Kruger, Percy Haskins, Henry Surniford, Bill McLane, Arthur Doody, Bill Segbers, Asa Baker, and Pat Tierney.

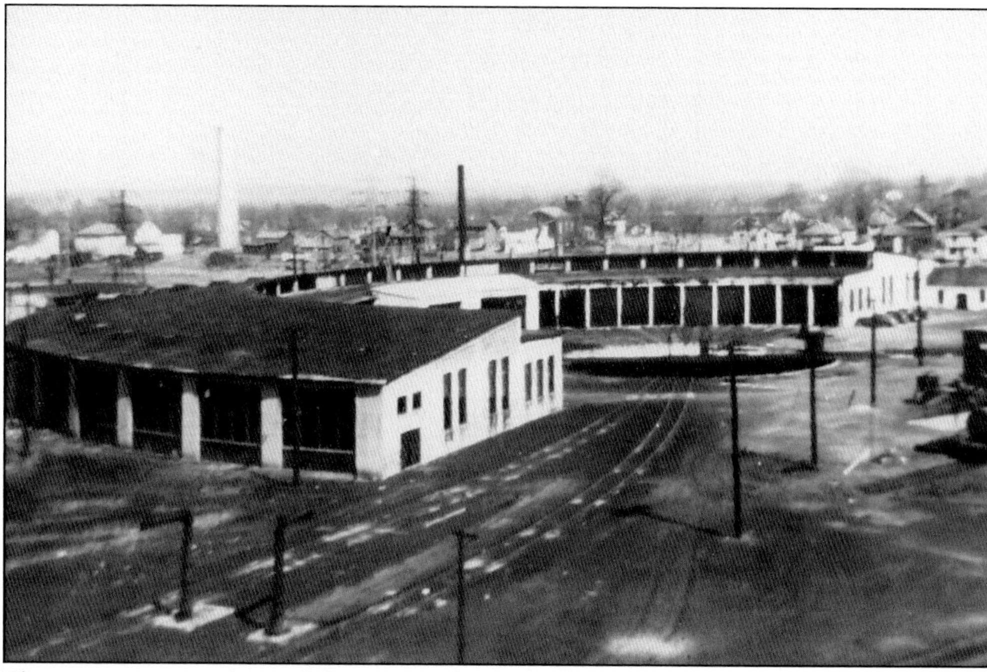

This western view of Manchester's roundhouse during the 1940s captures its commanding presence in the town. The roundhouse stored and repaired locomotives. It operated with the help of the turntable, which is shown in the middle of the roundhouse.

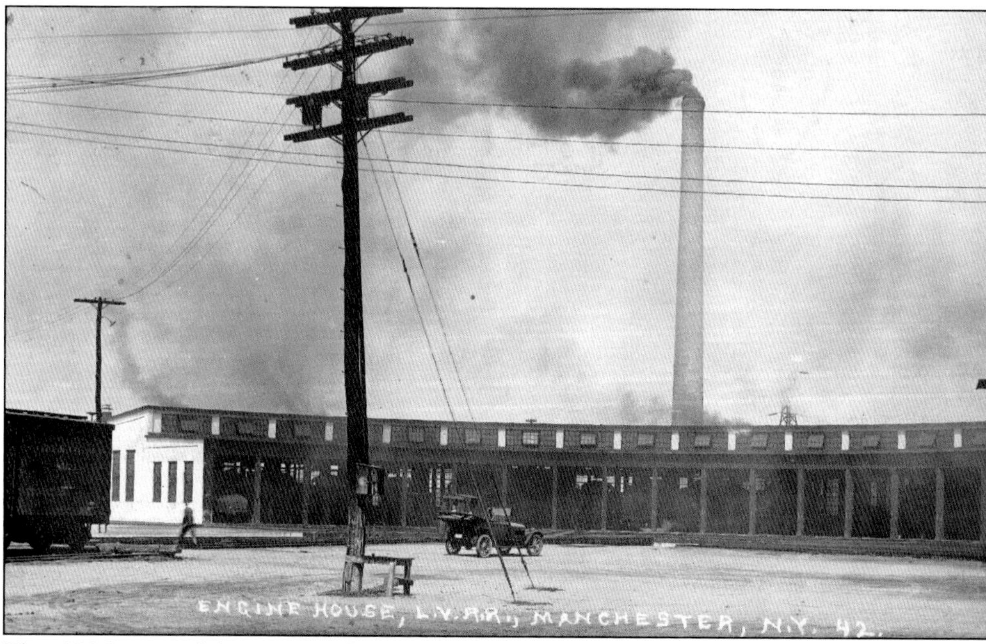

This 1916 state-of-the-art roundhouse was built with fireproof features in order to prevent the building from being destroyed the same way previous roundhouses had. It contained 35 accessible bays and a machine shop. The constant circulation of coal dust made hanging sheets a challenge for neighboring women, who had to be aware of westerly winds. This photograph was taken in 1923.

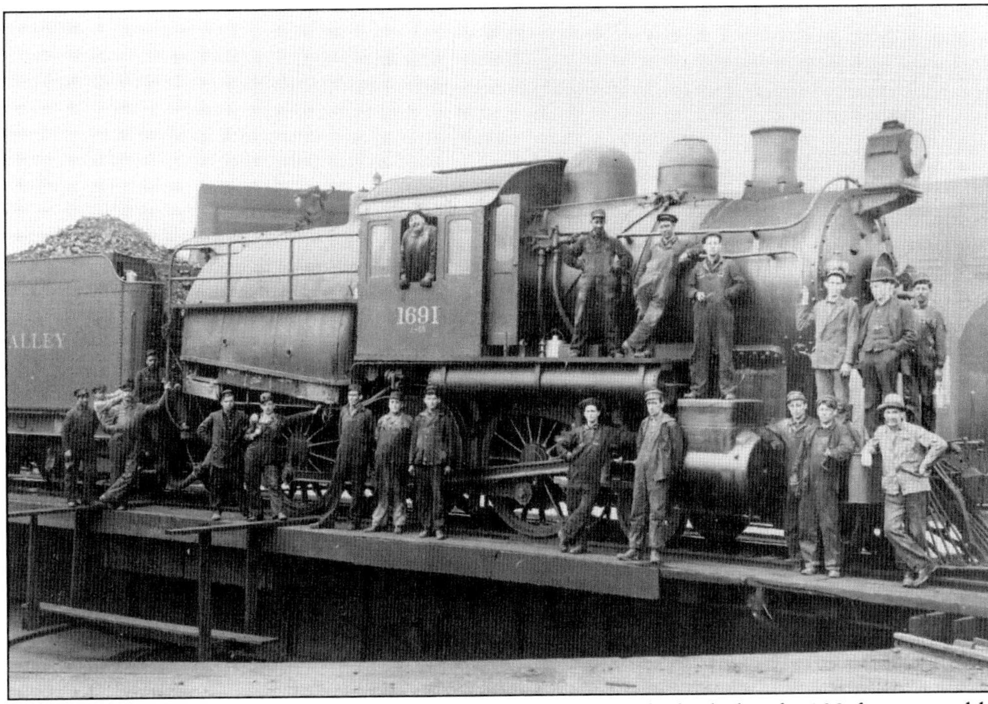

Locomotive 1691 is shown here being rerouted to Buffalo with the help of a 100-foot turntable and Manchester's roundhouse crew.

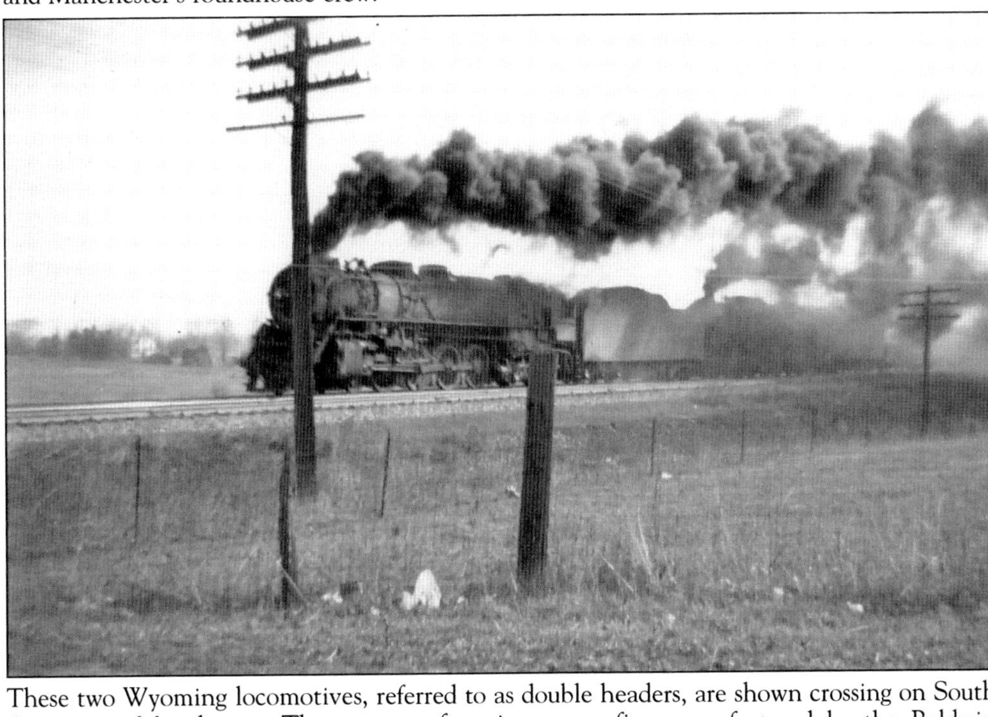

These two Wyoming locomotives, referred to as double headers, are shown crossing on South Avenue in Manchester. These types of engines were first manufactured by the Baldwin Company in 1862, the last of which were fabricated by the Alco Company in 1943. During this time, they were superseded by the growing demand for war tanks.

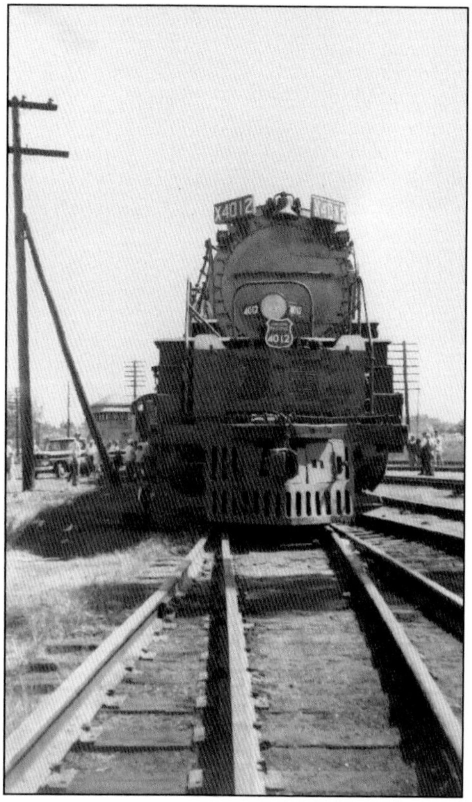

While passing through Manchester's yard in the 1964, this train's tender was derailed. Such an incident not only caused the train to be laid over for a week, but it also attracted an inquisitive audience. The train weighed more than 600 tons and was capable of achieving tractive power, which meant it could pull 111,600 pounds. It could carry 28 tons of coal and 28,000 gallons of water. The train was given the name "Big Boy."

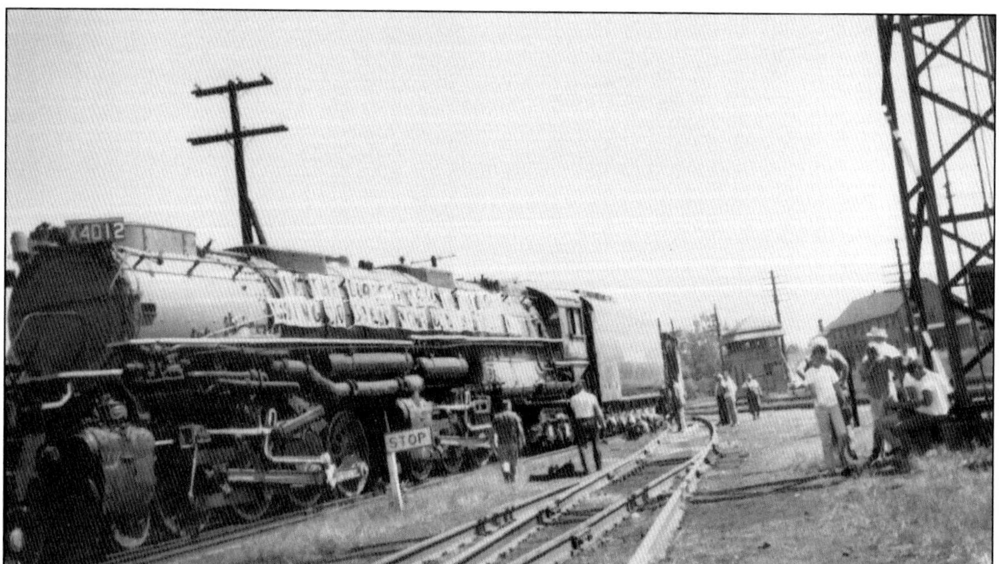

Such a view almost puts the 132-foot-long "Big Boy" into perspective. "Big Boy" is now on display in Steam Town USA, a national railroad museum located in Scranton, Pennsylvania. It is one of three trains to remain a relic of its time.

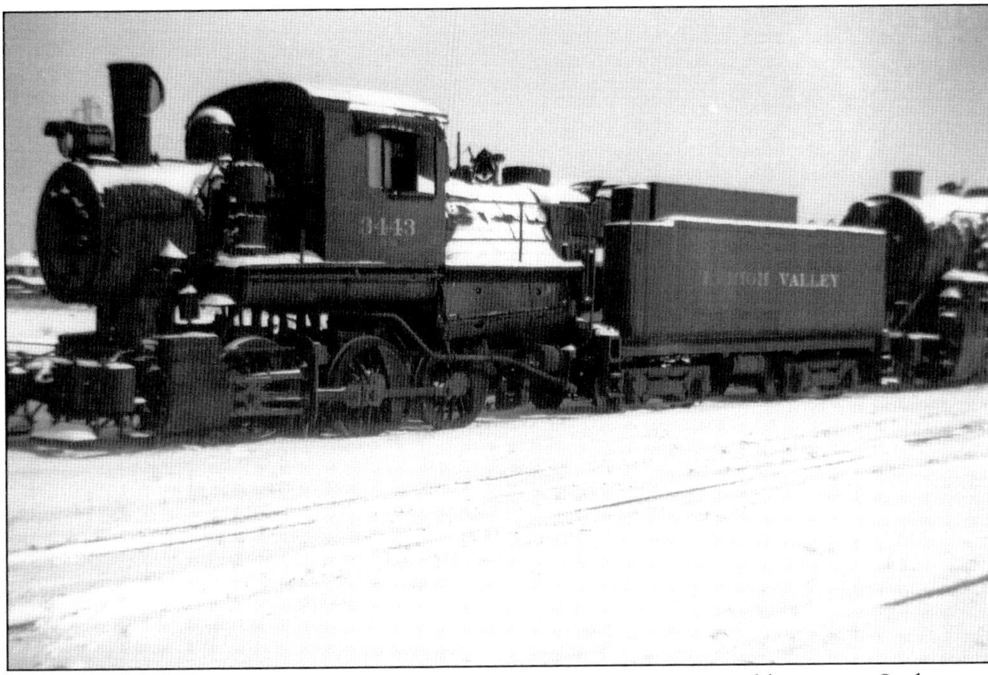

Snow-covered trains, like this Manchester steam locomotive, were seldom seen. Such trains were called "dead heads" and were taken to Buffalo for their final demise.

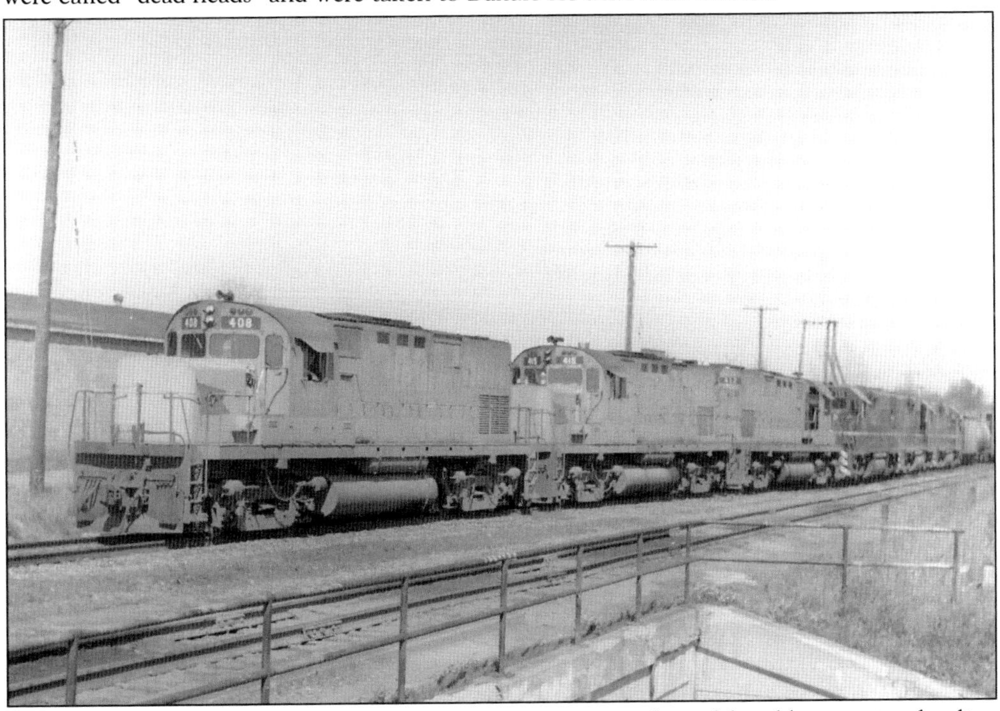

Passing over Manchester's underpass in the late 1960s is a tandem of diesel locomotives hauling freight. The underpass was constructed in the 1930s to separate car travel from heavy train traffic. Today, it is uncommon to see more than two trains passing over the underpass. Plans to remove the underpass have been scheduled to take place in 2002.

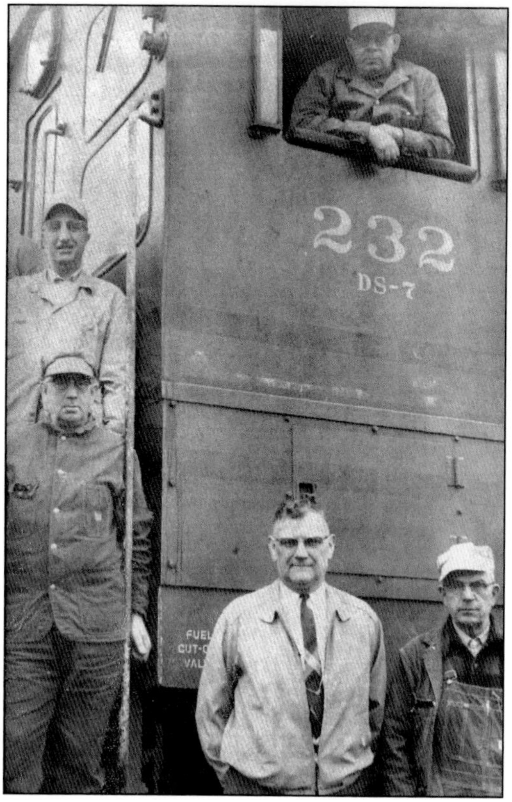

This April 30, 1964 picture captures a variety of railroad workers. Inside the cab is Charles Durrant, a 47-year engineer. At the top left is Jacob Hessney, a fireman for 21 years, and below him is Fay McCloud, who was a trainman for 39 years. On the bottom are Jack Quinter (left), who was a yardmaster for 42 years, and David Robinson, who was a conductor for 48 years.

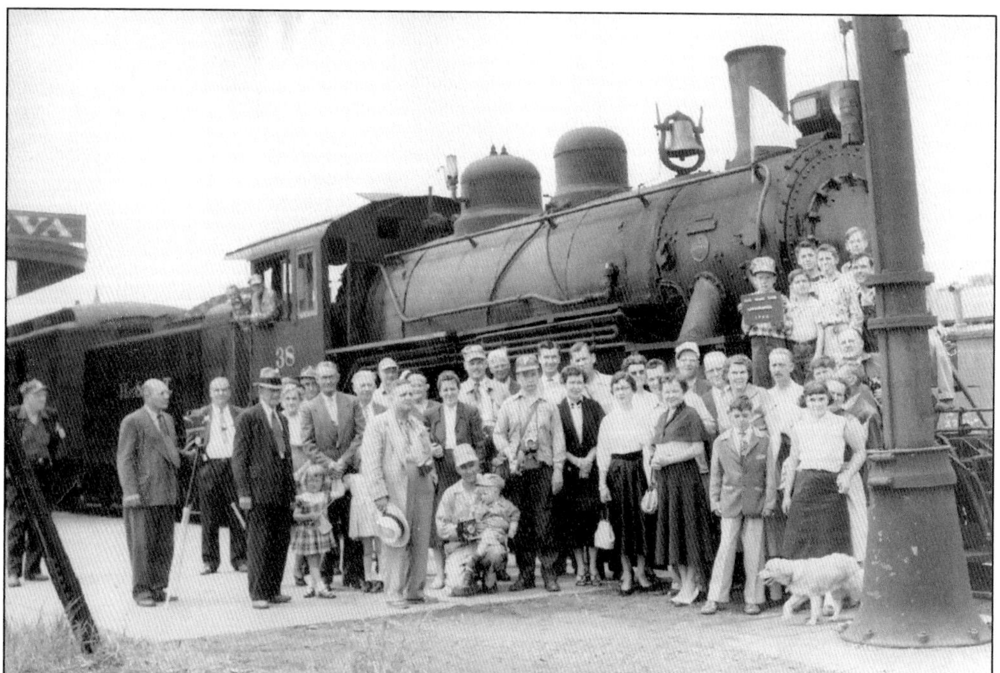

Surrounding civilians pay homage to the last steam locomotive to depart from the Geneva station in 1954. The last commercially produced steam locomotive was built in 1949.

Three

WATER NAVIGATION

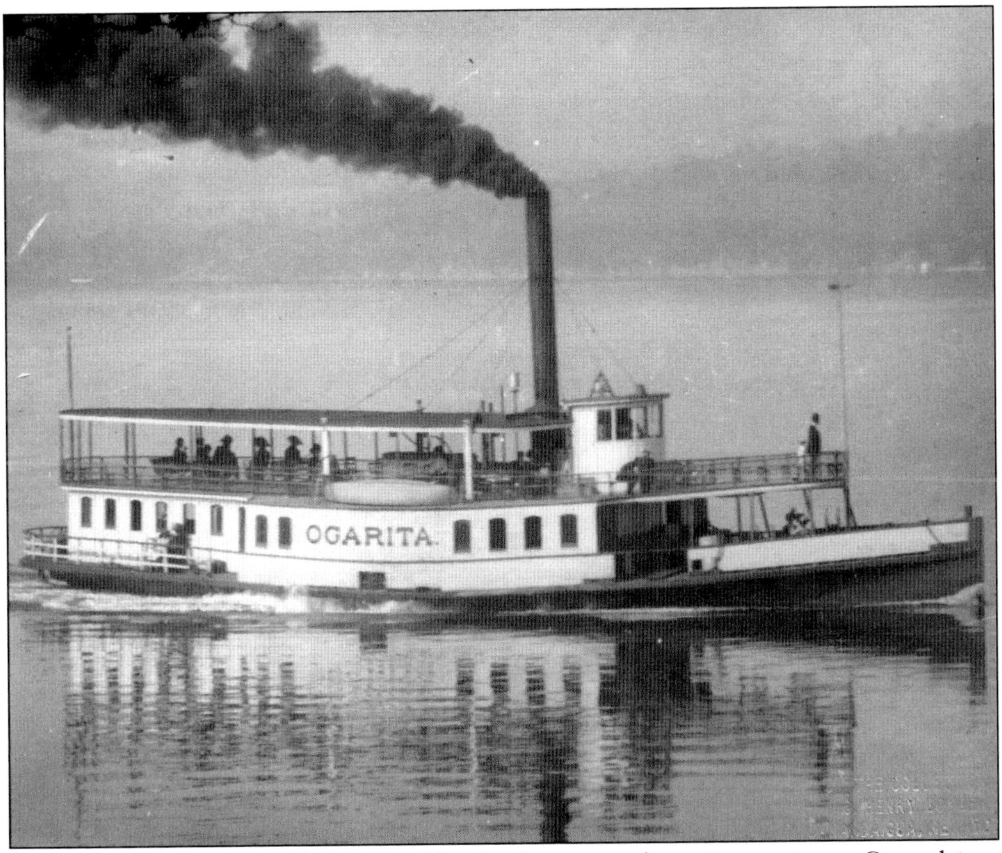

The *Ogarita*, which was the last steam side-wheeler to provide routine service on Canandaigua Lake, is shown here chugging its way through such waters. The Smith Concert Band, which was Manchester's official military band, was sometimes featured on the *Ogarita* during moonlight excursions. The steamboat era in the Finger Lakes began c. 1828 and almost came to complete expiration at the start of World War I.

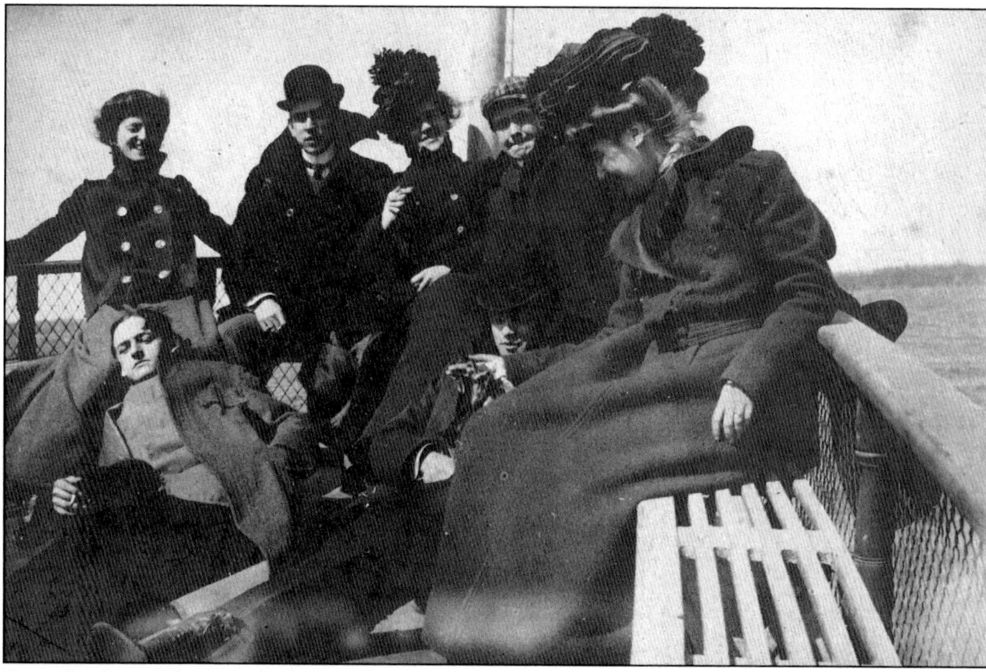

On a brisk, windy day, these people enjoy a ride abroad the *Ogarita*. The *Ogarita* could carry 300 passengers and 30 tons of freight. This picture was taken on April 24, 1901, on the bow of the boat.

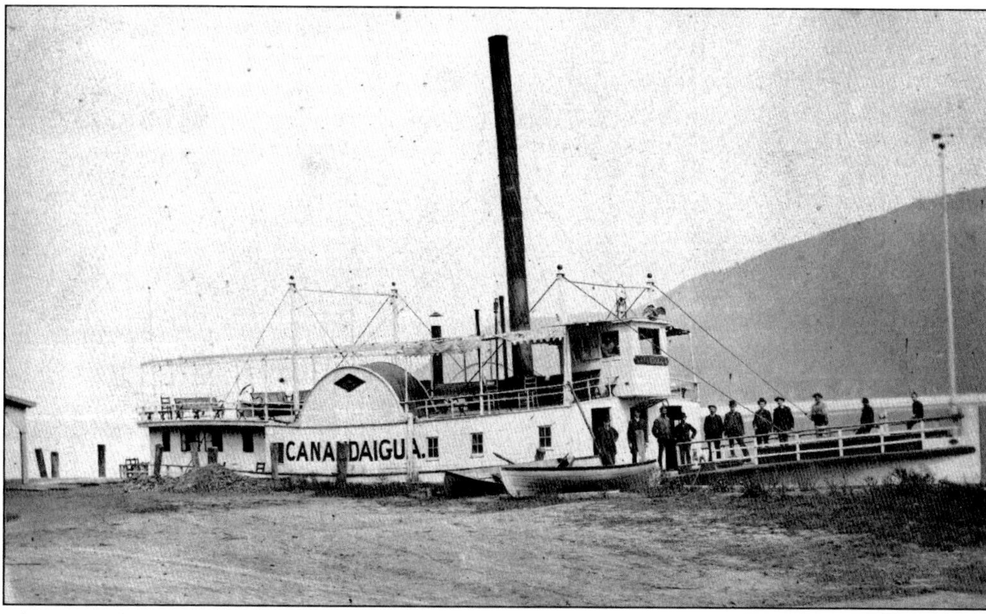

The steamboat era was stimulated after the appearance of the McKechnie brothers in 1867. Although beer brewers, the brothers furthered their ambitions to the water with their 110-foot-long, coal-burning side-wheeler named *Canandaigua*. Such a debut prompted competition with the wood-burning steamer *Ontario*, which was operated by Henry and Sales Standish of Naples. It has been said the two vied for the waters of Canandaigua Lake, as they were known to race to a passenger, or even to a load of grapes.

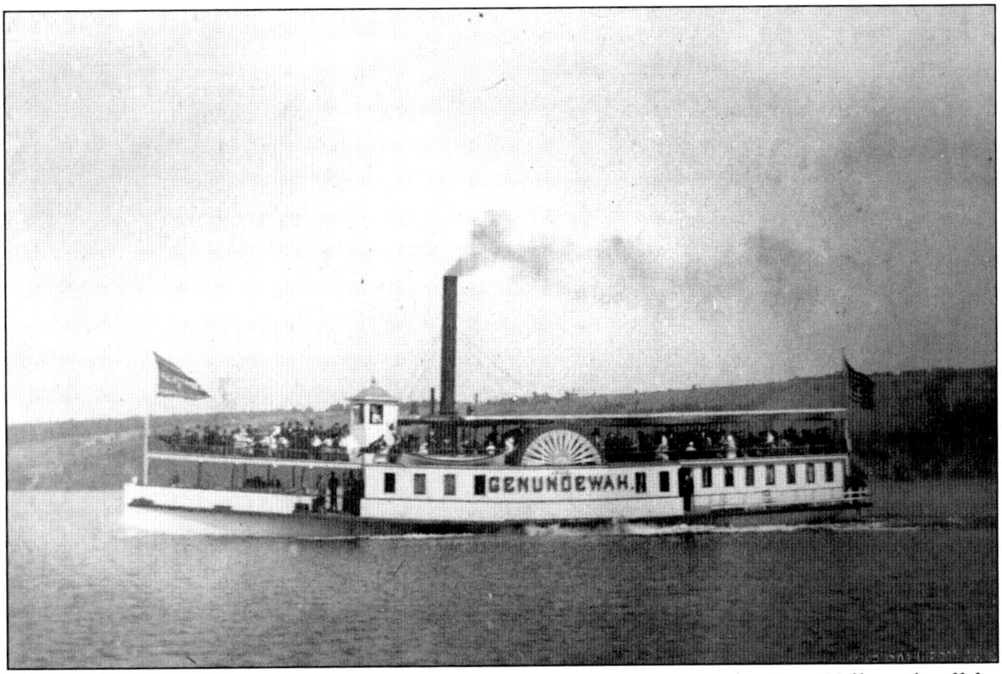

The *Genundewah*, which was named after the Seneca Indian name for Bare Hill, took off for the first time on May 5, 1889. It was regarded as one of the most beautiful boats and earned the nickname "Gee Whiz." It burned at the Woodville dock on December 8, 1894.

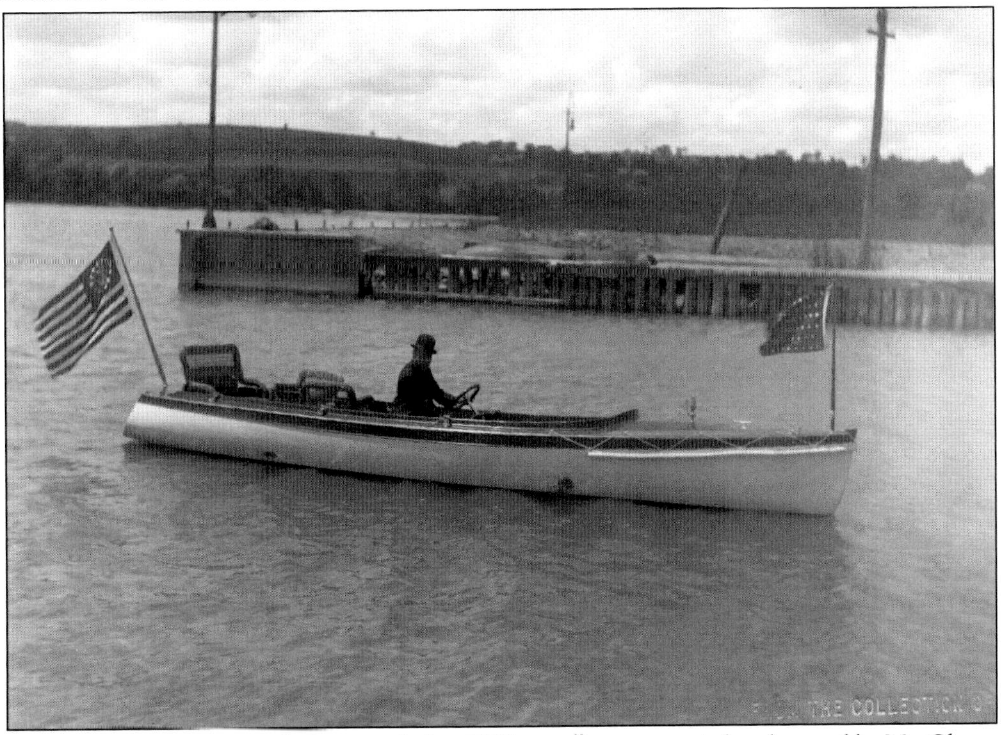
Known for its comparatively fast speed, this 1910 speedboat, occupied and owned by Mr. Clyne, passes by unpretentiously on Canandaigua Lake.

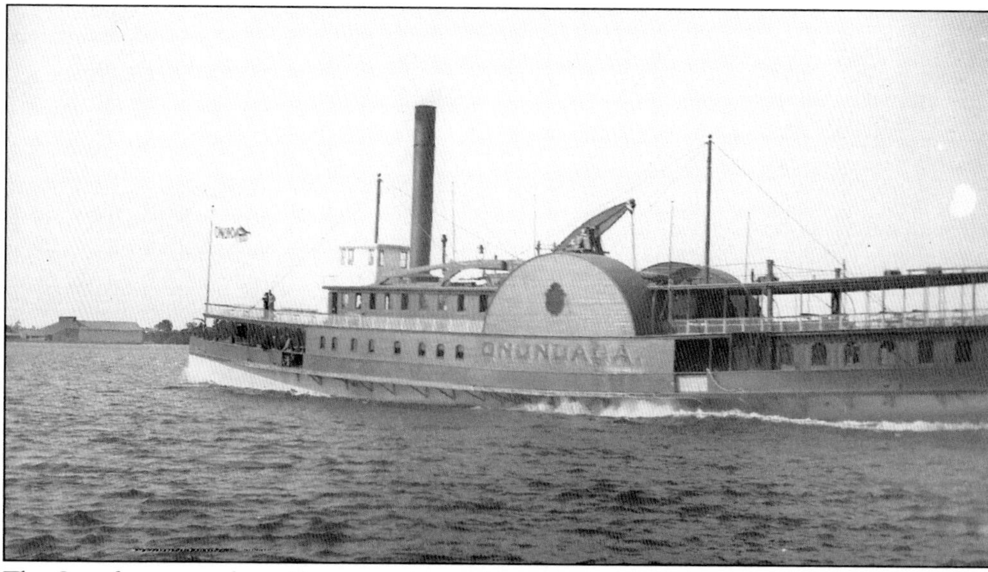

The *Onondaga* was a ship of beauty and one of notoriety as well. On May 21, 1898, the Joshua Simpkins Opera Traveling Company arrived in Geneva with its theatrical talent and a rumored case of smallpox. Because the atrocious epidemic was a great threat to everyone, the *Onondaga* was covertly quarantined from May 25 to June 24. During this time, conspirators planned to demolish the apparently infested ship and fabricated a credulous story to avoid panic. They had decided to claim that the ship's demise would be a reenactment, and thus a tribute, to the American battleship *Maine* that was destroyed in the harbor of Havana, Cuba, during a conflict between the Cubans and Spaniards. The ship blew to pieces on September 14, 1898.

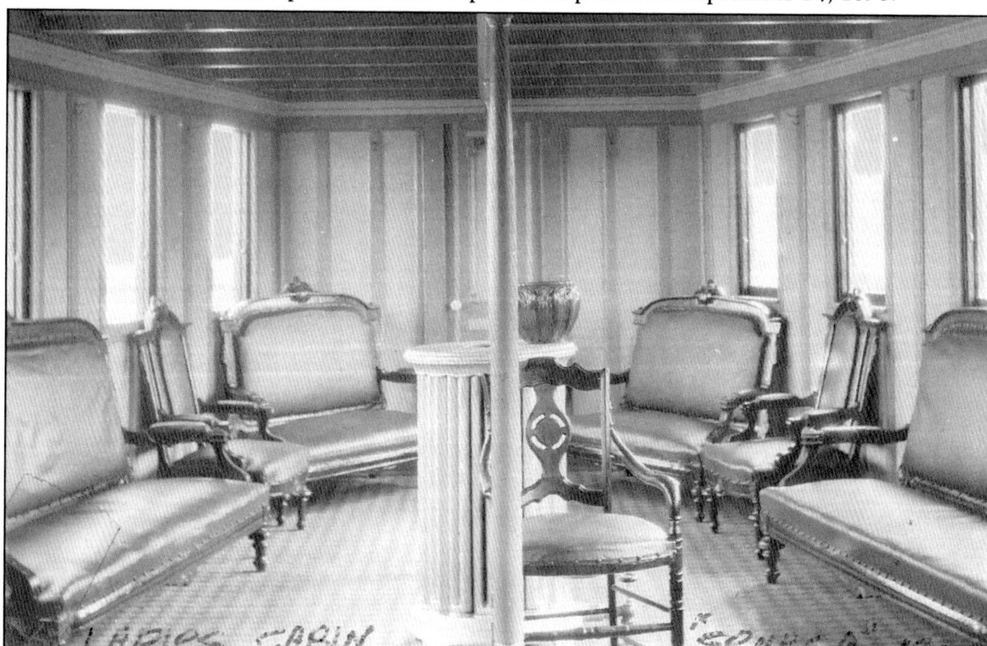

This 1906 photograph gives an inside perspective of the women's cabin in the *Seneca*. Women would come here to take refuge from the large whitecaps and to divide the time spent outside and inside during the four-hour trip from Geneva to Watkins Glen.

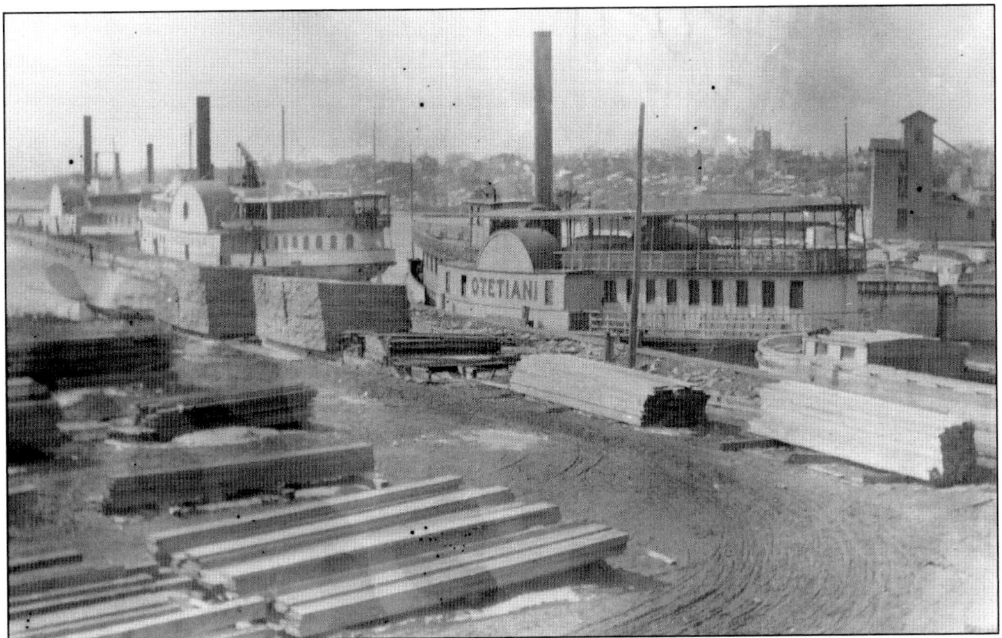

Shown here is a legion of steamboats moored to the pier of Geneva. Among them are the infamous *Onondaga* and the *Otetiani*. Both boats, along with other similarly sized steamboats, were capable of towing up to 38 canal boats.

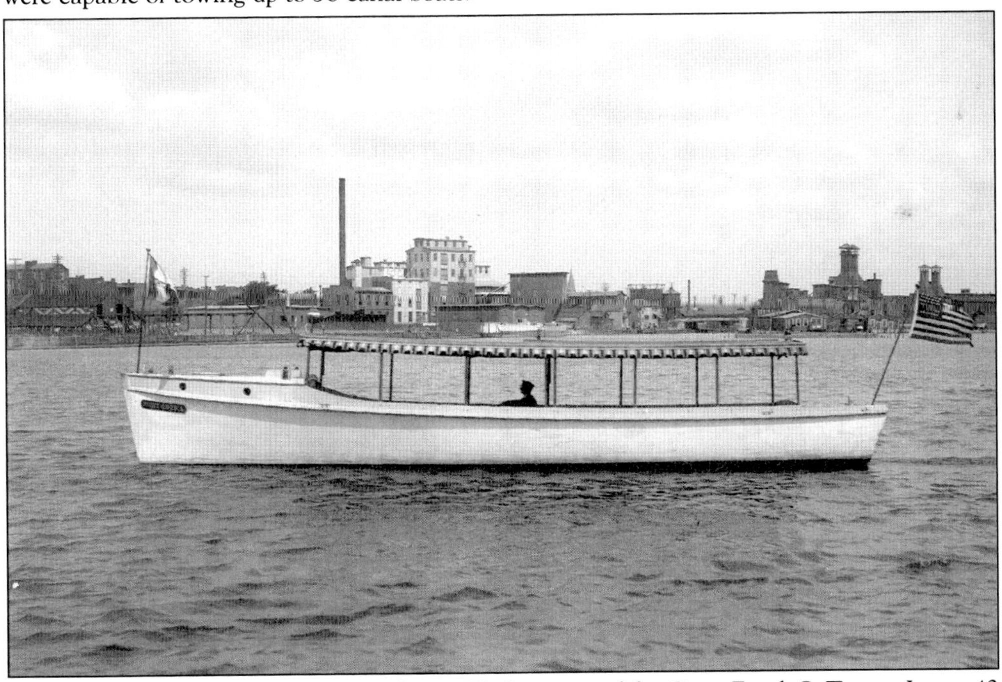

The *Portadora* was built in 1909 by Alonzo W. Springstead for Capt. Frank S. Tower. It was 43 feet long, had a capacity of 40 people, and was powered by a 30-horsepower gasoline Faybowen engine. It was the first gasoline-powered boat to run a regular schedule on Seneca Lake. In 1929, it was sold to New Yorkers for bootlegging alcohol. Soon after, the *Portadora* was seized and destroyed by federal revenue officers.

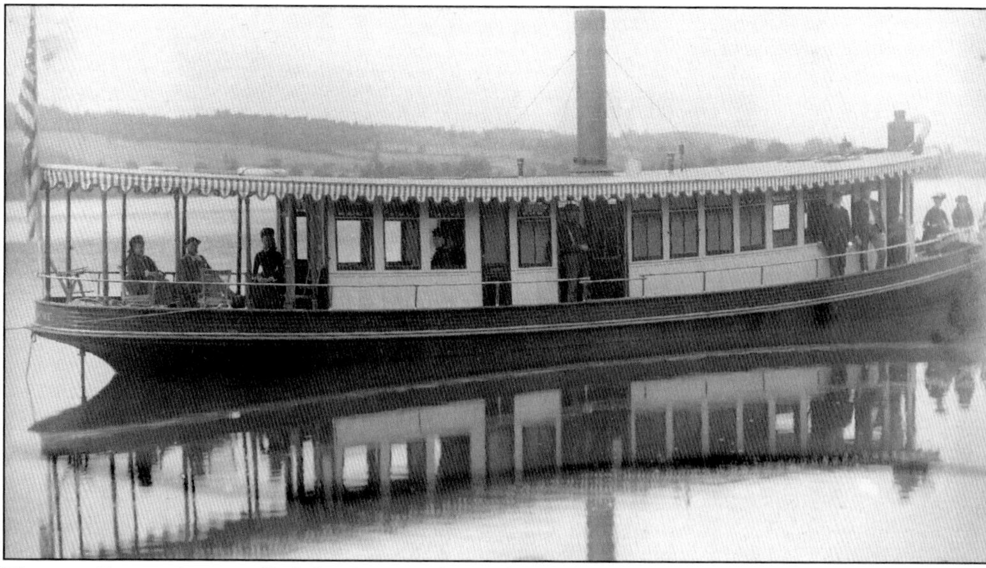

This small steamboat, called the *Scot*, is shown being beautifully replicated in the calm waters of Seneca Lake in the latter part of the 19th century.

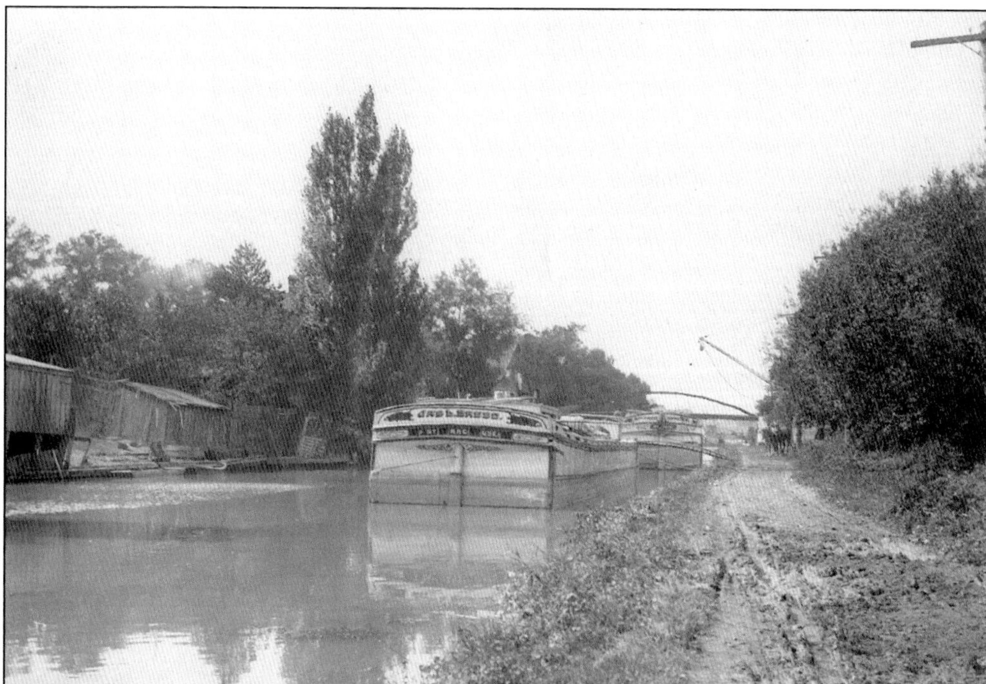

In 1819, the Seneca Lock Navigation Company made the Seneca-Cayuga canal operational. In 1823, the barge (similar to the one shown in this picture) was first introduced in Geneva. In 1830, the canal engendered so much prosperity that there was an influx of contentious canal drivers who would fight for favorable positions. At the end of 1830, the barge had carried a total of 214,000 bushels of wheat, 4,000 barrels of whisky and gin, and 30,000 barrels of flour.

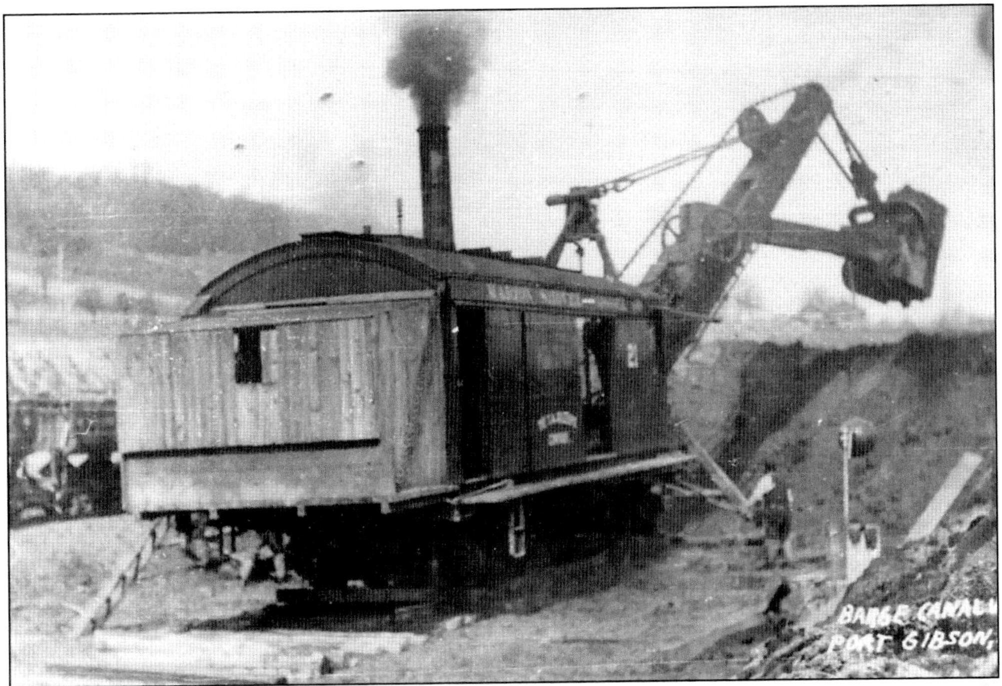

This 1905 photograph depicts a Marrion steam shovel digging the Barge Canal, the 34-mile route of which extended from Port Gibson to Rochester.

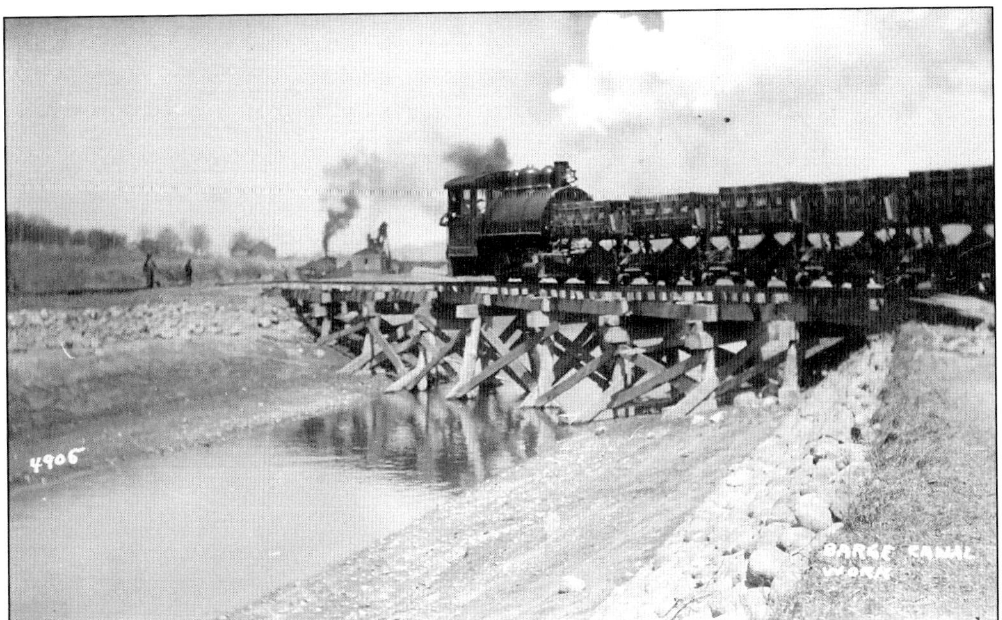

This 1905 view shows a portable short line transporting dirt derived from the building of the Barge Canal. The short line was implemented only for this purpose. The Barge Canal system was formed in 1918.

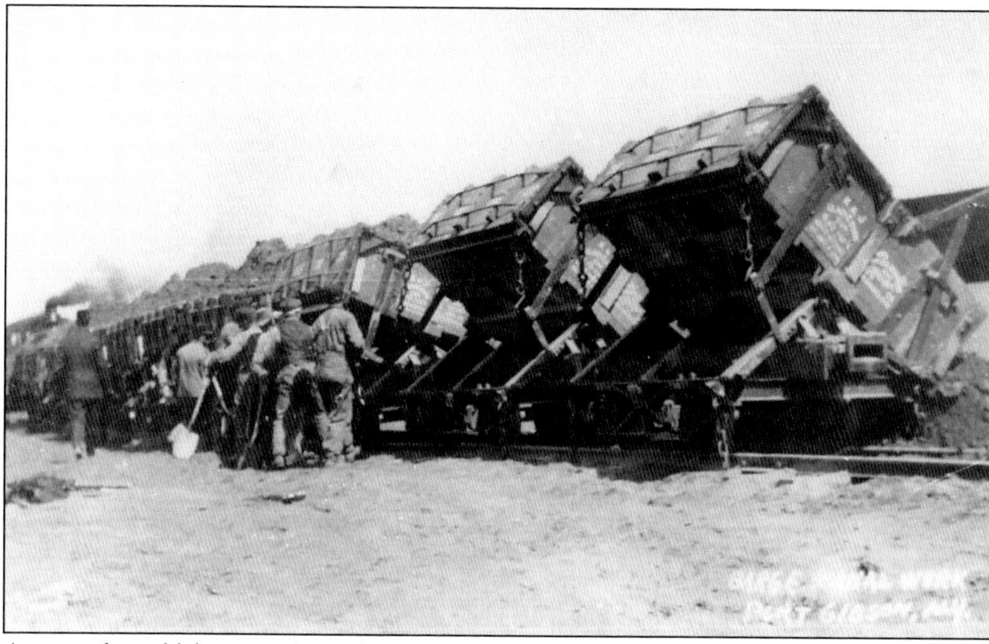

A team of canal laborers is shown here lifting a dirt-filled dump car. Today, the very mounds of dirt that were deposited by the workers in this photograph can be seen in Port Gibson.

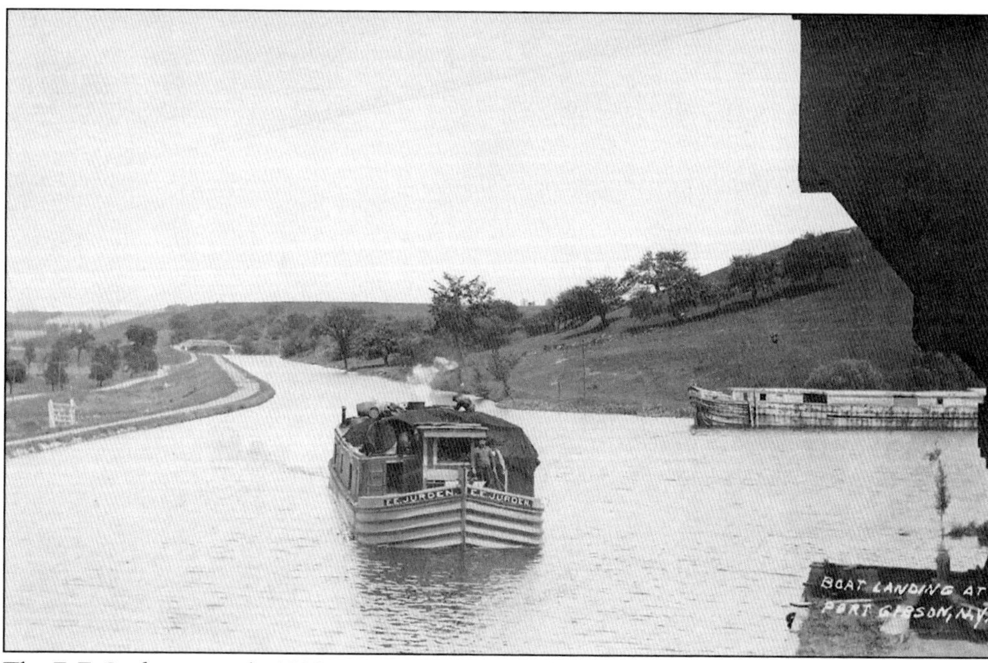

The *E.E. Jurden*, an early-1890s steam engine powerboat, cruises down the Erie in Port Gibson. The water level is almost flush with the land because the lock was closed.

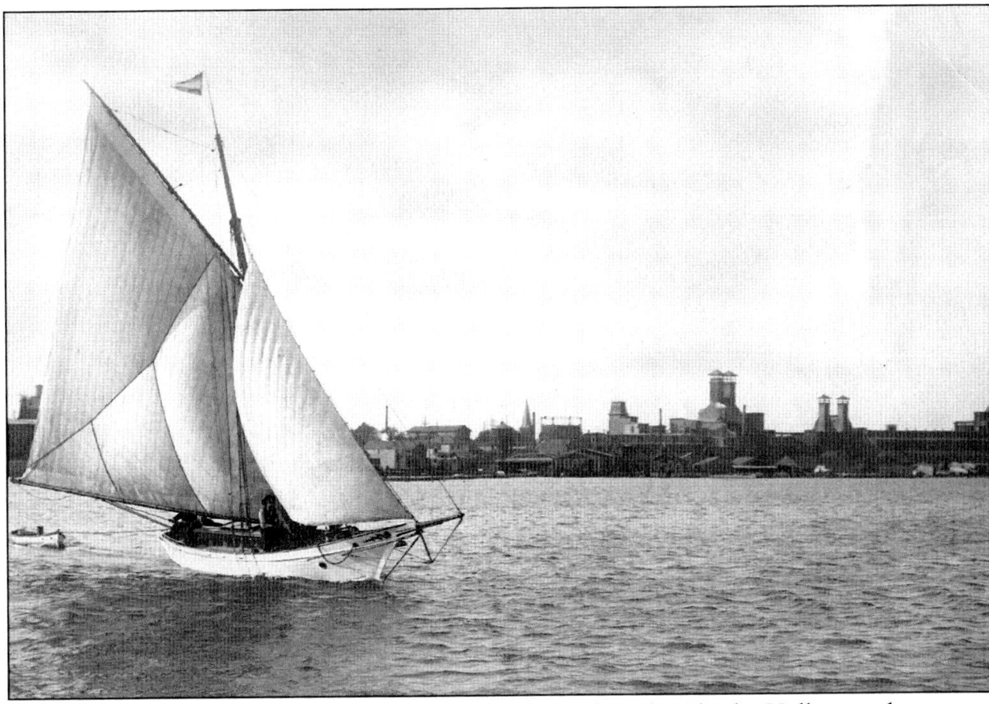

The 1908 sailboat *Petrel*, which was brought over from Ithaca by Charles Hall, is catching a gust of wind on the Geneva harbor. Note the towering malt houses in the background.

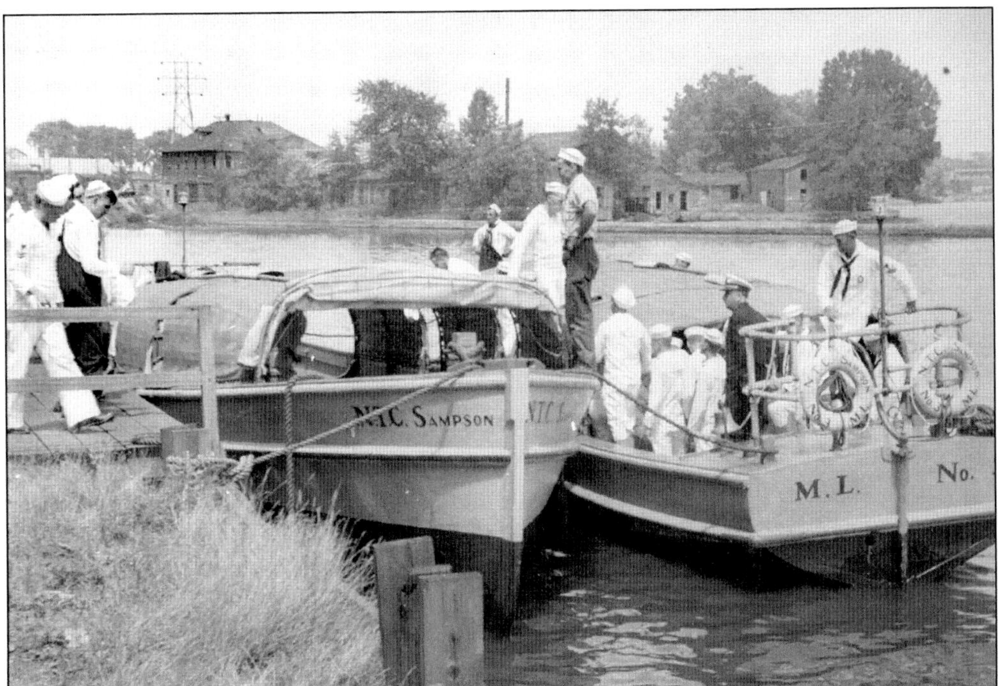

In this 1943 photograph, World War II naval recruits return from Sampson naval base. The recruits anticipated their revelry on the way to Geneva, or as some called it, "Liberty Town."

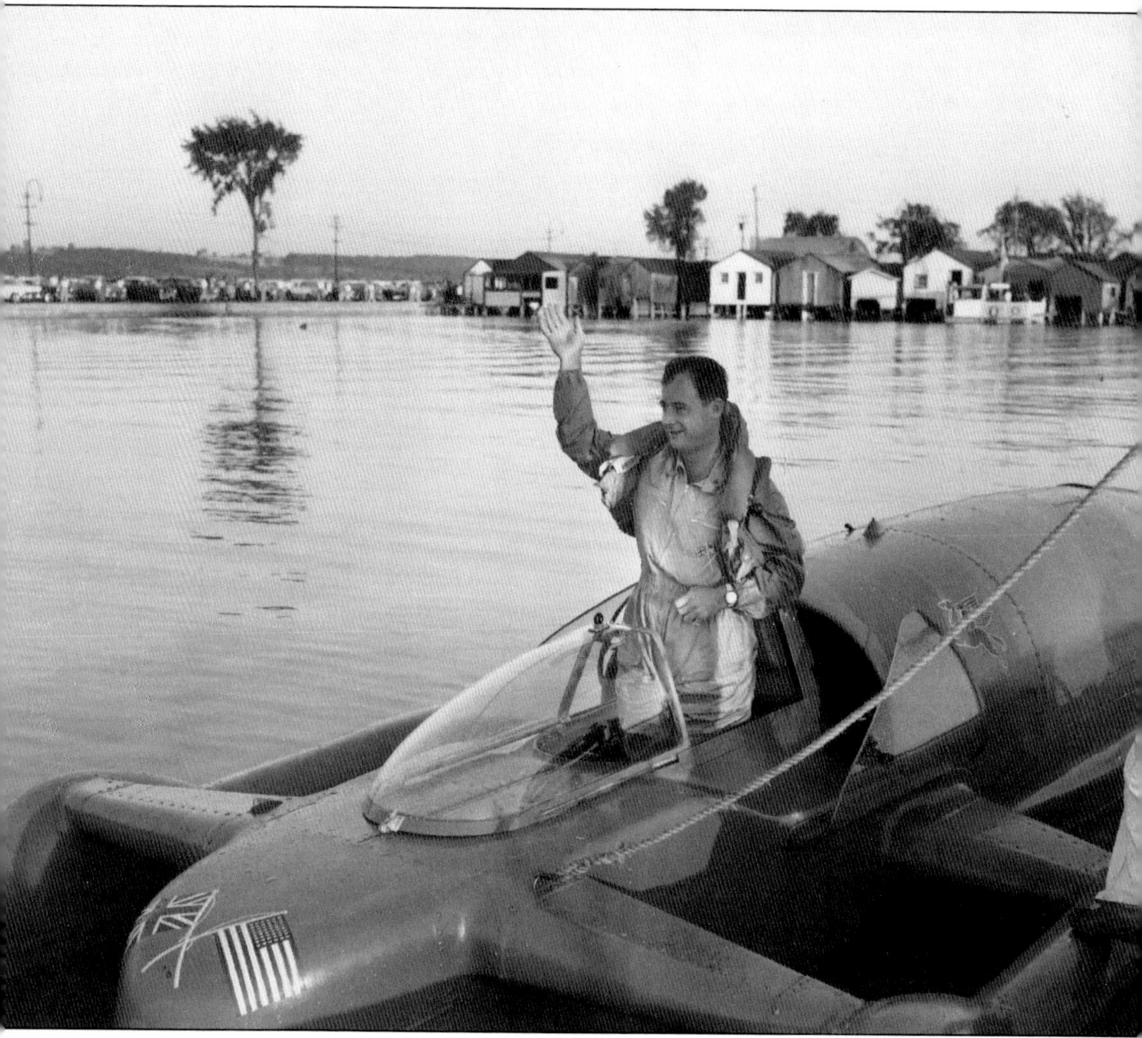

Donald Campbell waves to a Canandaigua audience before attempting to surpass his previous world record of 225.63 mph for the mile distance in 1957. Some 34 years later on March 9, 2001, Donald Campbell's boat and remains were excavated from the depths of the Coniston Waters in England. Speculation suggests that Donald was attempting a similar record to the one in Canandaigua.

Four

Trolleys

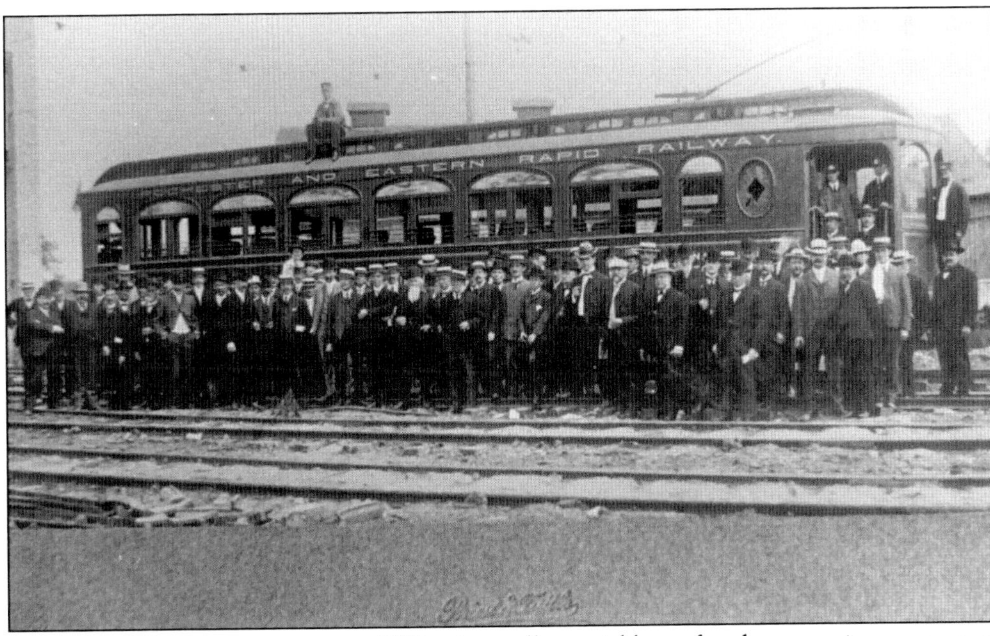

With the fall of its ancestors *c.* 1883, the trolley quickly surfaced as a unique means of transportation. No longer was it commonplace to see the cabriolet, the omnibus, and the mail coach as the predominant form of travel. Rather, the incipient trolley could be seen roaring down the road claiming its new supremacy. With the genius of Frank J. Sprague, a colleague of Thomas Edison, multiple-unit control was possible. This major development earned him the title of "the Father of Electric Traction." In 1900 and 1901, the Rochester & Eastern Rapid Railway was organized and chartered. From 1902 to June 1904, 43 miles of track that extended from Rochester to Geneva was laid down. In this 1904 view, employees stand in front of an early trolley.

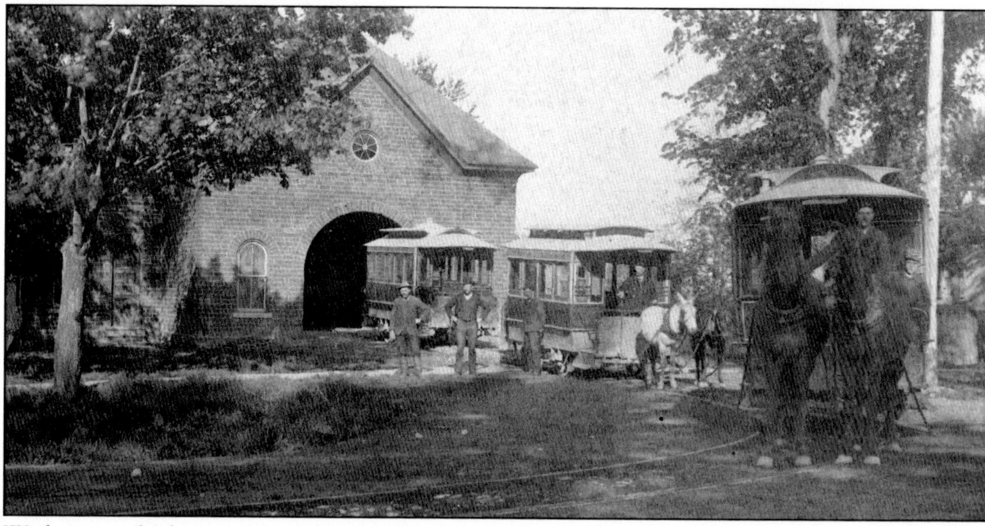

With its gradual expiration, the omnibus was slowly replaced by horse railways, which added not only comfort to the ride but speed as well. Its engaging features and unprecedented luxuries—including solid-bronze brake handles, perforated wood seats, and coal stove heaters—won the preference of the people. Its increasing popularity allowed for the 500-horse car railway lines that extended in about 300 cities around the United States. The horses were expected to work four- to five-hour days, at an average of between 12 and 15 miles, and consume 30 pounds of food, which often yielded large quantities of manure. Although profitable, the manure became a dreadful nuisance. In July 1887, the Canandaigua Street Railroad Company constructed its trolley barn at 404 North Main Street.

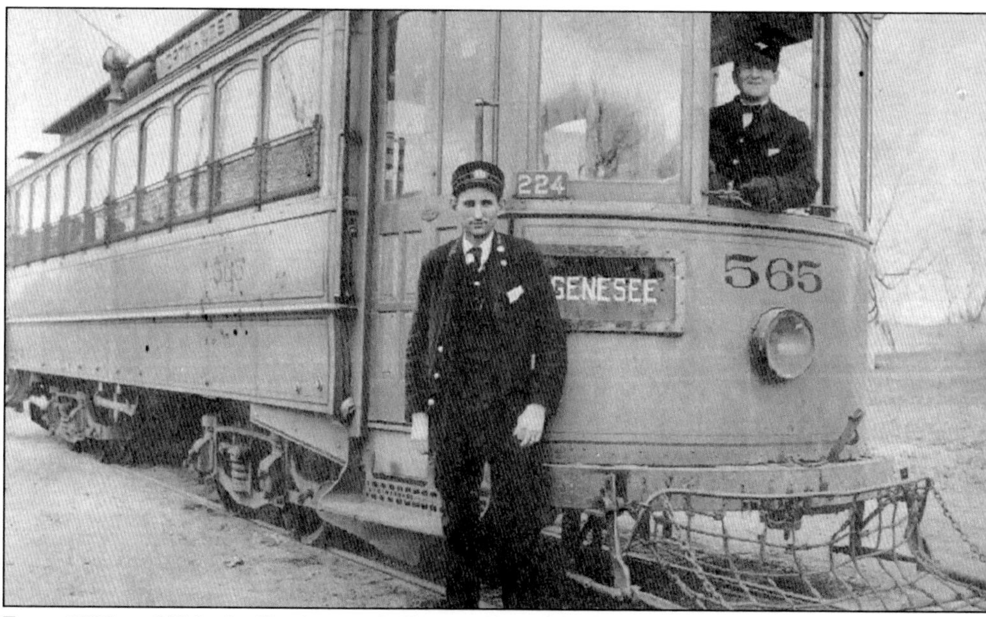

From 1903 to 1930, the Rochester & Eastern Rapid Railway offered electric trolley service to Ontario County as a unique form of transportation. Unlike passenger trains, they provided the passengers with an opportunity to view the passing scenery through the considerably larger windows. In this 1906 photograph, conductor John M. O'Burke stands before car 565 while motorman Jim Blane poses in the window above.

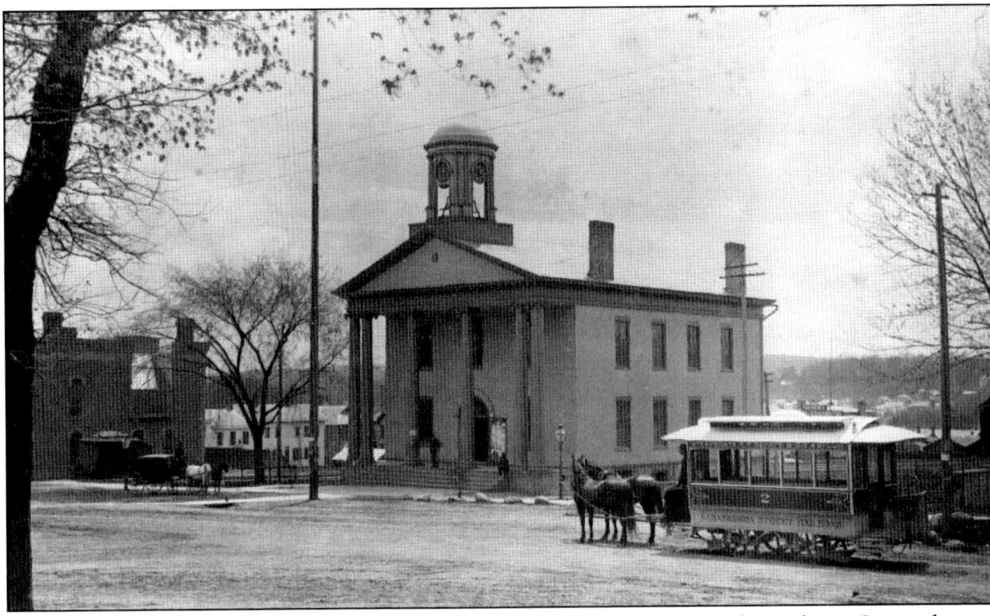

From 1887 to 1893, horse-drawn trolleys were a common appearance throughout Canandaigua. They were capable of reaching speeds of up to 5 mph, and drivers would receive $1 a day. Seen here at the top of the hill, a horse-drawn trolley passes by the town hall en route to the lake. In similar situations, trolley companies would place the horses on the rear platform for the return trip downhill, which conserved the horses' energy.

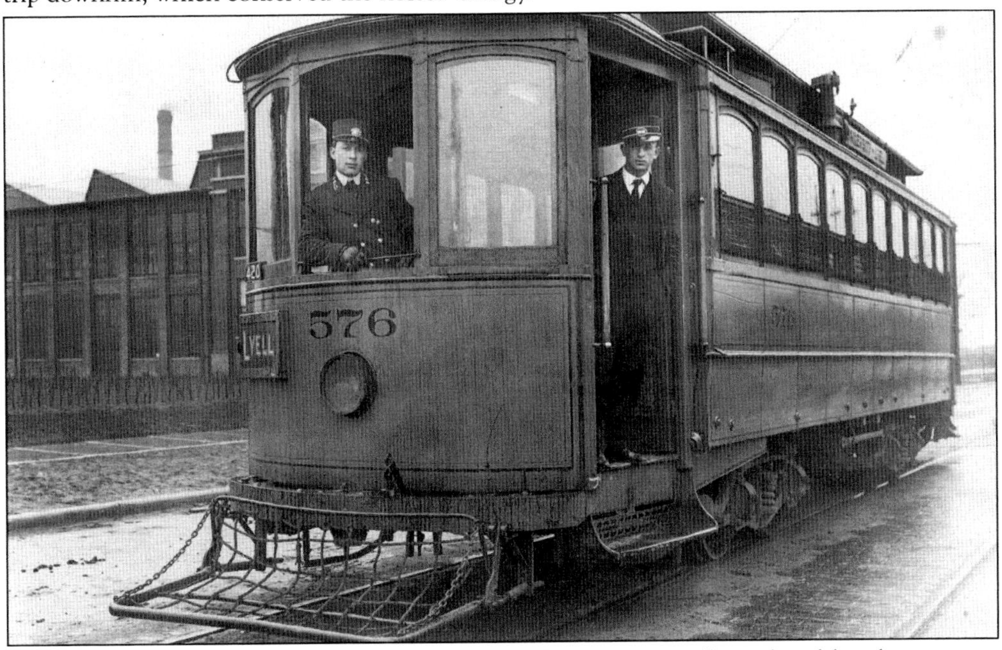

By October 5, 1893, horse cars were removed and were eventually replaced by electric cars. Seven years later, A.L. Parker, a former resident of Naples, announced his plans of constructing a 43-mile interurban trolley line from Rochester to Geneva. It would later be known as the Rochester & Eastern Rapid Railway. This 1910 photograph of a trolley, whose route ran on Lyell Avenue, was taken by the Clark family of Phelps.

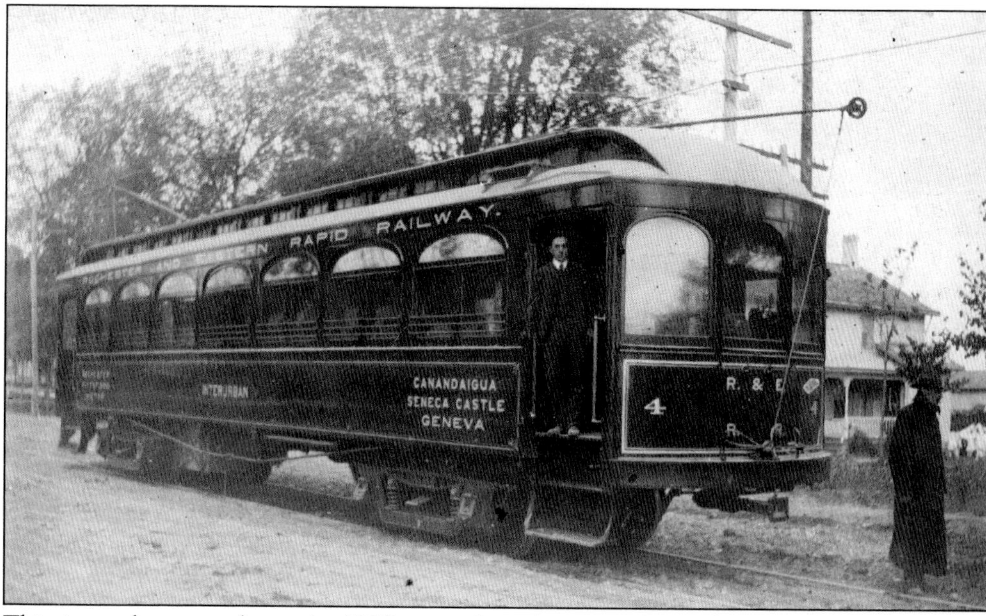

This interurban car, shown in 1910 somewhere between Canandaigua and Seneca Castle, stopped at the following communities: Canandaigua, Seneca Castle, Geneva, Mendon, Victor, and Bushnell's Basin. Although it was one of the smallest communities in Ontario County, Seneca Castle had a trolley station, which was located on Gates Road.

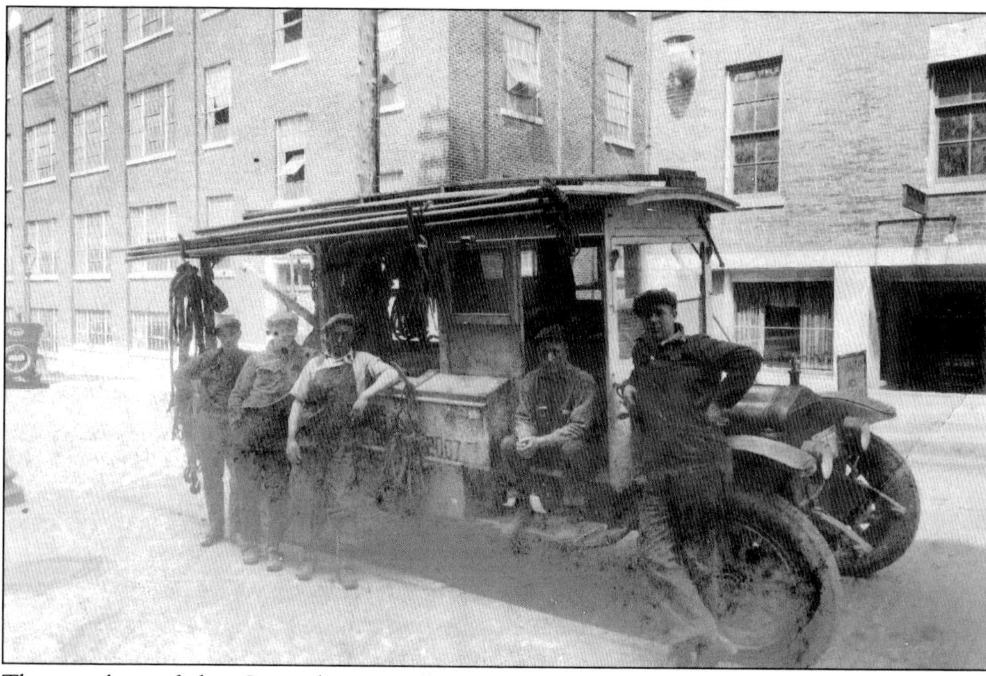

The members of this Canandaigua trolley maintenance crew are, from left to right, Fiere, Smalley, Arnold, Moore, and Ferguson. Known as linemen, the workers were responsible for jobs ranging from derailments to clearing trees that obstructed pathways. It was said that the crew dreaded the winter months, for they had to work feverishly to keep the rails ice-free. Their 15-hour workdays often led to 100-hour workweeks. This picture was taken on Chapin Street.

This October 21, 1924 photograph captures a rare glimpse of the Canandaigua powerhouse and E. Dobbins, the substation operator. The building housed two 1,000-pound Williams Vertical cross compound engines and two Westing house 380-volt alternators. This technology provided power for the Rochester & Eastern Rapid Railway.

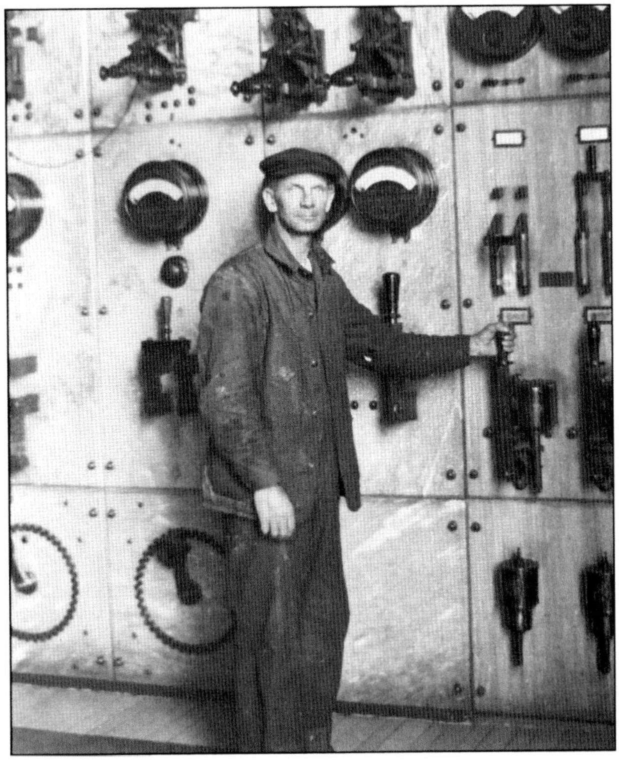

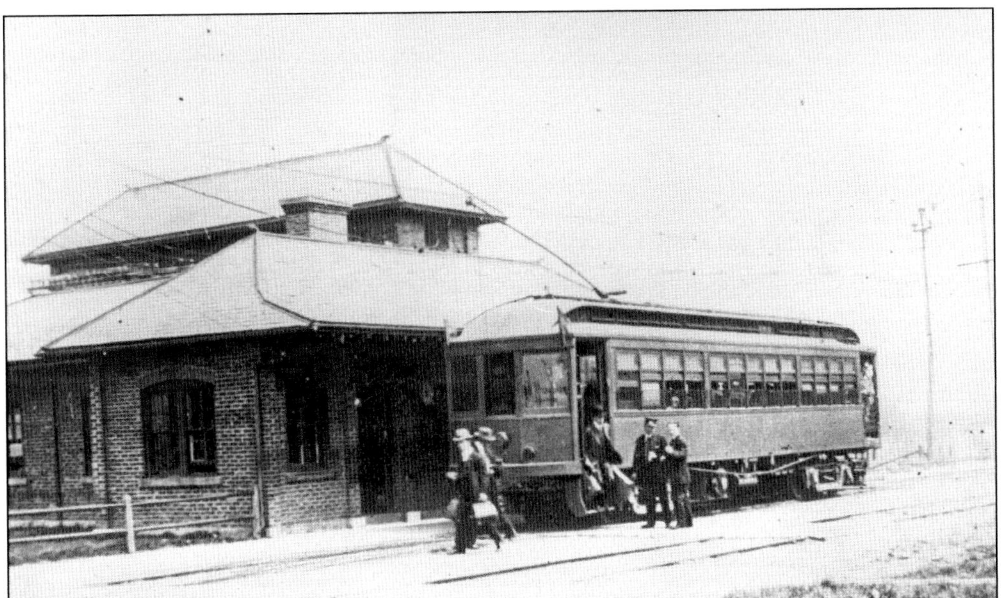

Shown in 1904, this Rochester & Eastern trolley station (on Maple Avenue in Victor) was the stop for the Orange Limited, a service that ran exclusively for Pittsford, Victor, and Canandaigua. It consisted of 16 orange colored trolleys. Each trolley was 52 feet long with mahogany interiors, water coolers, electric lights, heaters, and restrooms. Capable of reaching speeds of up to 60 mph, the trolleys were able to shuttle people more efficiently than the railroad, sometimes stopping 21 times a day.

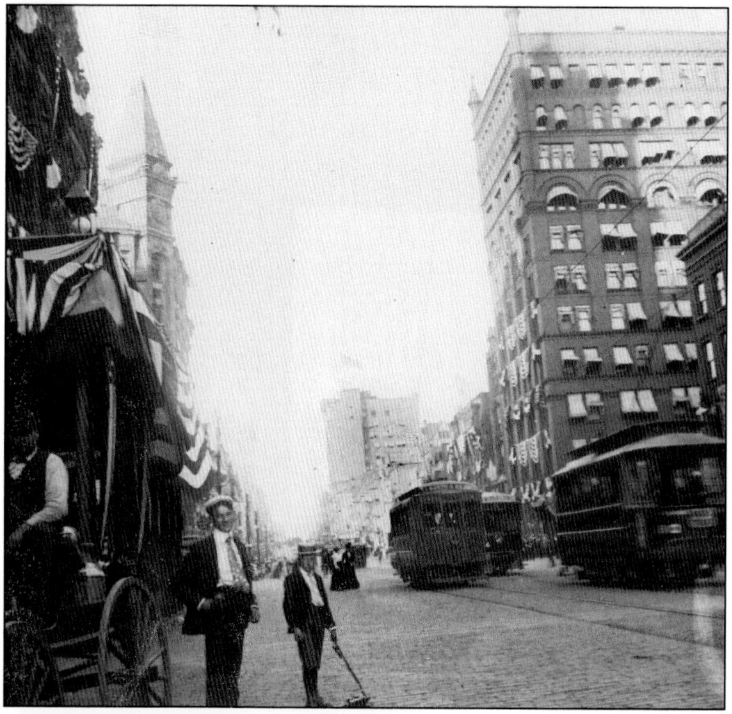

For some during the 1900s, the Fourth of July was a day of tradition and celebration. People would often use the Rochester trolleys to attend baseball games at Culver Field or enjoy a day in the sun at Charlotte Beach.

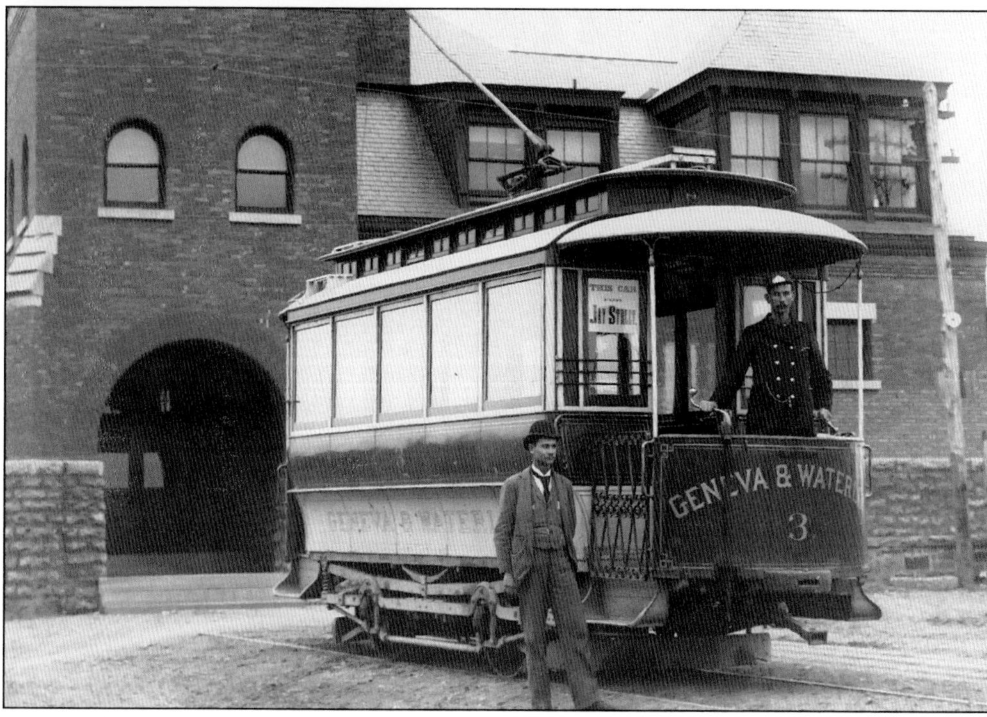

By the 1890s, Geneva had organized three trolley lines: the Geneva Surface Railway, the Geneva & Waterloo Railway, and the Waterloo, Seneca Falls, Cayuga Railway. On June 29, 1894, Geneva introduced electric trolley service. The trolley shown here was used to pick up travelers at the Lehigh depot on Sherrill Street and drop them off on Jay Street.

This photograph shows an early Geneva trolley passing by the North Presbyterian Church on Lewis Street, near the Genesee park bandstand. The North and First Presbyterian Churches merged in 1989. The present-day minister of the Presbyterian church is Rev. Jim Gerling. The Faith Community Church is now in this building.

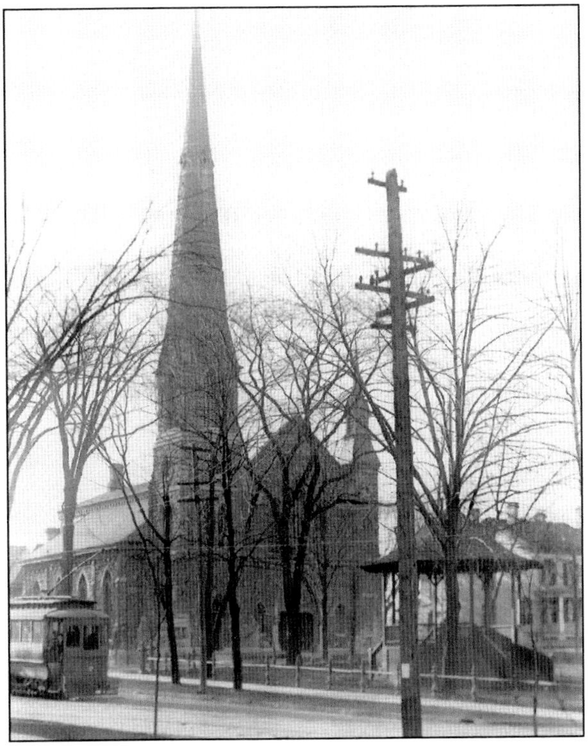

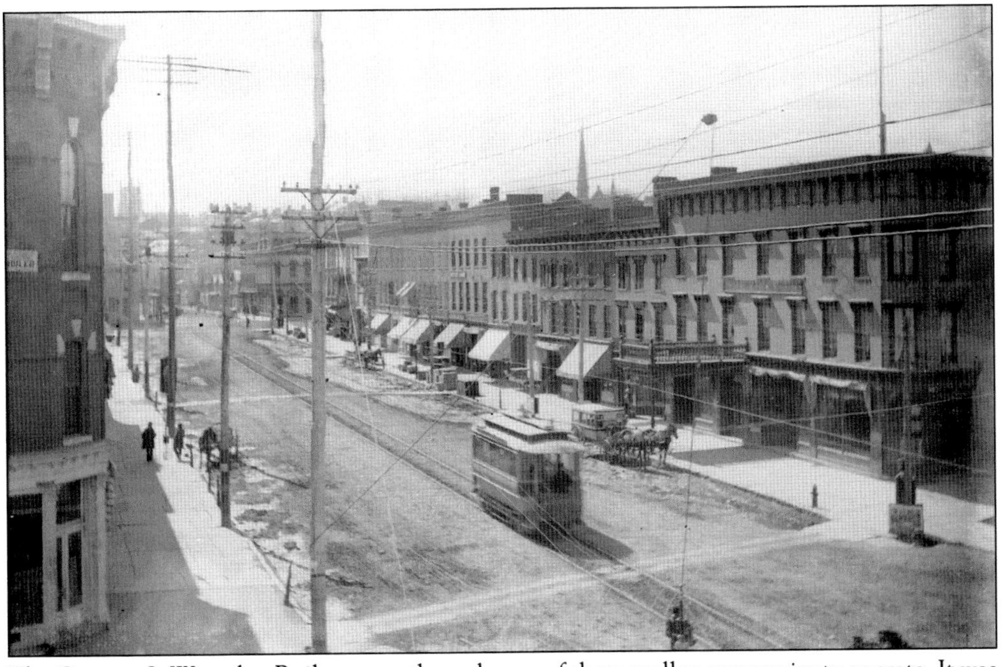

The Geneva & Waterloo Railway was the only one of three trolley companies to operate. It was controlled by the Bush Electric Company of Cleveland, Ohio, which also operated the electric utility of Geneva. The Geneva Electric Light & Power Company was located at 547 Exchange Street. This was the source of power for the Geneva & Waterloo trolley. This picture was taken from the Nester Building on the northeast corner of Exchange and Castle Streets.

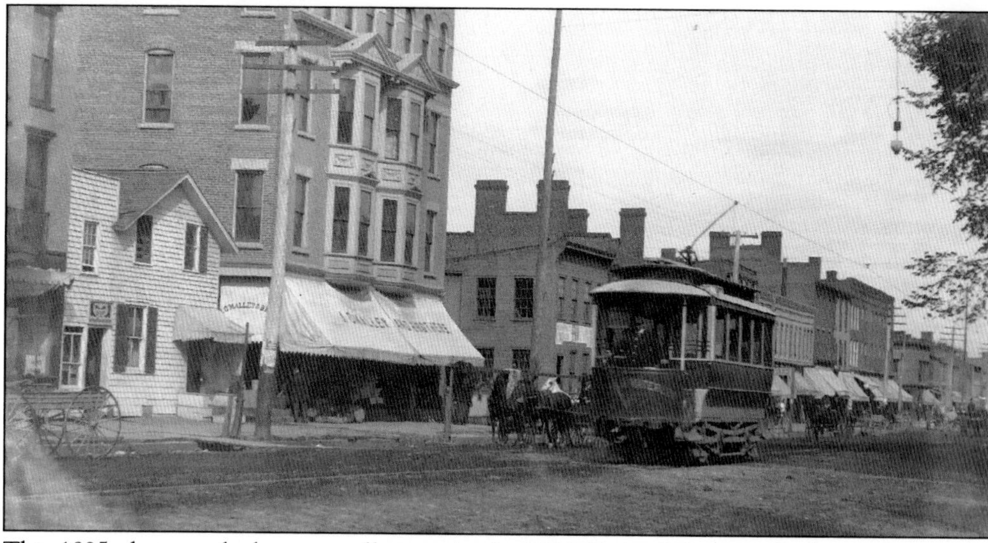

This 1895 photograph shows a trolley passing by O'Malley's of Geneva. Exchange Street, the road on which this trolley is shown, was the very road that led to a conflict between the Geneva & Waterloo Railway Company and the New York Central Railroad. The dispute was over the legality of the trolley lines passing through the railroad. On July 30, 1895, Geneva & Waterloo disconnected power long enough for a team of horses to pull their streetcar along the New York Central tracks. Coming to no compromise, the two companies resolved the matter by going to court. The trolley company won and was awarded the right to cross New York Central Railroad lines.

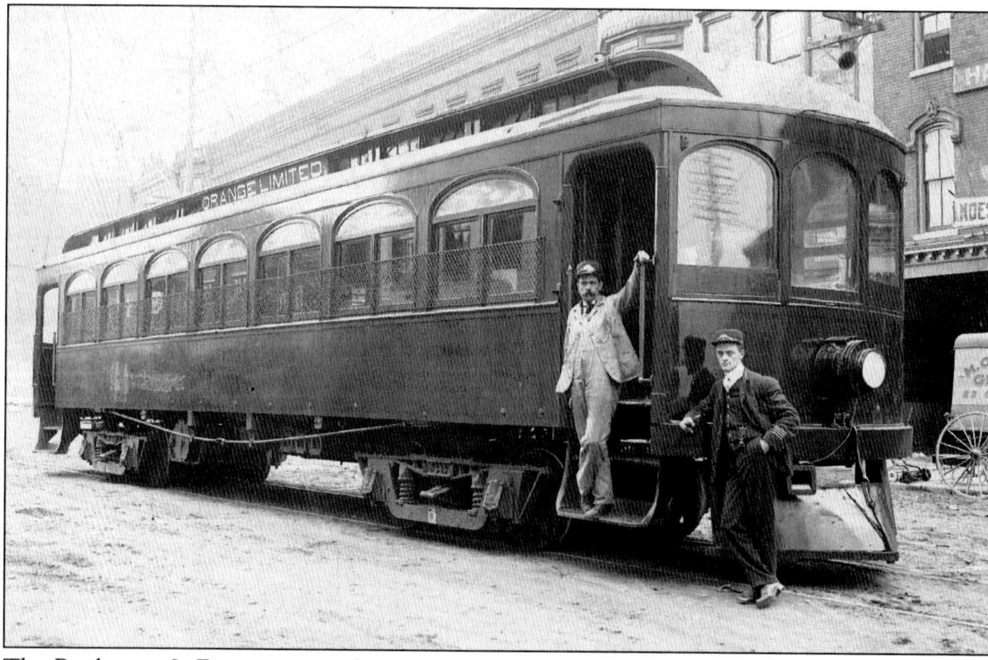

The Rochester & Eastern entered Geneva on June 15, 1904. This May 12, 1905 photograph shows conductor Earl Holcomb and motorman Harley Hancock preparing to board passengers on one of the stylish trolleys of the Orange Limited. Despite the trolley's sophisticated features and first-class services, the workers were paid a meager 8¢ an hour.

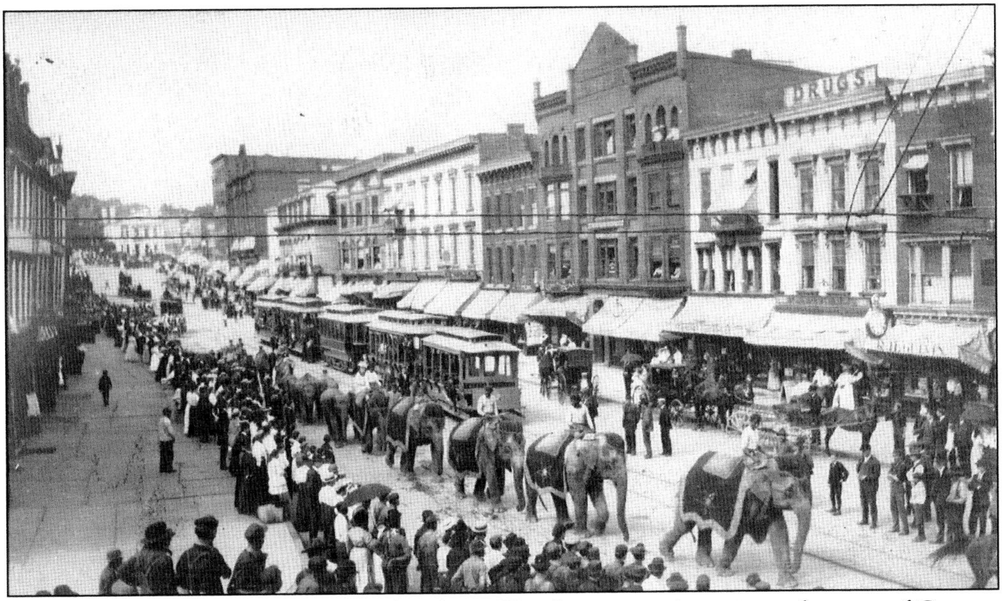

This early-1900s photograph, taken by Eloise Wood, portrays the animated streets of Geneva during the coming of the circus.

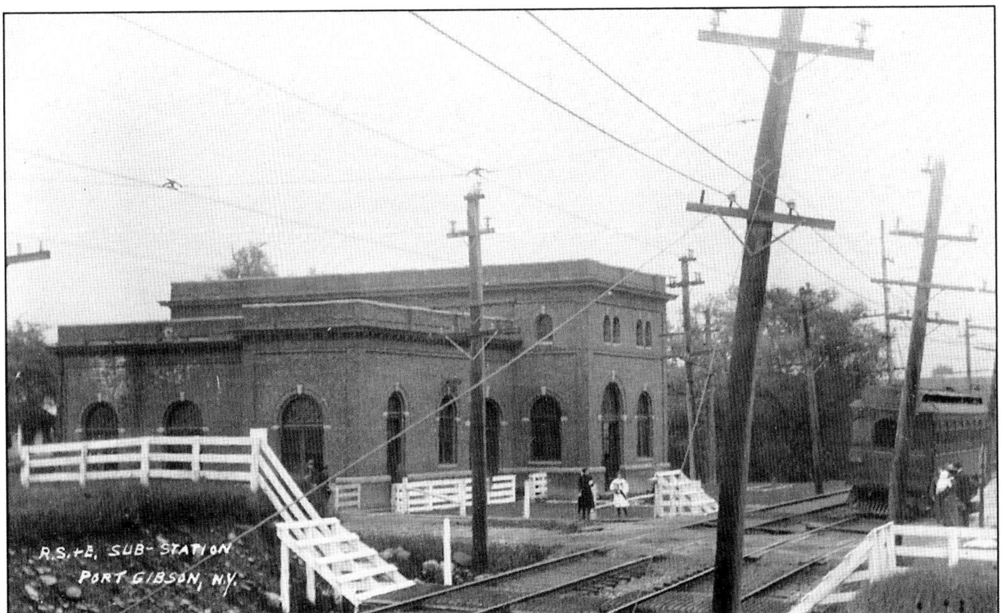

The Rochester Eastern & Syracuse Trolley opened a station in Port Gibson in 1906. The purpose of the station was to provide trolleys that would shuttle people and take them on recreational excursions, one of which was the ever-popular city of Syracuse, located no more than 59 miles away. Today, the station is owned by Walt Wandigus.

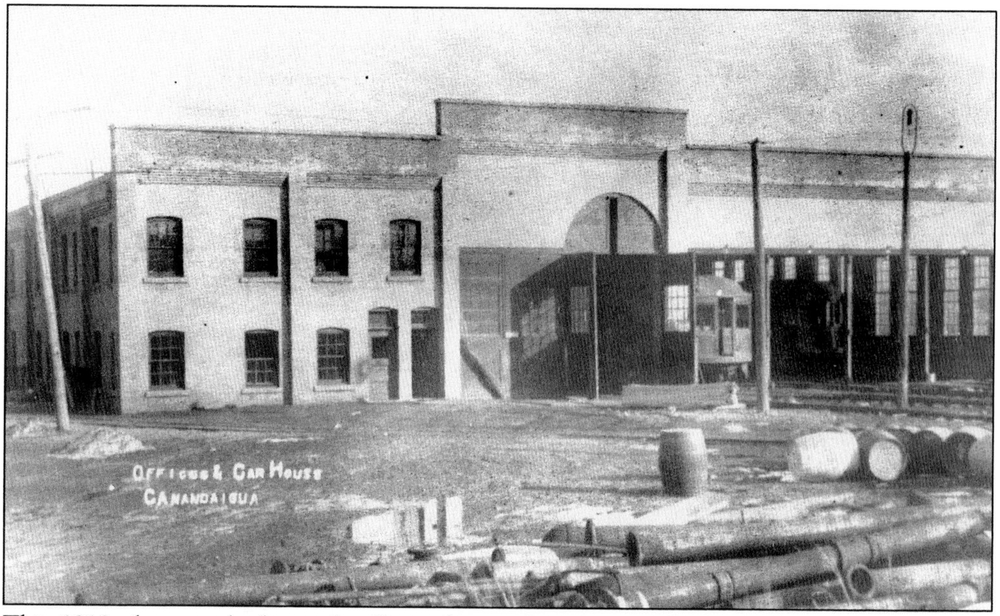

This 1910 photograph shows the Canandaigua Car House, which accommodated about 20 trolleys. It was located on South Main Street and Lakeshore Drive.

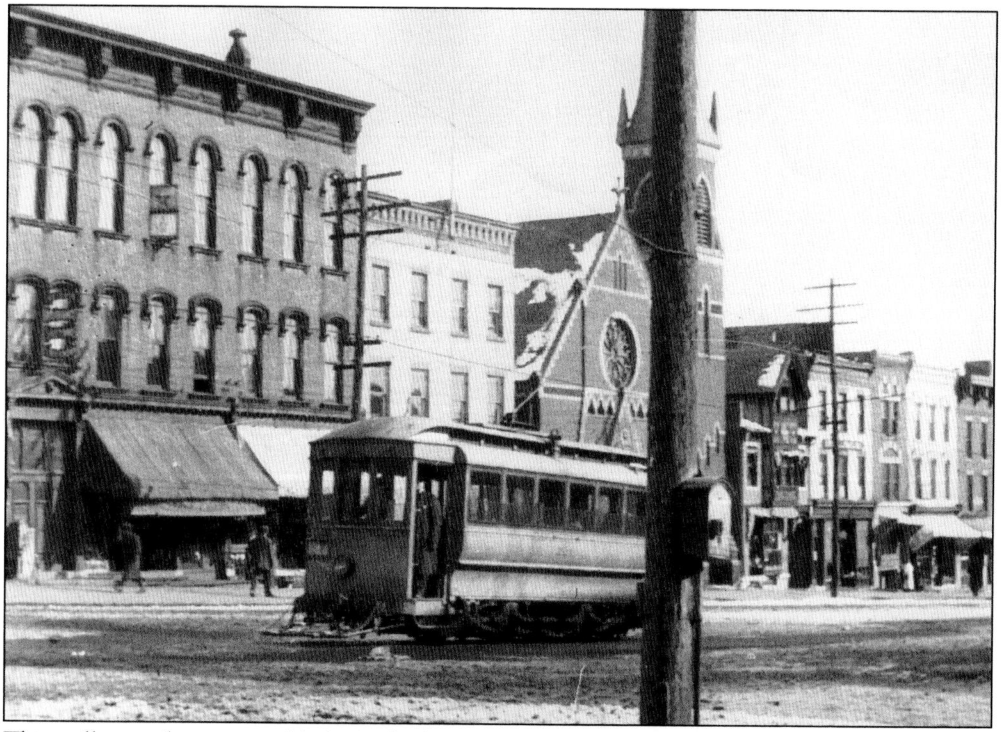

This trolley was known as a "dinky," which ran along Main Street in Canandaigua. George Pruner was the motorman for the trolley until 1930. The early Canandaigua trolley line was chiefly a passenger line. However, the conversion to Rochester & Eastern in 1904 became controversial when it proposed a freight franchise. In an attempt to prevent such actions, Mrs. F.F. Thompson offered to donate $10,000 to oppose the transport of freight through Canandaigua.

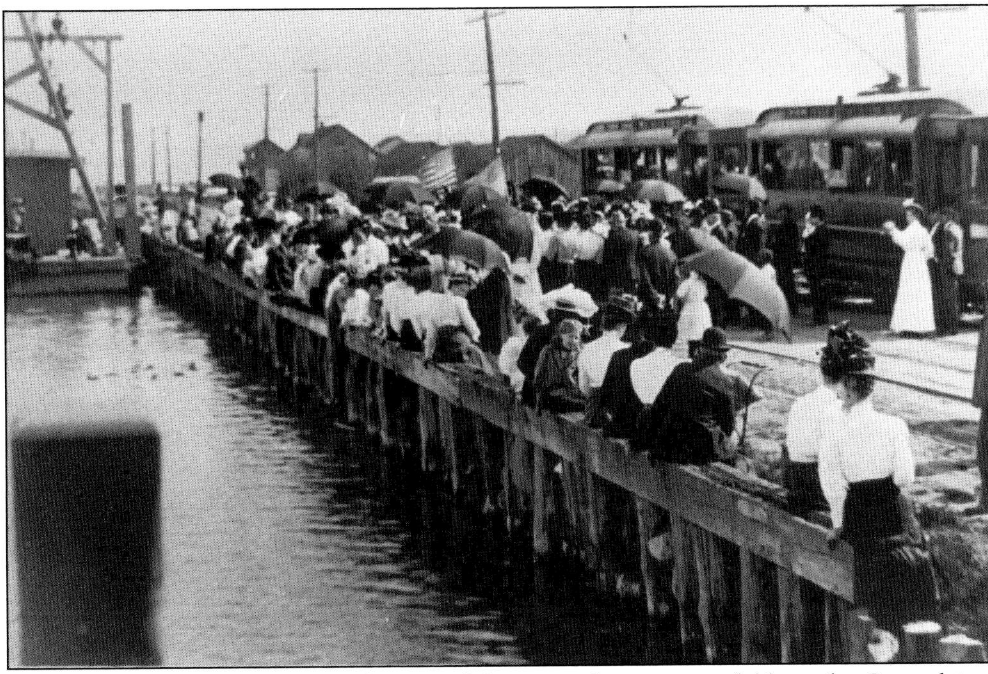

This July 4, 1905 picture depicts the annual festivities that were available at the Canandaigua pier. After being dropped of by one of the many "dinky" trolleys, people would often set sail for an enjoyable ride out to the south end, only to return to a brilliant sky illuminated by fireworks.

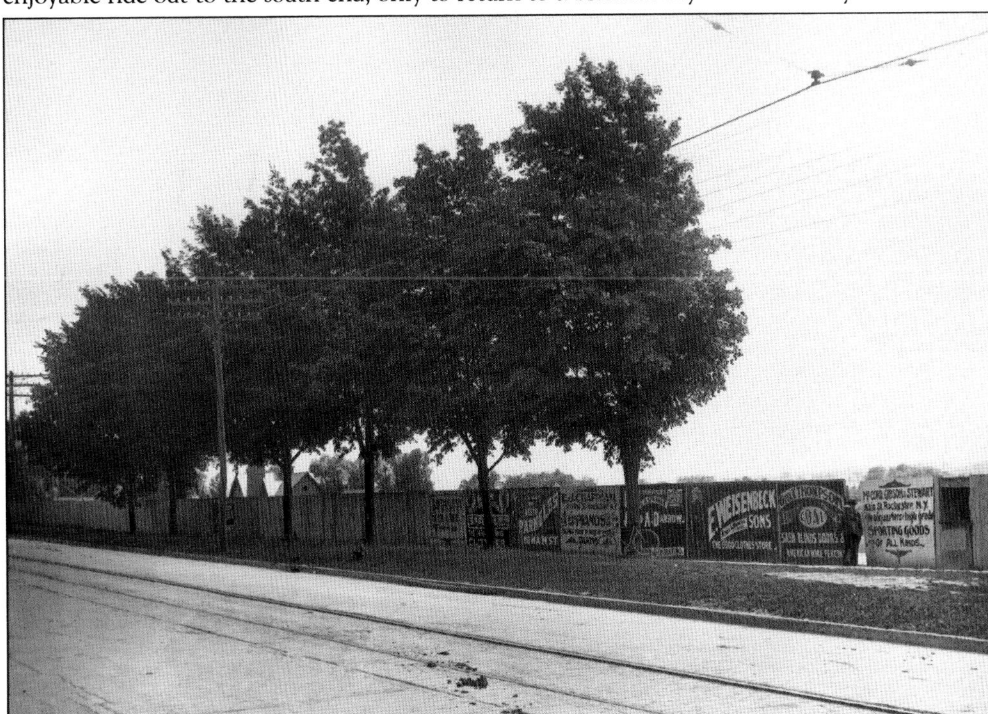

In the early 1900s, Canandaigua businesses took advantage of the open scenery of trolley routes, as they often advertised using seven-by-nine-foot billboards by the Miller Advertising Company.

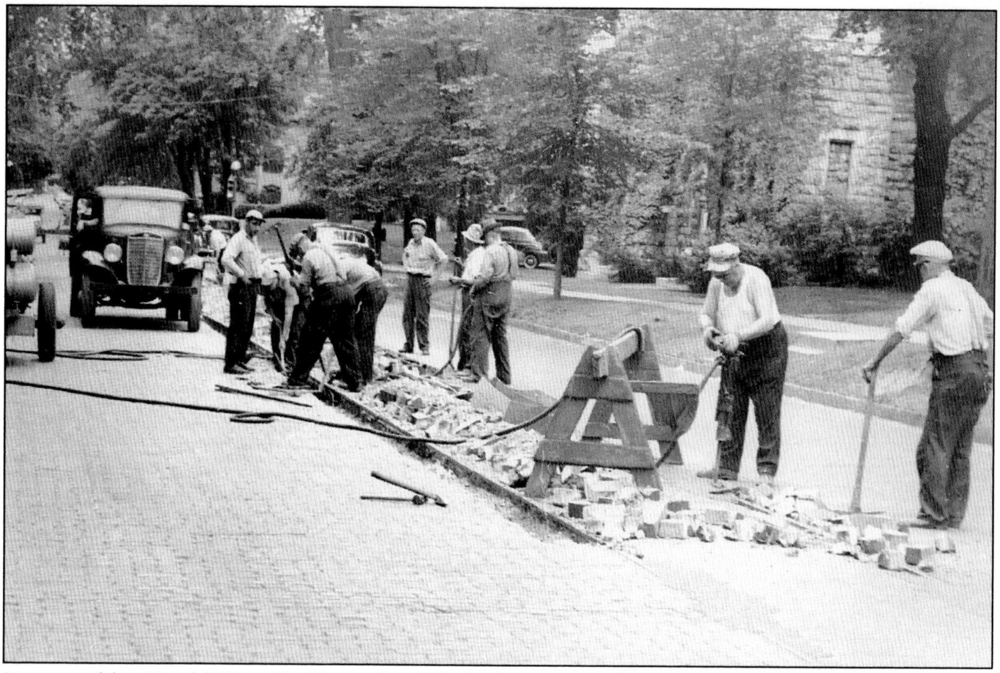

Prompted by World War II efforts, this Works Progress Administration (WPA) crew is shown eradicating the streetcar rails that were once part of the 17.75 miles of track on Genesee Street in Geneva.

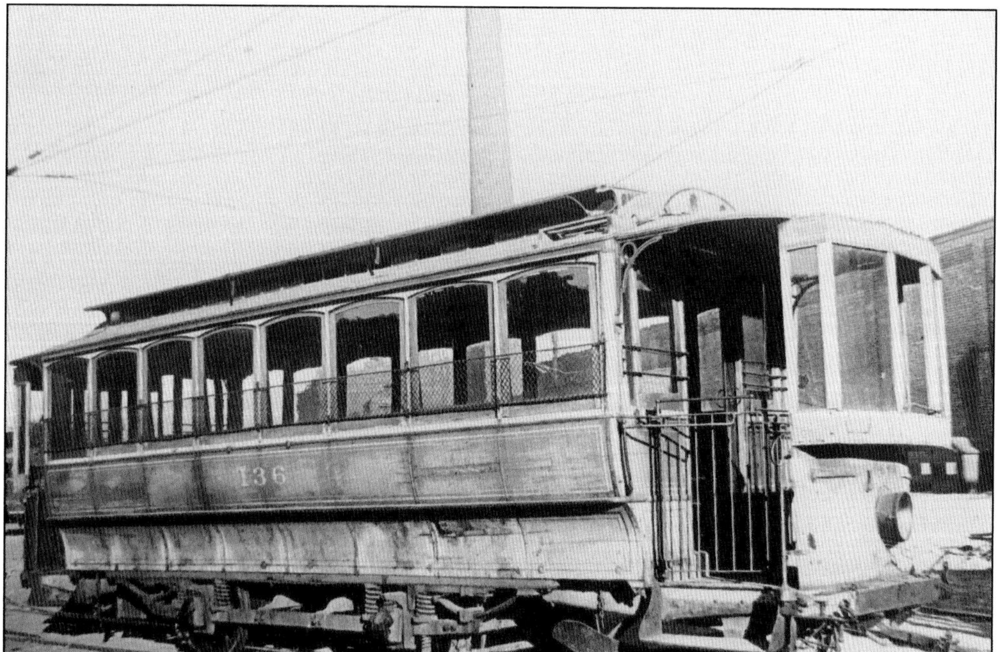

With the furthering of technology, the once-useful and popular means of transportation were becoming superseded by automobiles. Steamers became extinct, and Rochester trolleys were banned in 1922. On July 31, 1930, the midsummer rides to the Smith Opera House became a distant memory, leaving behind tarnished bronze brake handles.

Five

Automobiles

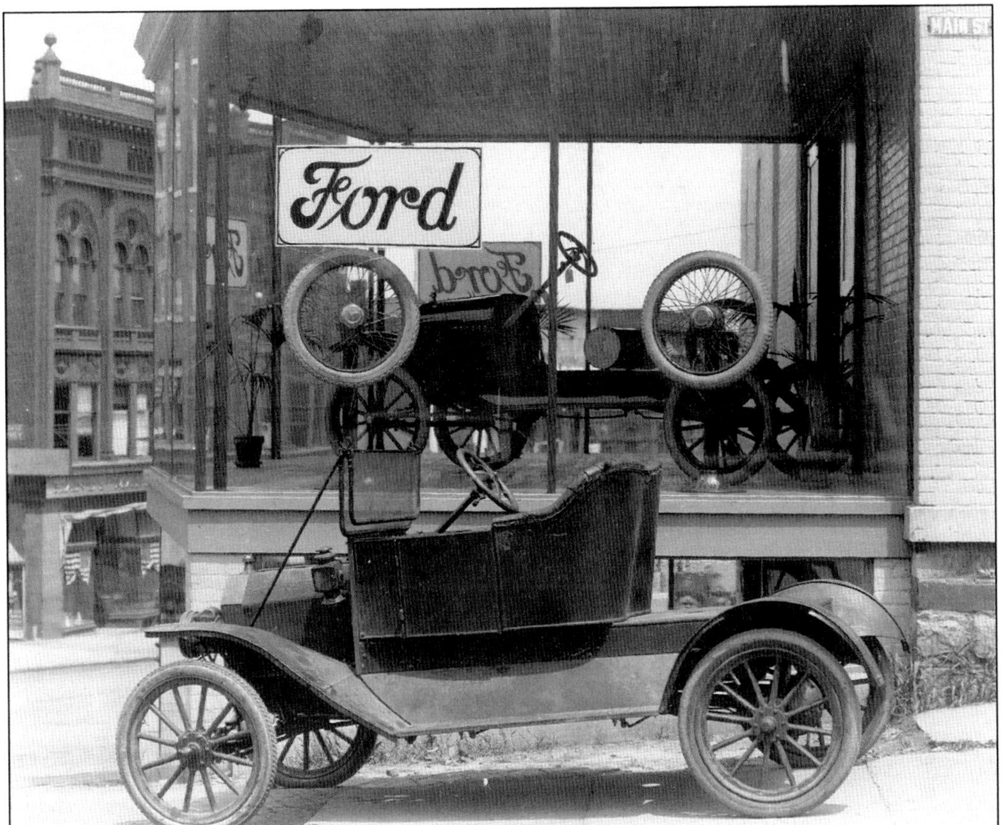

This idle 1918 Ford is parked before Adam's Garage, located on South Main and Seneca Streets in Geneva. In 1918, Ford's Model T accounted for more than half of the cars in New York. They could be purchased at an enticing $400 and bore the motto "You can paint it any color." Automotive pioneer John North Willys, a native of Ontario County, contributed to the evolution of the automobile.

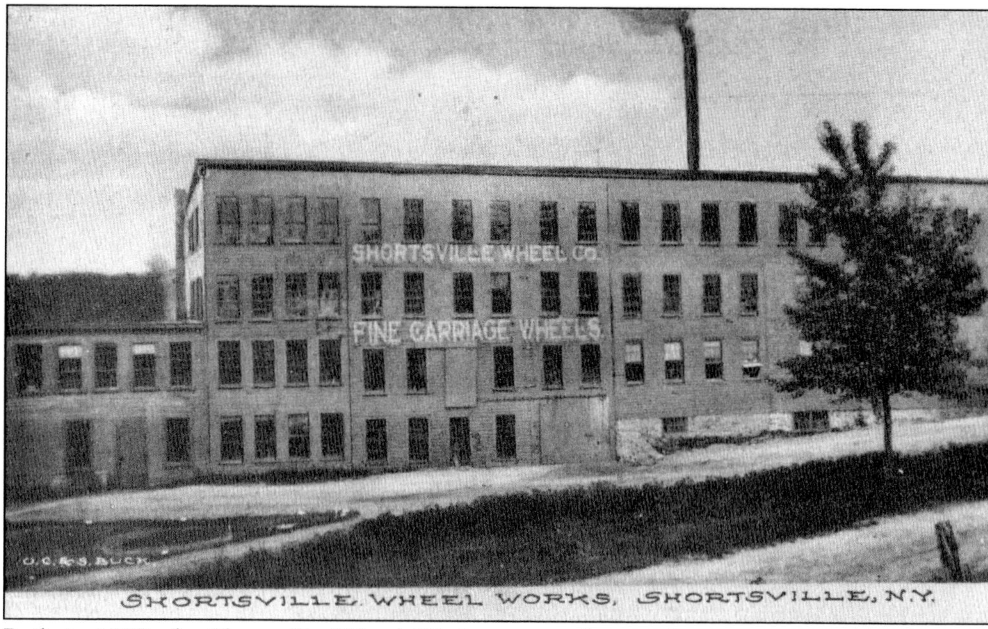

Built in 1879, the Shortsville Wheel Works occupied more than two acres of land. It was located on the Auburn branch of the New York Central Railroad, 30 miles east of Rochester and on the main line of the Lehigh Valley Railroad. Before the advent of automobiles, the Shortsville Wheel Works was a manufacturer of horse-and-buggy wheels.

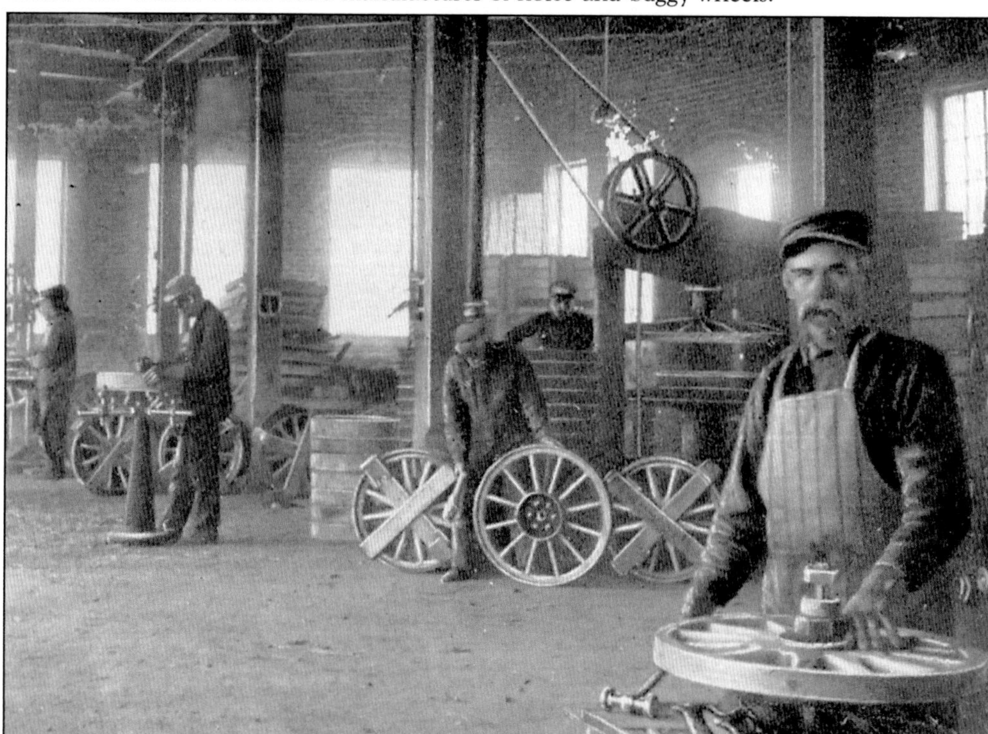

This 1909 photograph is of the automobile wheel department at the Shortsville Wheel Works. The man on the right is involved in a process that ensures a wobbling-free tire.

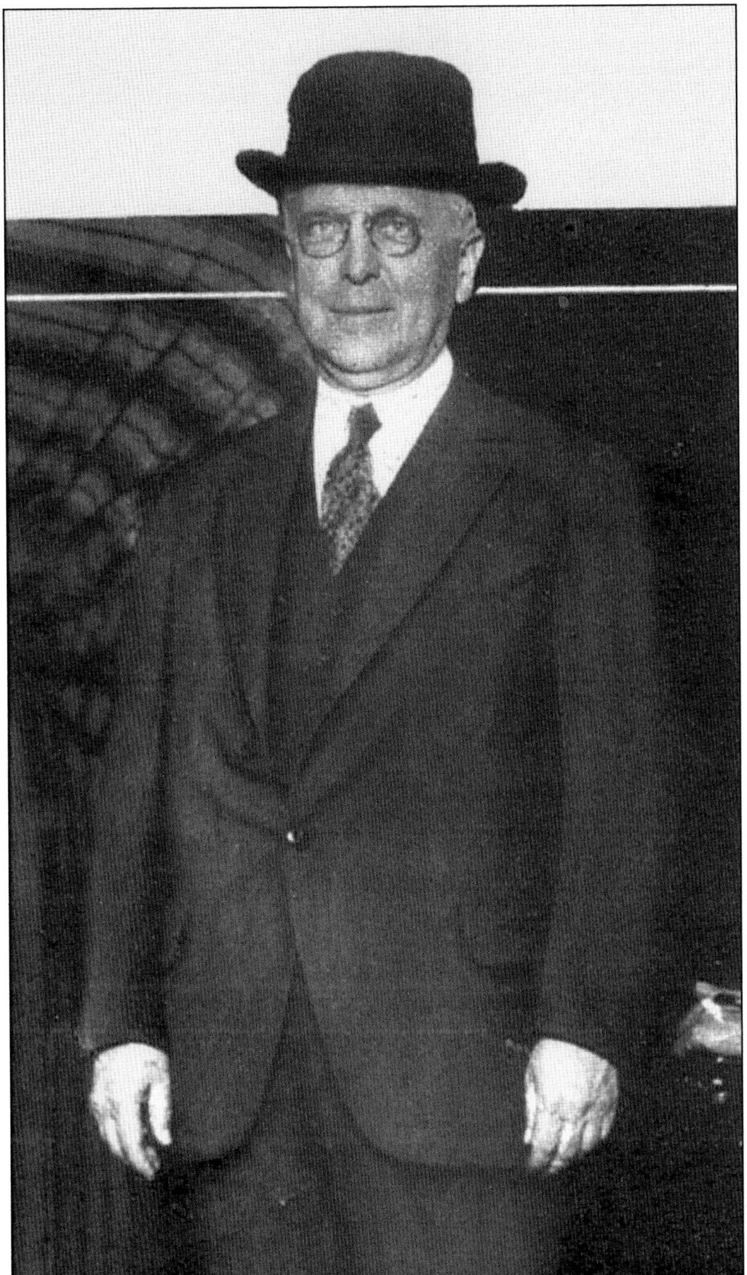

Born in Canandaigua in 1873, John North Willys was to become an eminent man in the automotive world. Before venturing into automobiles, Willys began as a bicycle salesman in Geneva. In 1907, after moving to Toledo, Ohio, Willys formed the Willys Overland Company. In 1914, the Willys Knight, which had a special sleeve engine, was developed. In 1918, the second generation of a Willys car was developed and was named the Whippet, which cost between $535 and $735. Its sales soared so high it was placed second to the Ford. From 1930 to 1932, Willys was Poland's ambassador. After his death in 1935, his company was responsible for manufacturing army jeeps. Such responsibilities paved the way for domestic-owned jeeps.

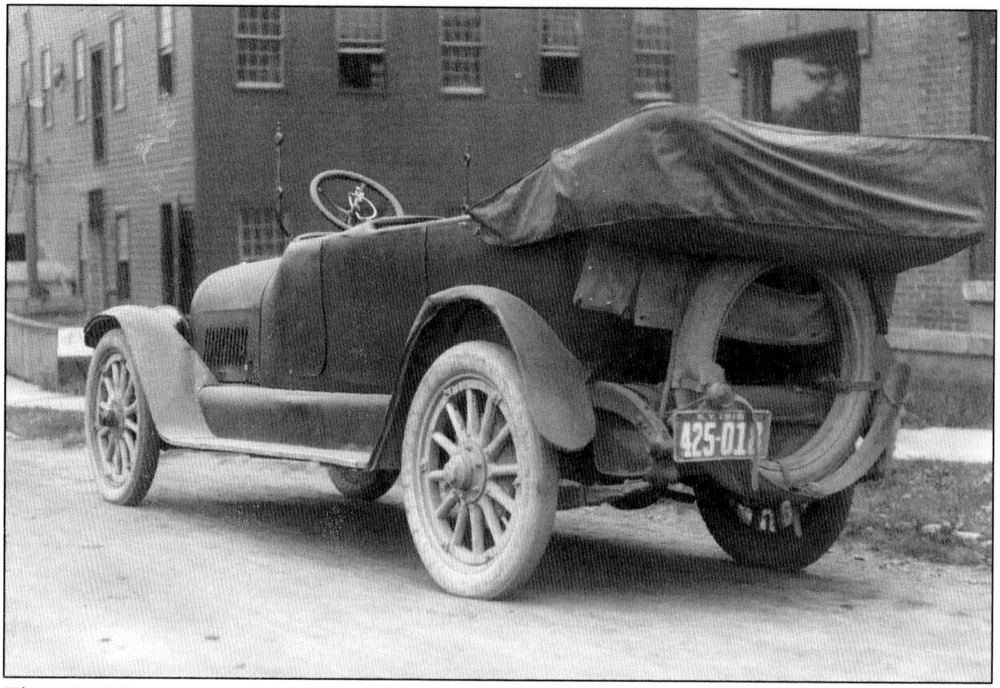

This 1918 Patterson sedan belonged to Ward Preston, the owner of the Papec farm machine company that was located in Shortsville.

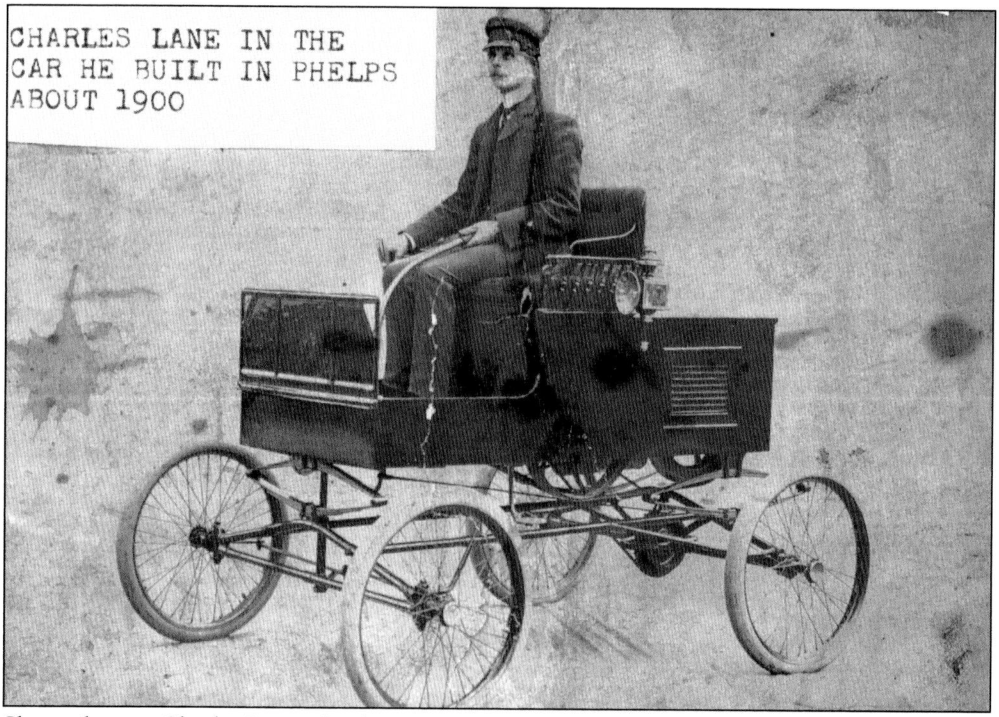

Shown here is Charles Lane, the first automotive mechanic in the town of Phelps. The 1943 novel *Excuse My Dust*, written by Tom Hunter, is based on Lane's early automobile adventures.

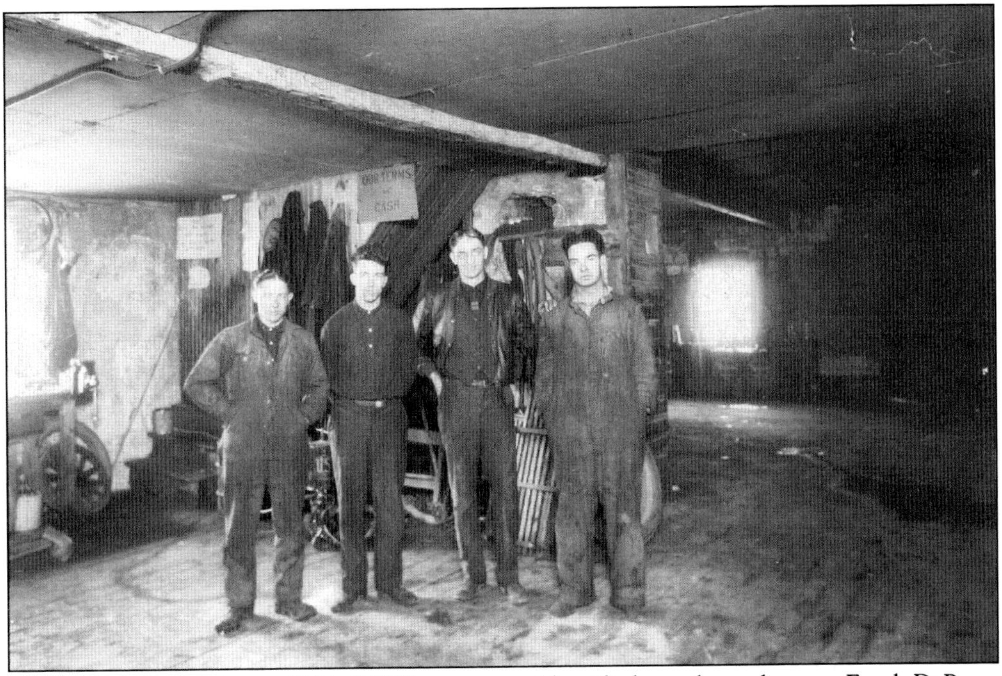

From left to right, Merton "Mike" Tiffany, two unidentified people, and owner Frank DePauw stand proudly inside DePauw's Garage in Phelps for this 1923 picture. The garage later became a restaurant.

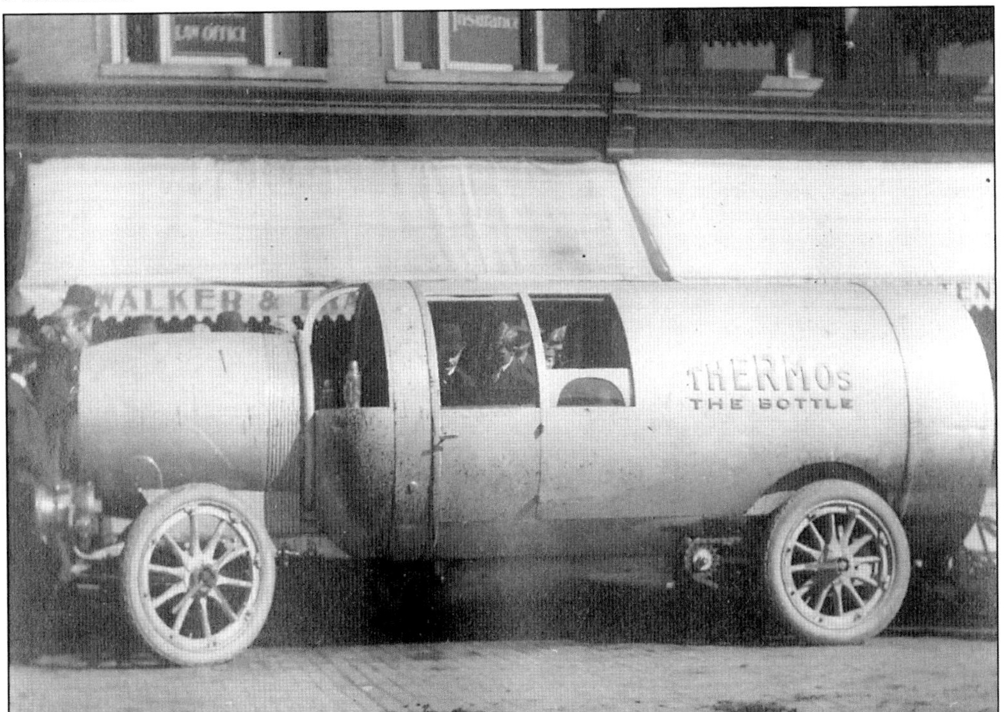

This 1928 thermos car stops to deliver food to a Canandaigua consumer. Its most popular products were ice cream and fish.

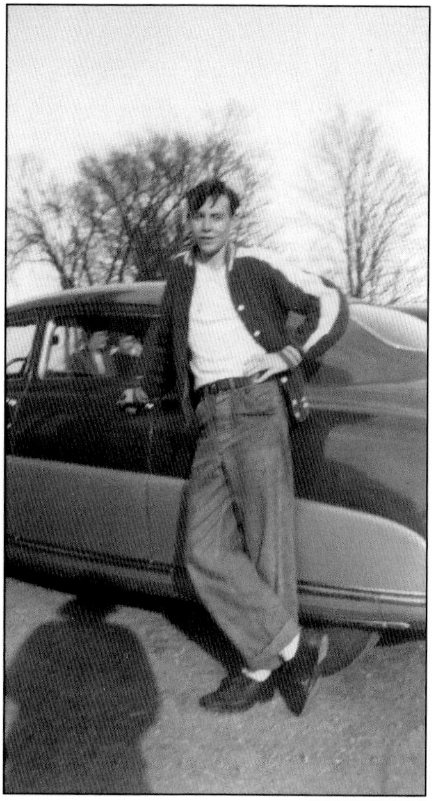

Robert "Bobby" Warner poses before his father's 1947 Hudson in the Manchester High School parking lot.

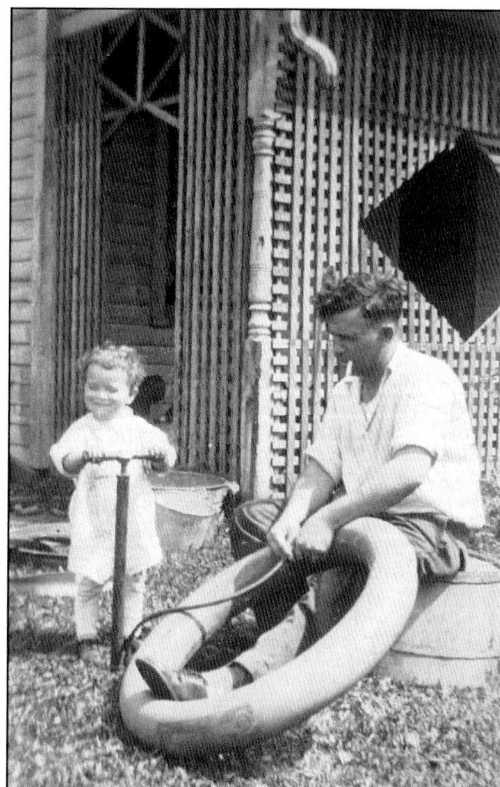

Mr. Record and his son, residents of Shortsville, pump a pneumatic tire for their Model T before taking a Sunday drive.

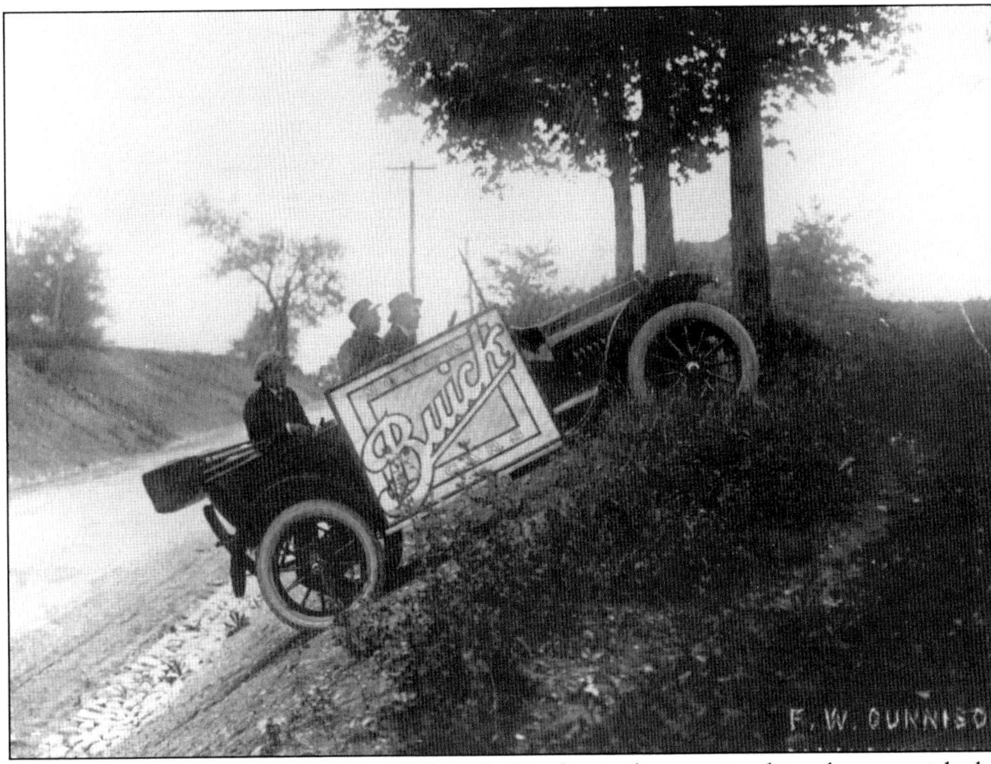

Buick-Welch car dealership owner William J. Hawley is shown using his salesman tricks by proving to his clients that the car can not only scale Arsenal Hill (a common test used to measure the power of a car) but can also climb a tree. Hawley's dealership was established in 1901 and was located at 221–229 South Main Street in Canandaigua.

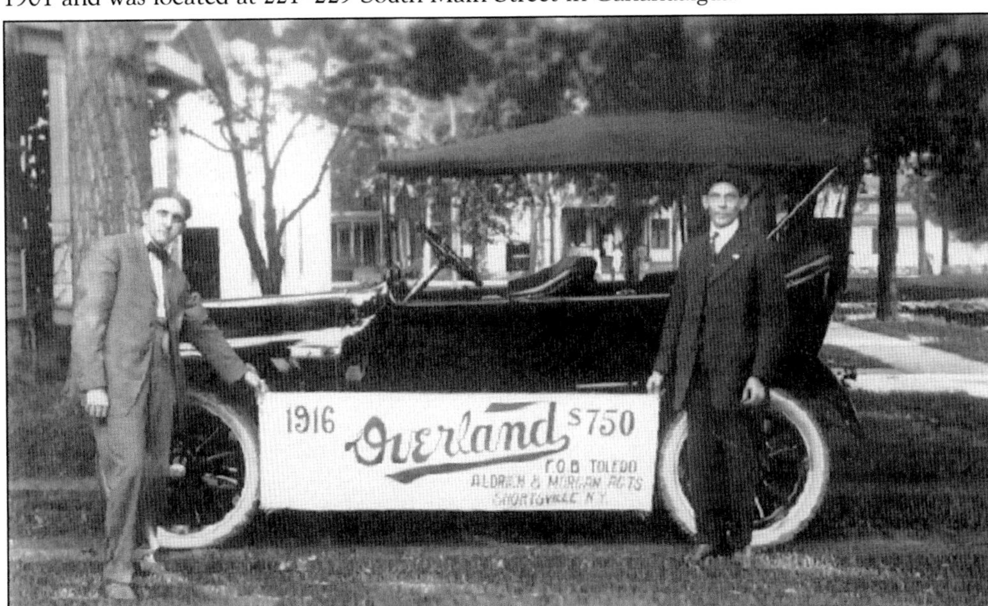

This 1916 Overland is being formally introduced by Howard D. Aldrich (left) and Walker Morgan in Shortsville.

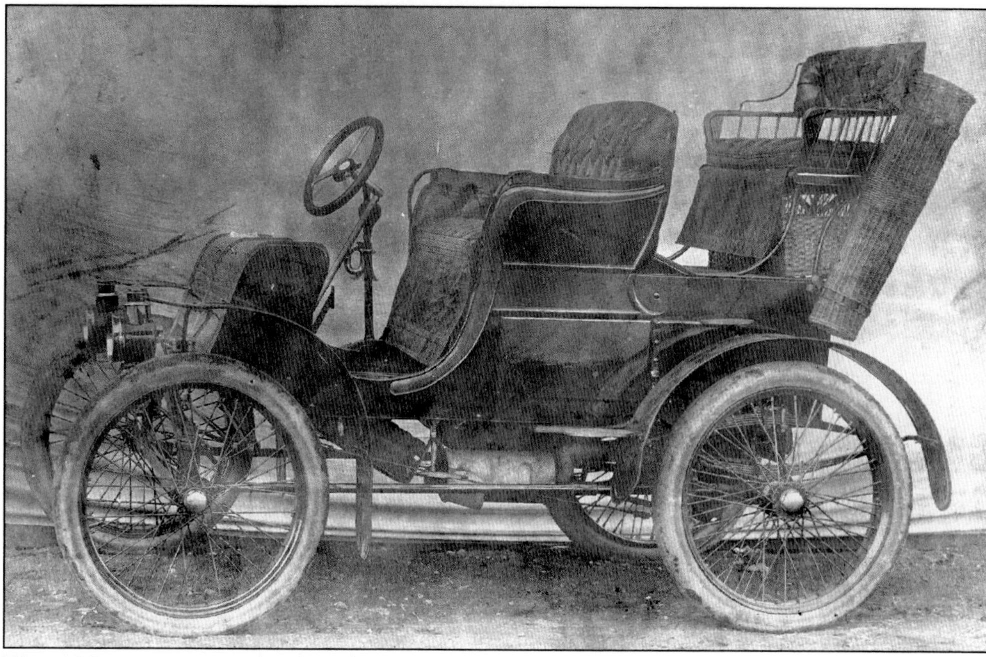

This 12-horsepower Packard made in 1900 was the first automobile owned by Hugh Rose of Geneva. There were only 81 of its kind manufactured and it was considered the "quiet man's luxury car." They were valued at $1,500.

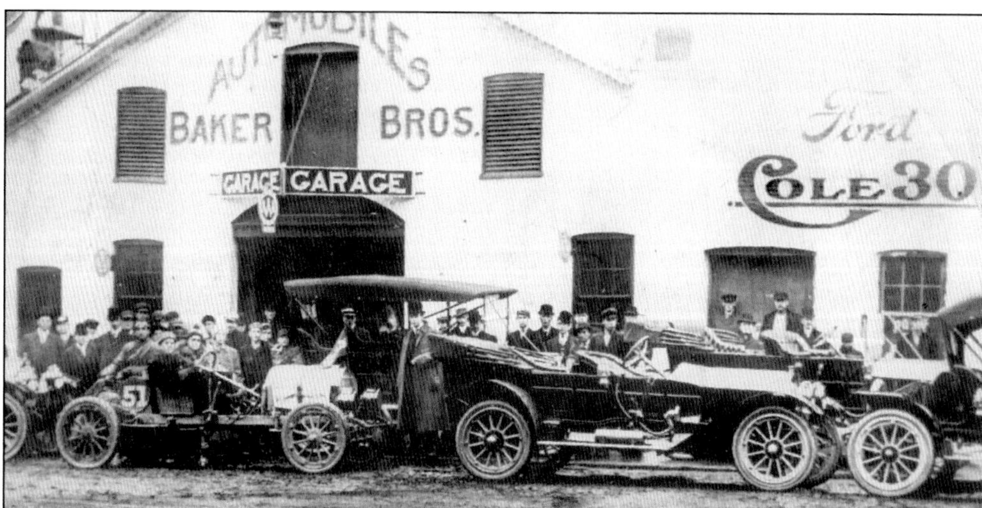

The Vanderbilt Cup Race, named after William Vanderbilt, was held in Massapeque on October 1, 1910. The event attracted 50,000 spectators, who were said to have witnessed the race from the periphery of the 24-mile triangular course. Representing Geneva's Baker Brothers Garage was Henry F. Grant, who contended for first place against Lewis Chevrolet. On the seventh lap, team Chevrolet was involved in a tragic incident that killed one of its mechanics. The misfortune allowed Henry to take victory.

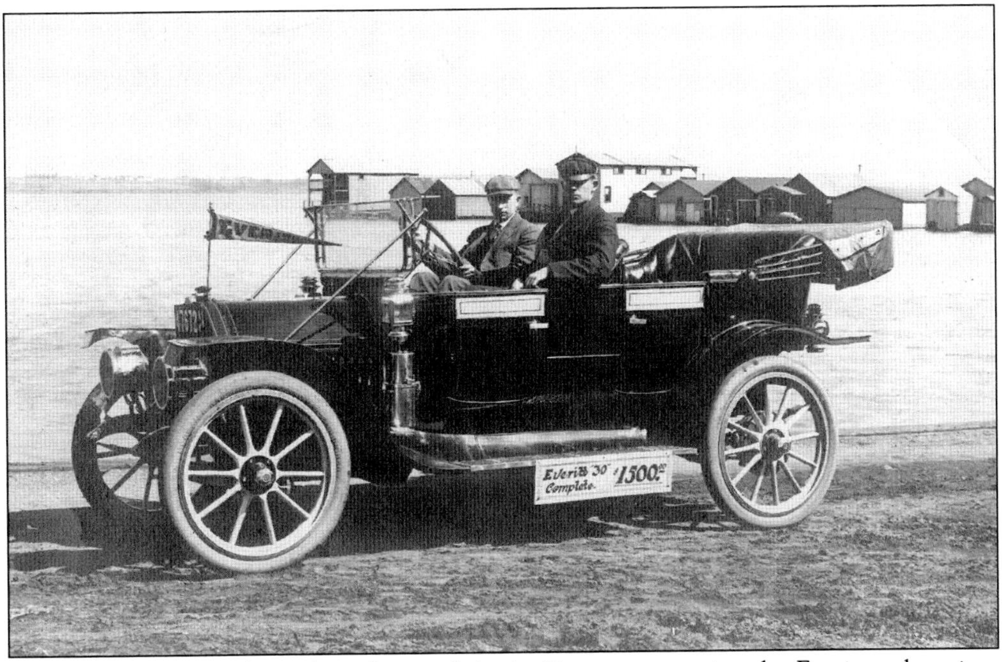

Company employees drive along Seneca Lake in Geneva promoting the Everitt, a luxurious commodity in its time. Note the price on the running board.

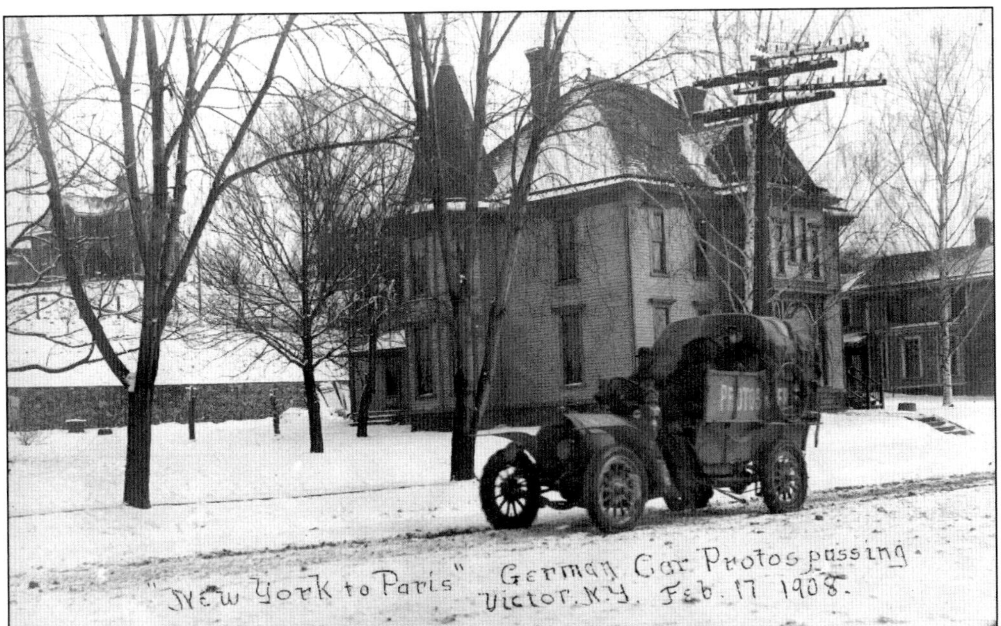

Passing by the "doctor's house," which is located on East Main Street in Victor, during the Great Transcontinental Race on February 17, 1908, is this German Proto's car. The race extended from Paris to New York.

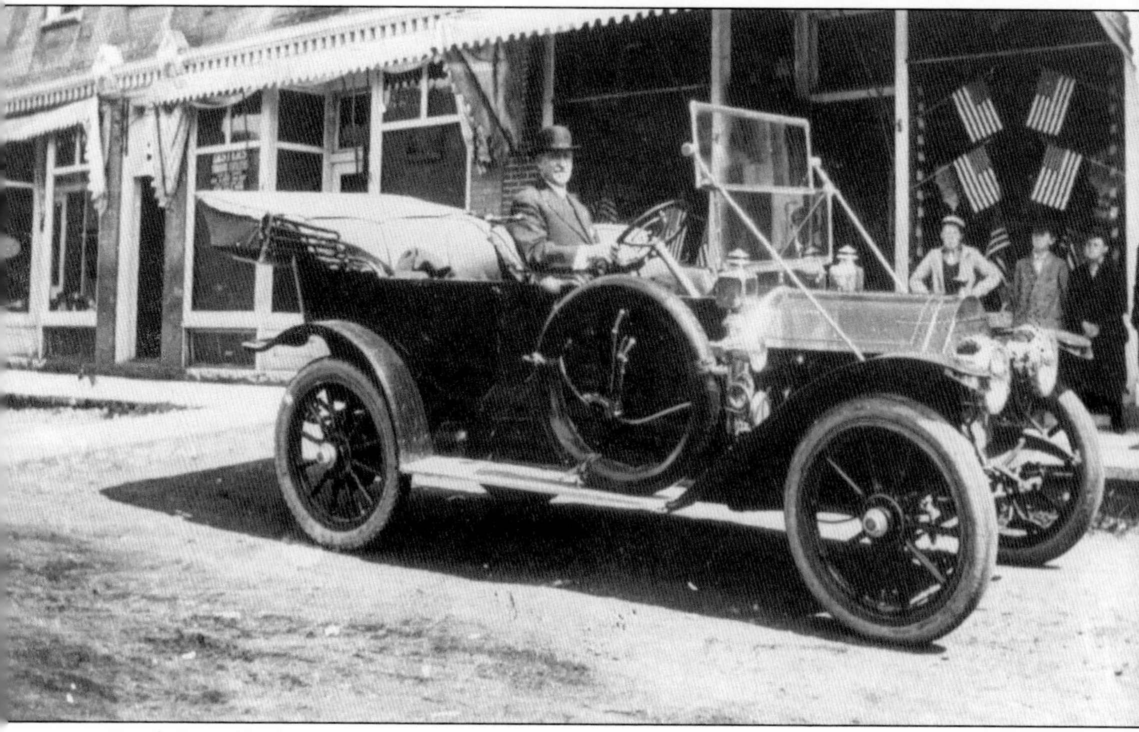

Frank E. Cobb shows off his 1911 Cadillac on the streets of Victor and draws the attention of a group of young boys. Cobb was the owner of a drug and stationery business established in 1884. His gregariousness went beyond the store, and he was a well-liked man.

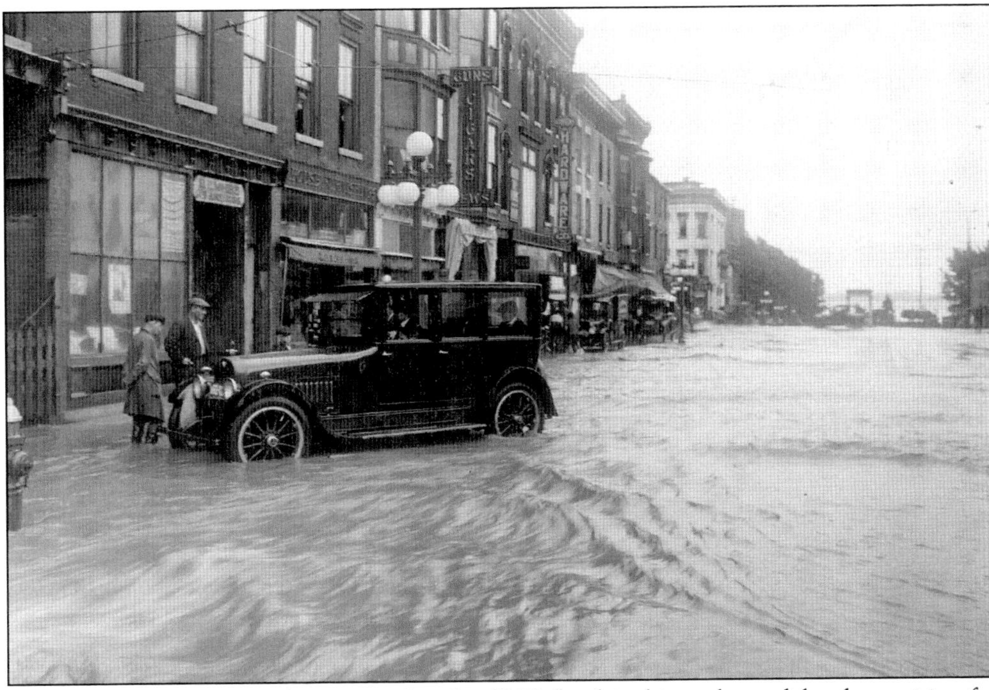

Parked on Castle Street of Geneva after the 1922 flood is this early-model sedan waiting for the cascading currents to subside.

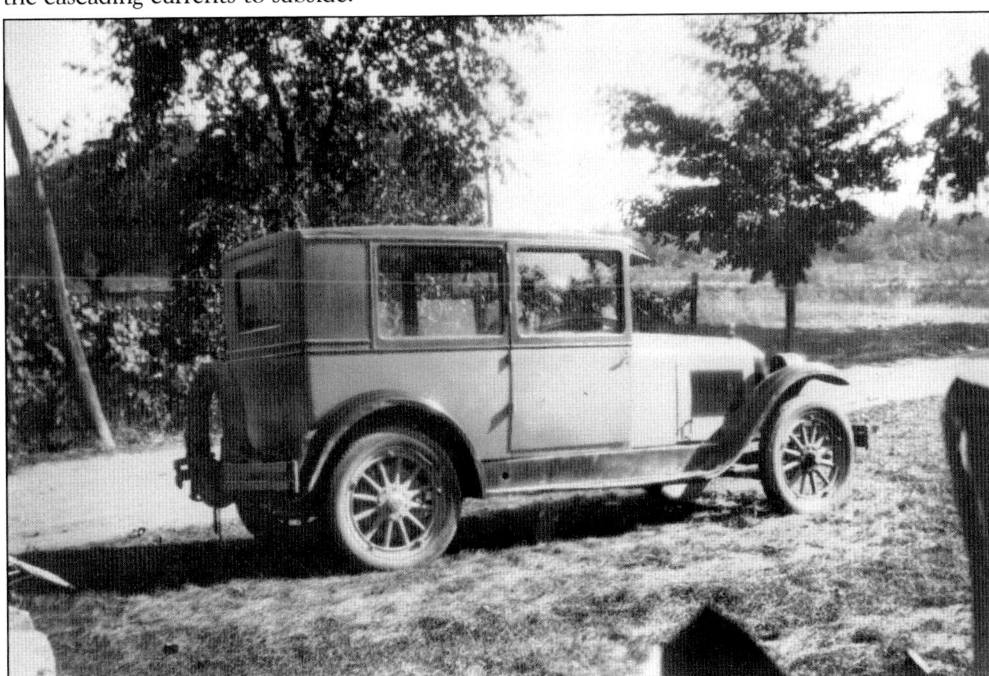

Shown here is a Manchester resident's Essex automobile. In 1919, the manufacturers of Essex introduced an all-steel-body model that cost only slightly more than the Ford. In 1932, Essex fabricated yet another state-of-the-art car, which offered a six- or eight-cylinder engine. Essex was known for its hill-climbing, speed records, and economy runs.

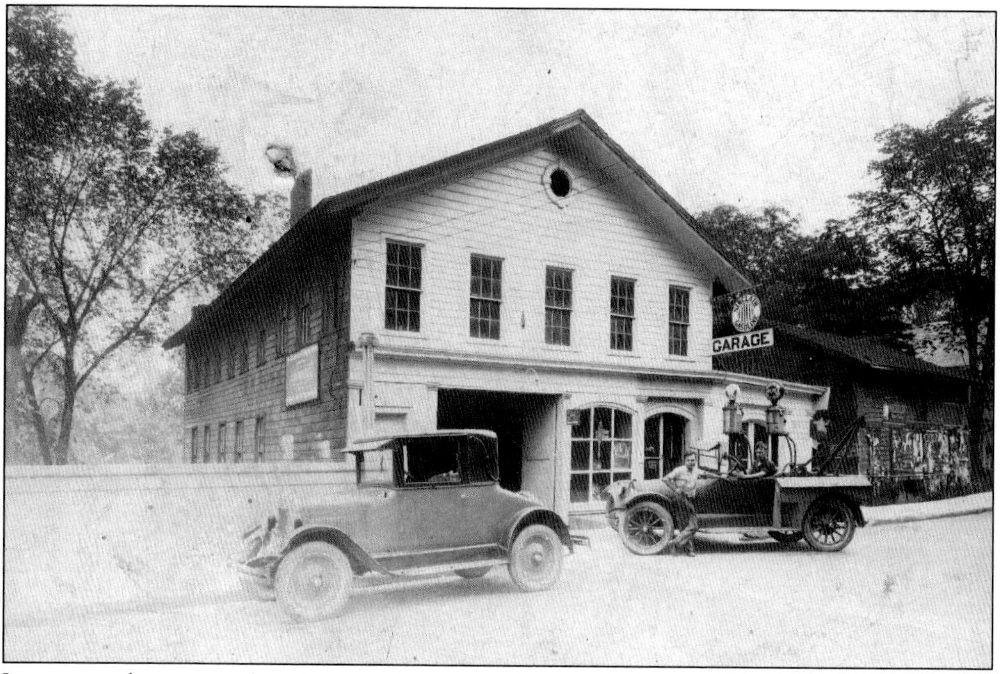

Leaning on his tow truck in front of his garage is Leonard Sabin in this late-1920s photograph. Before it became a garage, the building was the Bowker Carriage Factory. The Phelps Carwash stands there today.

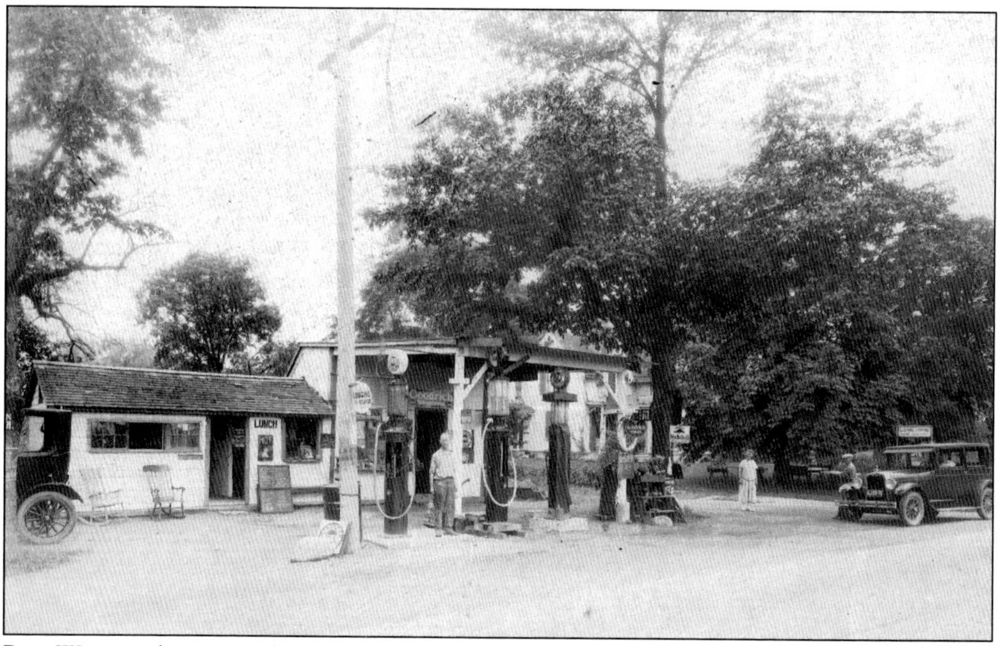

Burt Warren, shown standing between two pumps in this 1925 photograph, offered what quite possibly was the precursor to the convenient store. Not only did he sell Mobil oil and Sinclair gasoline, which cost a mere 18¢ per gallon, but he also had a supply of food and accommodated passing travelers in his own spacious house. Warren's store was located across from what is now the new Magnus Company in Phelps.

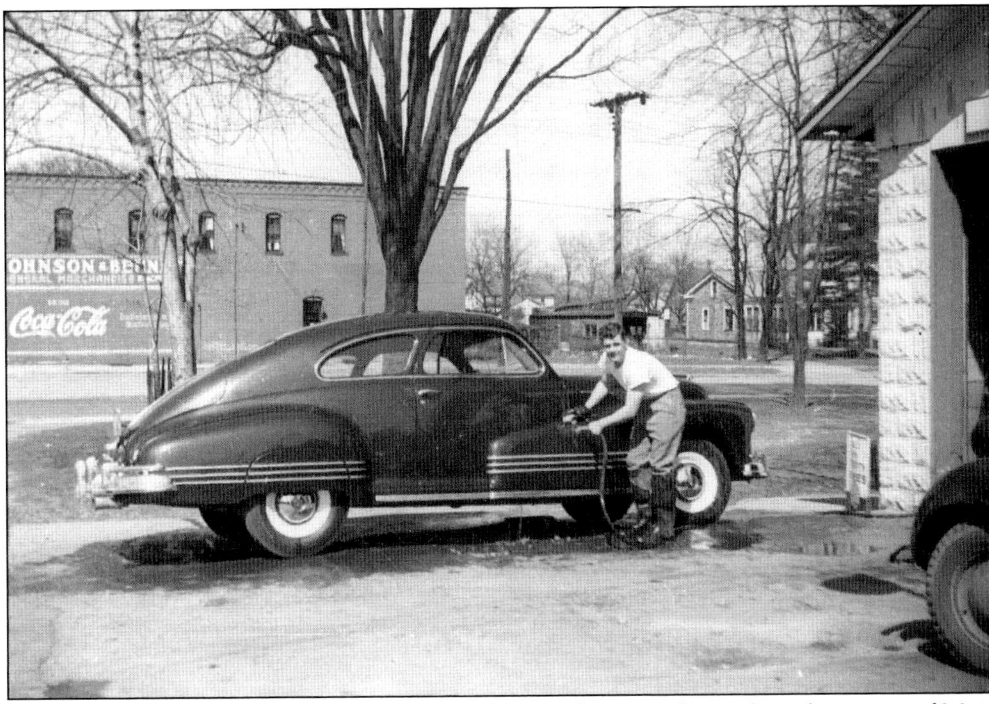

Seen here is a 1948 Pontiac parked in the driveway of a garage located on the corner of Main and Clifton Streets in Manchester. This particular type of car was called either the Silver Streak or Silver Torpedo. Also in 1948, Pontiac produced 245,019 cars, offered optional handicap controls, and was ranked fifth among other car sales.

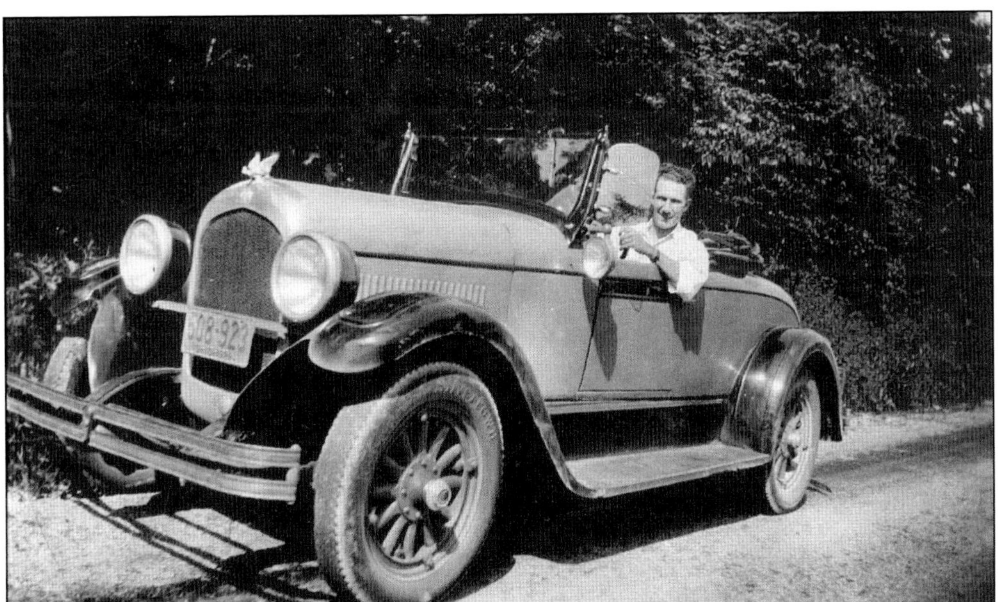

An unidentified Manchester man cruises along in this 1925 Chrysler; it was capable of reaching speeds of 58 mph.

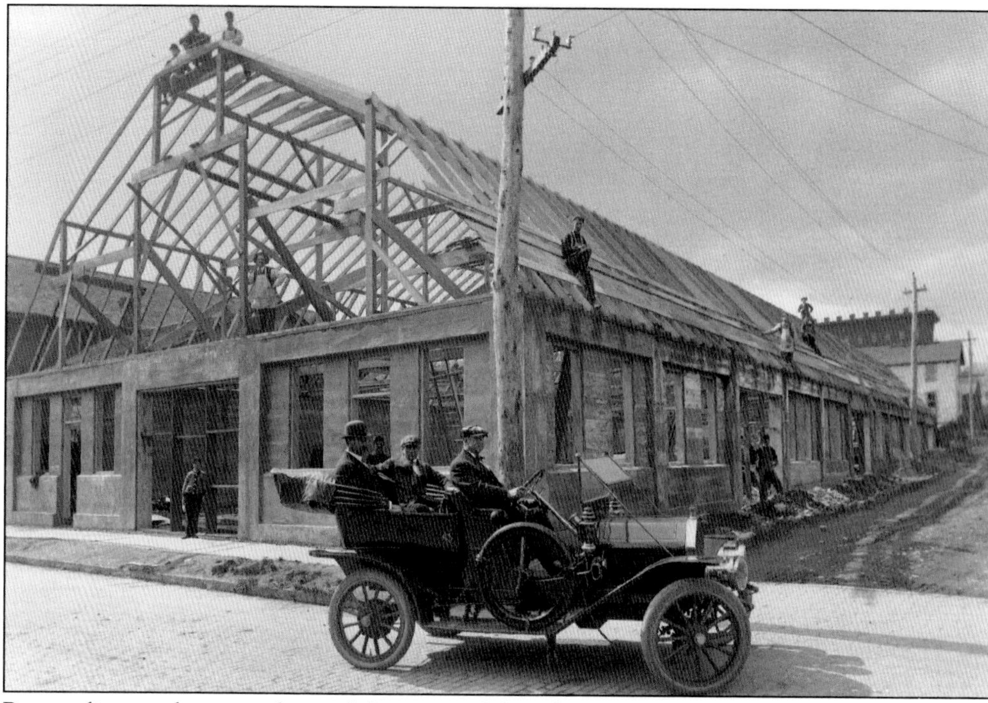

Responding to the great demand for automobiles, the Seman brothers built a garage on the corner of Phoenix and Lafayette Streets of Canandaigua in 1909. Its dimensions were 57 by 166 feet, and it was safeguarded by a fireproof frame. Besides automobiles, the garage sold motorcycles and canoes.

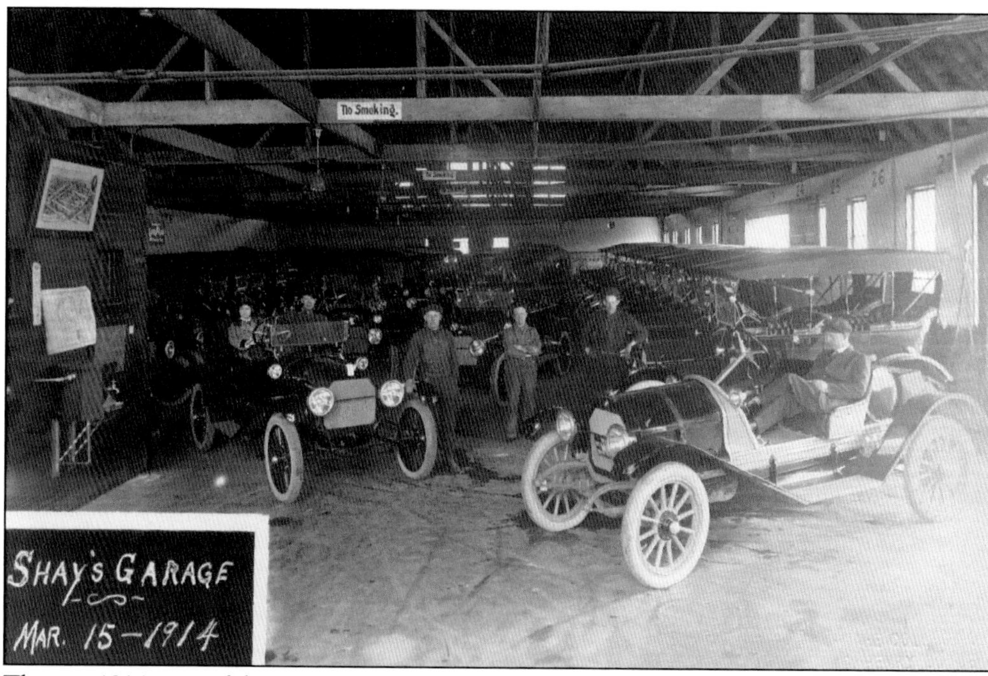

This is a 1914 view of the inventory inside Shay's Garage in Canandaigua. From 1908 to 1927, 15 million Model Ts were sold.

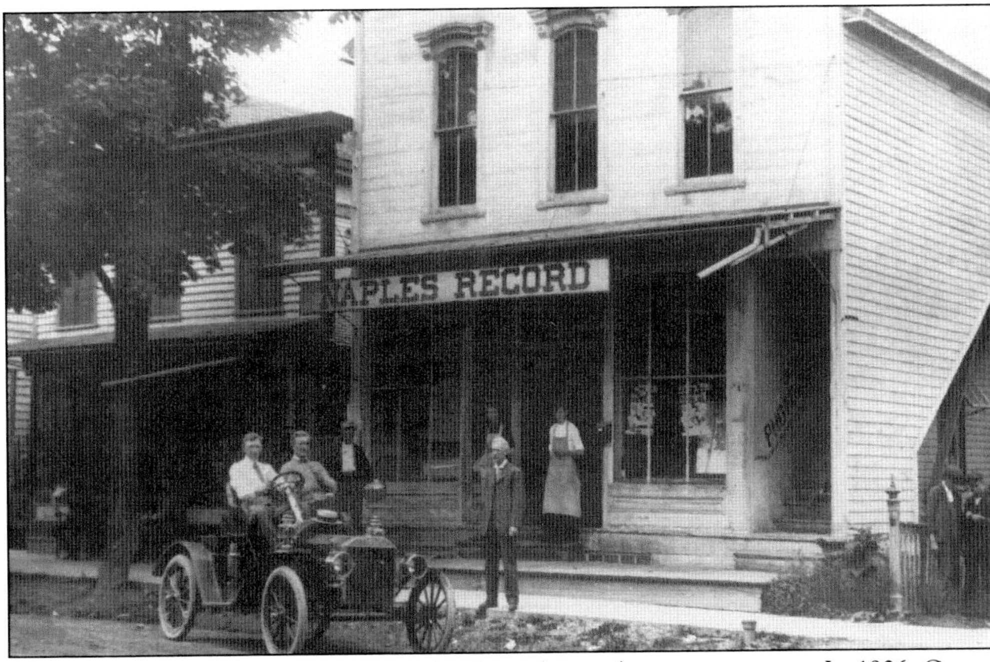

This early-model car drives by the Naples Record to pick up a newspaper. In 1906, George B. Hemingway was one of the first people in Naples to purchase an automobile. In 1907, the village of Naples imposed a 10-mph speed limit for automobiles. In 1914, the once-dirt roads of Naples were replaced with brick.

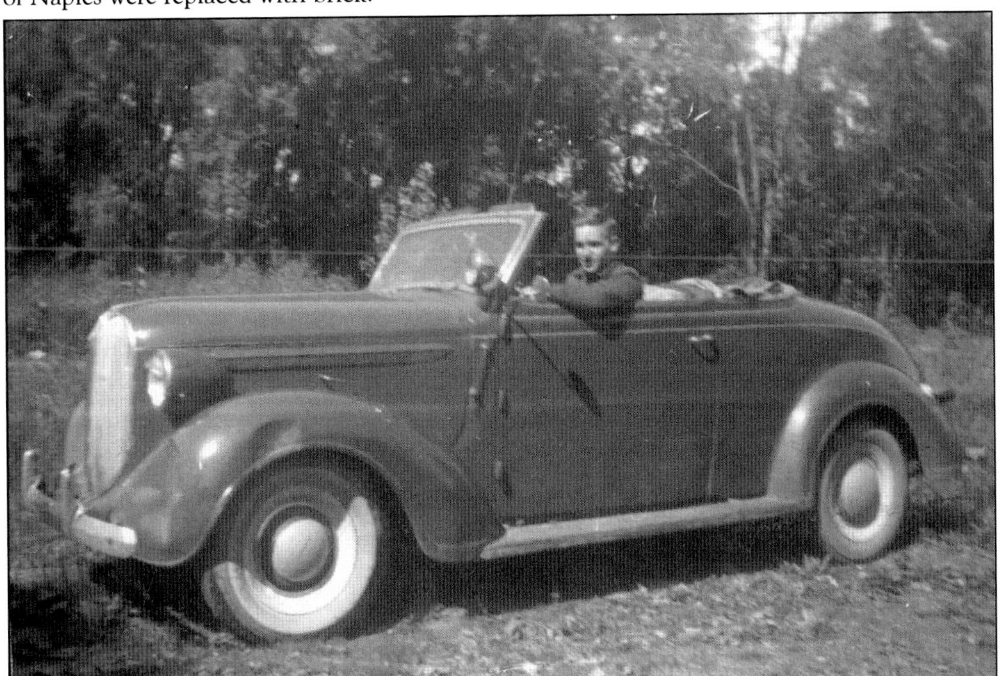

Photogenic Zeke Daley poses for a picture inside his 1937 Plymouth. On June 1, 1928, Plymouth produced its first car. Today, the D'Amico Chrysler-Plymouth dealership, located in Geneva, offers a large selection of Chrysler and Plymouth automobiles.

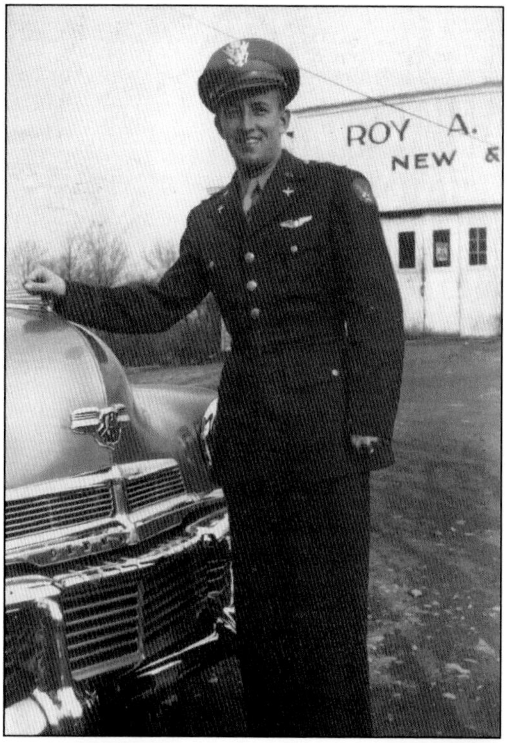

Standing proudly in his World War II uniform behind his home at 8 Palmyra Street in Shortsville is Roy J. Farnsworth, who is commonly known as "Bud." In 1918, Roy Alonzo Farnsworth, Bud's father, established the family automotive business. Bud joined the business in 1946 and built a showroom and offices at 16 Canandaigua Street in Shortsville in 1951.

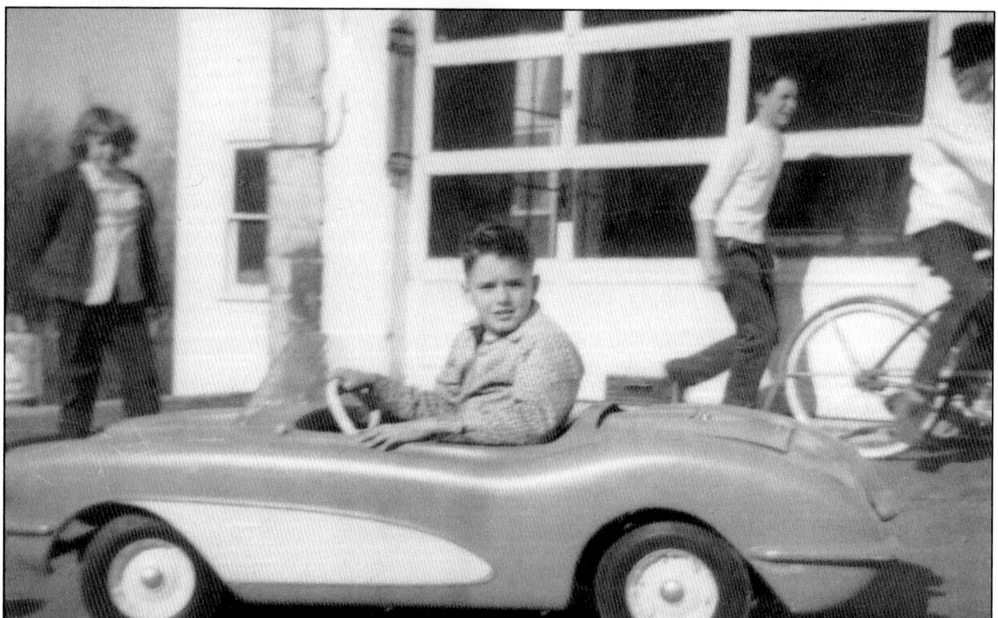

Randall Farnsworth's innate interest in cars, as shown in this May 1961 photograph, paved the way for his future career. Today, Randall Farnsworth and his wife, Margaret, hold the positions of president and vice president at the Farnsworth Group dealership, located on Route 332 in Canandaigua. It is the largest dealership in Ontario County and offers a wide selection of cars from Oldsmobile, Pontiac, Buick, Cadillac, Chevrolet, and GMC.

Six

FIRE COMPANIES

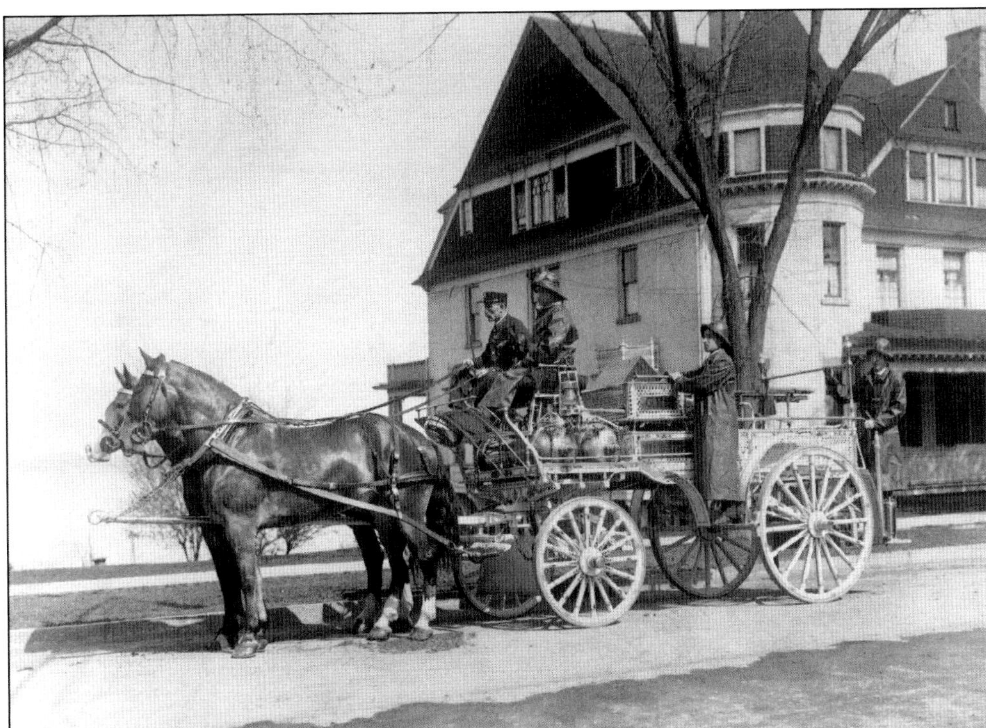

Before fire trucks had been invented, firemen were transported to fires by horse and carriage. In this late-19th-century photograph, horses Sunshine and Lightning lead Geneva firefighters of the Hydrant Hose Company to the fire.

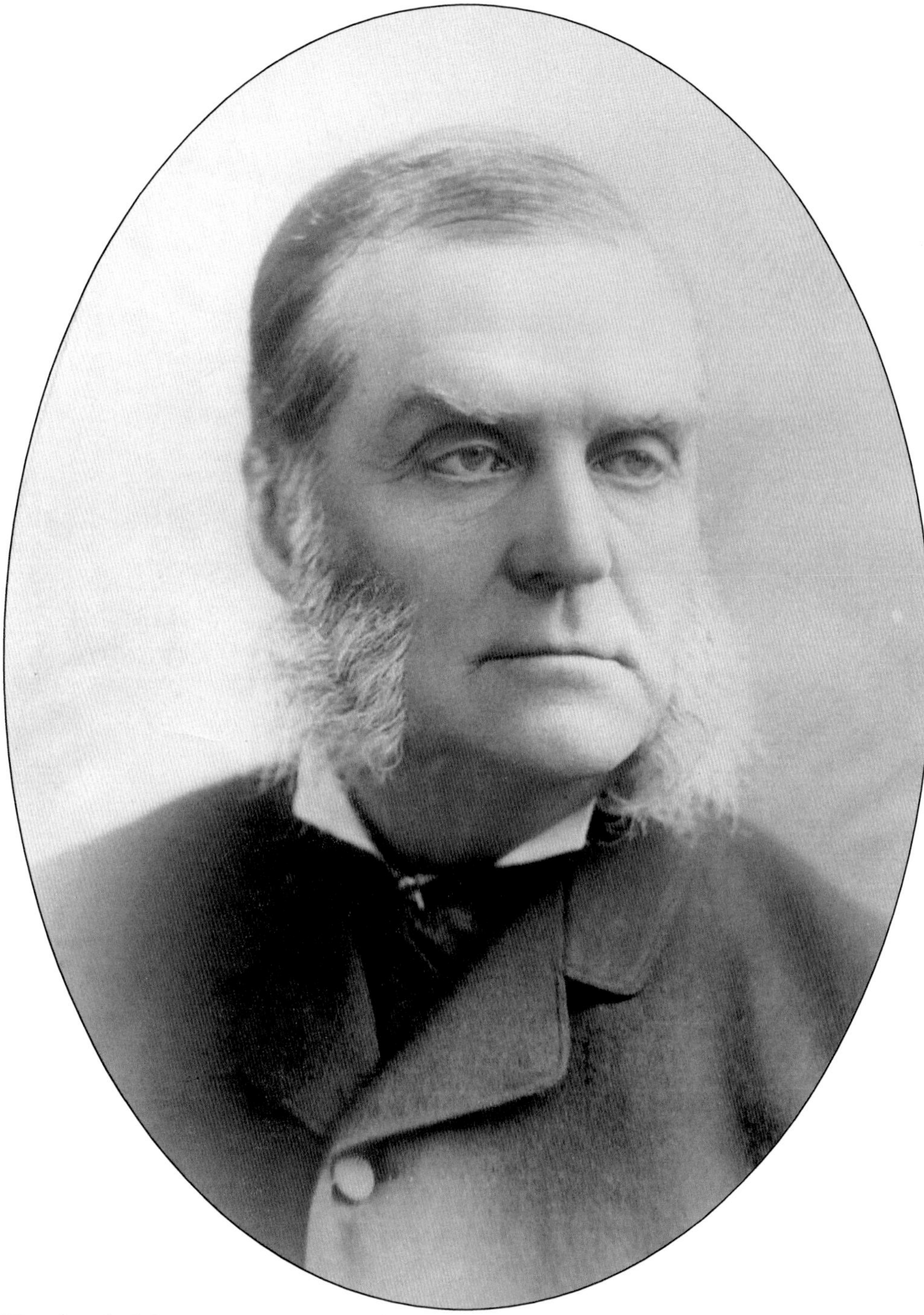

This dignified Geneva man is none other than Charles J. Folger. He was born on Nantucket Island, Massachusetts, on April 16, 1818, and was the secretary of the Treasury under Chester Arthur. Folger brought his leadership and skill to Geneva when he organized a fire company that was named after an outdated piece of fire equipment, known as Outcast No. 5. It was later named the Folger Hook and Ladder Company. Folger died on September 4, 1884, in Geneva.

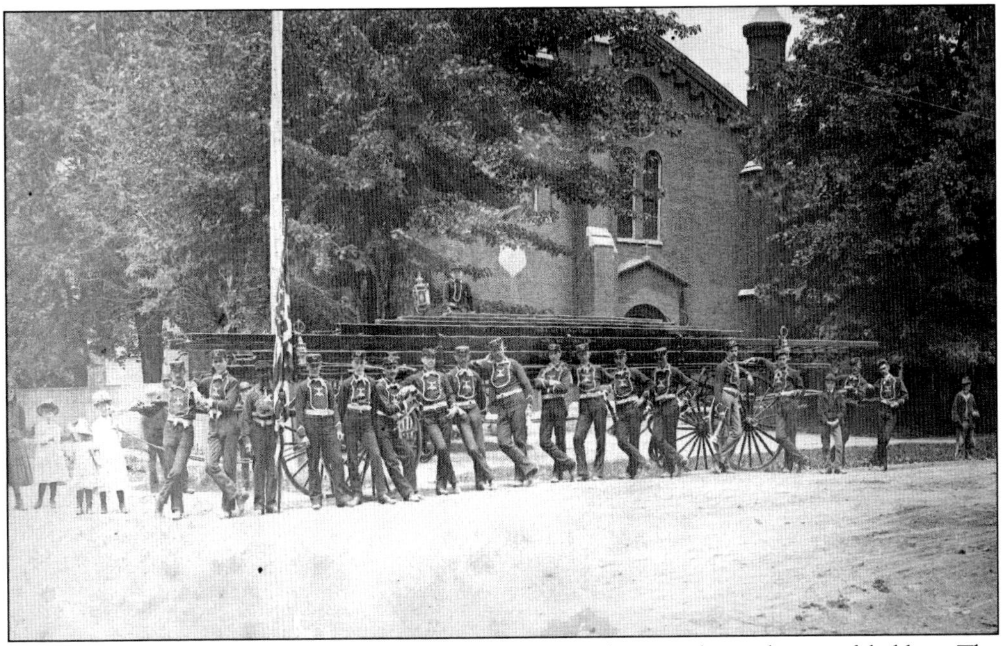

Stacked behind the Mutuals of Geneva in this 1885 photograph are heaps of ladders. The varying lengths of the ladders allowed the firemen to reach the height of just about any Geneva structure.

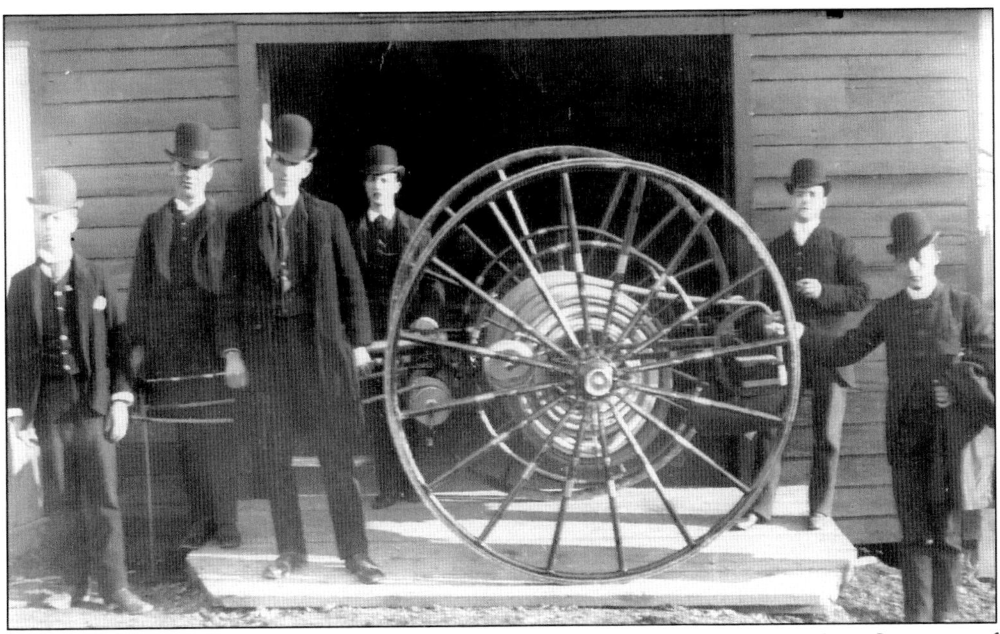

Standing around the first hose cart in this 1894 photograph is the Ogoyago Hose Company of Geneva. Early officers and charter members of this company were Jay George Stacey, William Millerd, Patrick H. Glynn, Edward McDonough, John Brennan, Frank Fox, and Albert Nichols.

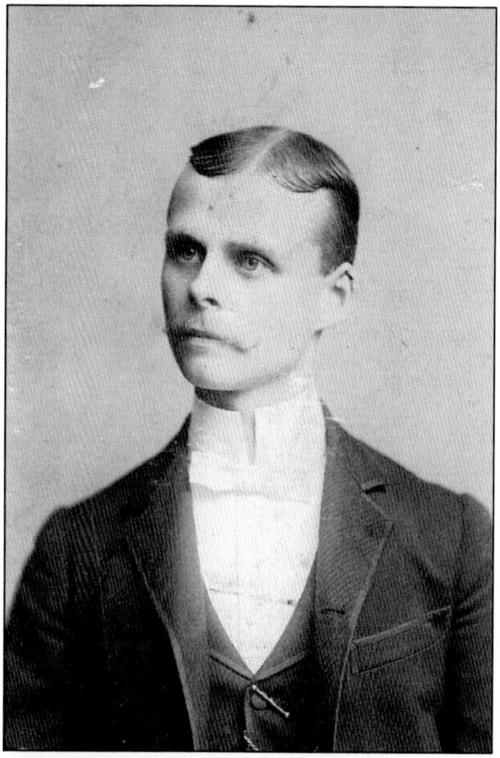

Charles A. Lane built the first pumper truck in the town of Phelps on a Ford Model T chassis for the White Hose Company.

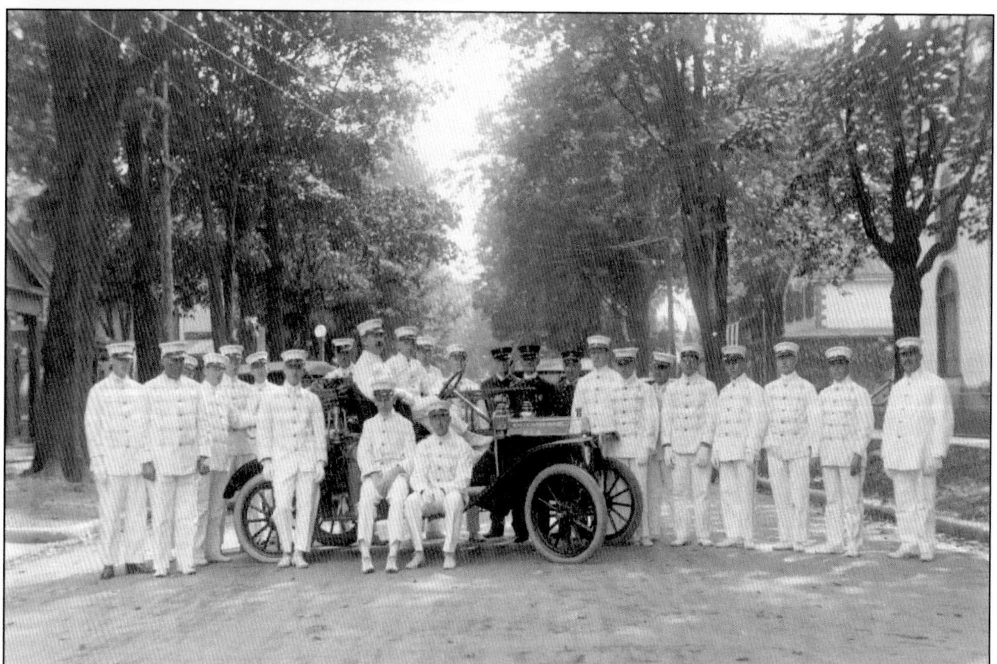

In their traditional white uniforms, the White Hose Company poses for this September 29, 1917 photograph around the pumper truck. The chief of the fire company, Charles A. Lane, can be seen sitting on the right of the running board of the truck he built.

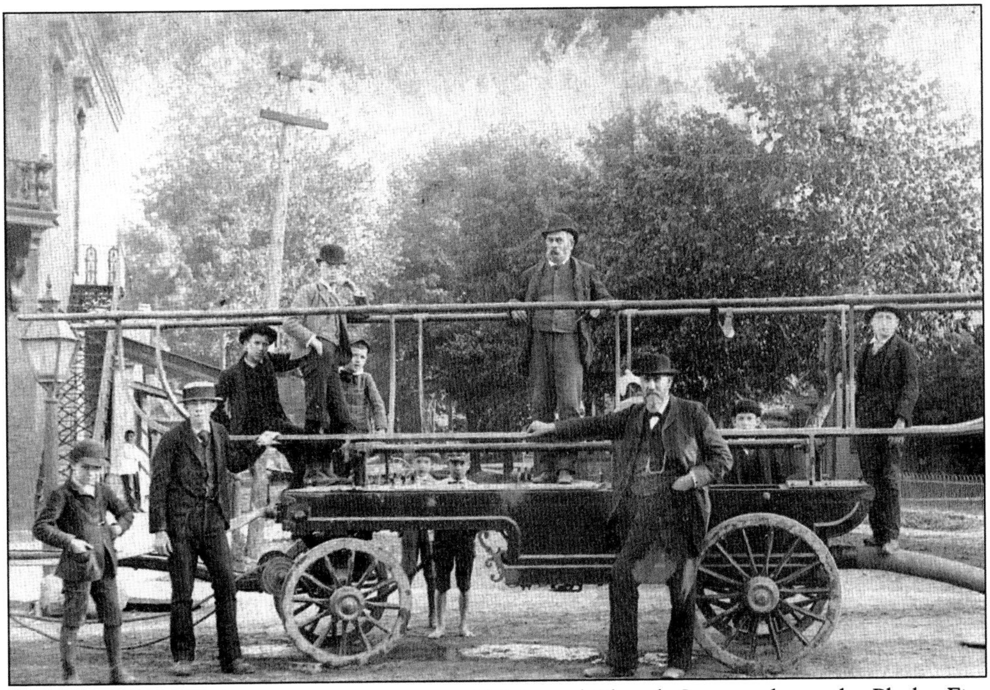

This 1864 photograph, taken at the corner of Main and Church Streets, shows the Phelps Fire Company in action. The large hose going into the street is heading into a reservoir built after the great fire of 1864.

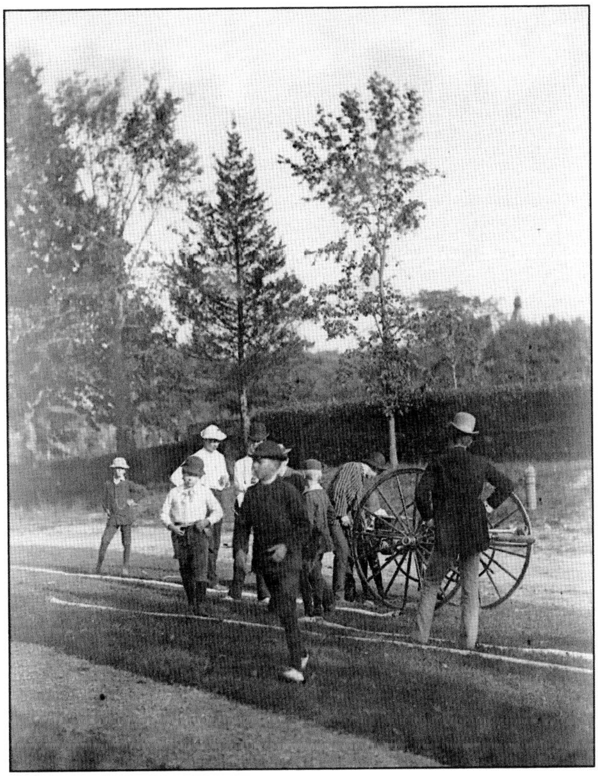

Shown in this 1885 photograph is Frederick Ferris Thompson's private fire company, whose service covered merely the Sonnenberg mansion.

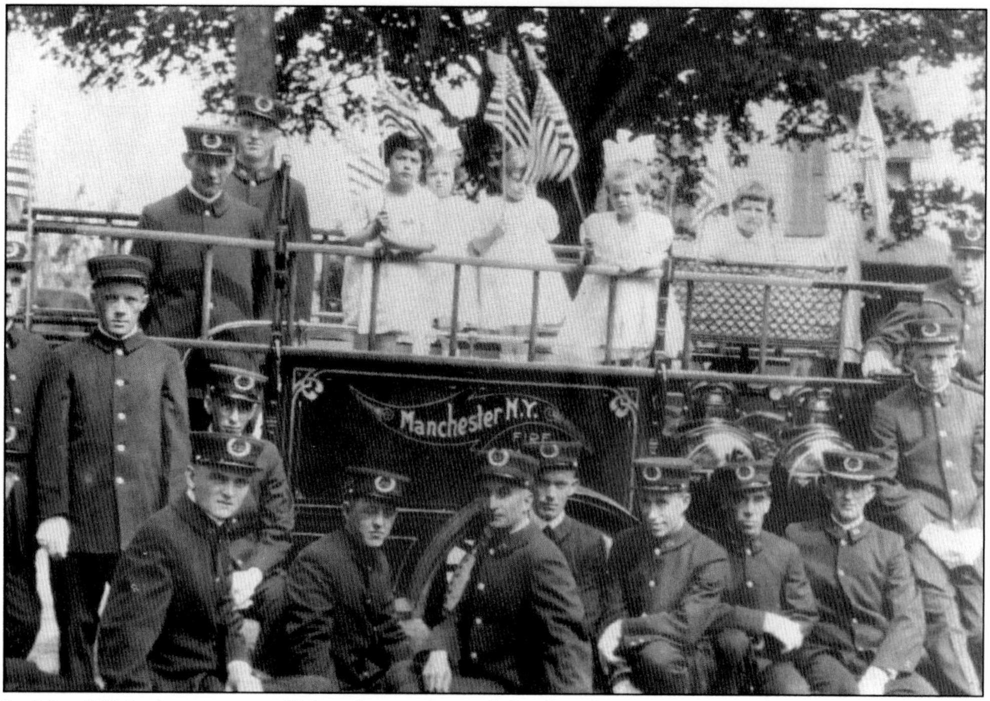

In May 1911, the citizens of Manchester formed the first fire company and elected Jacob Malter as chief, George Shaw as president, and George Sheppard as secretary. Shown from left to right are the following: (front row) Elmer VerPlanck, Henry Tobias, Frank Lyke, Leon Cooley, Floyd Gilman, Joe Meehan, Elmer Hyde, Charles Craig, John Robinson, Ernest VanDyne, and William Davidson; (back row, on the truck) John Gilman, Edward Murray, Lucille Dalberth, Mary Ryan, Mary Howland, Marie Tobias, Rita Proechel, and Eddie Smith (driver).

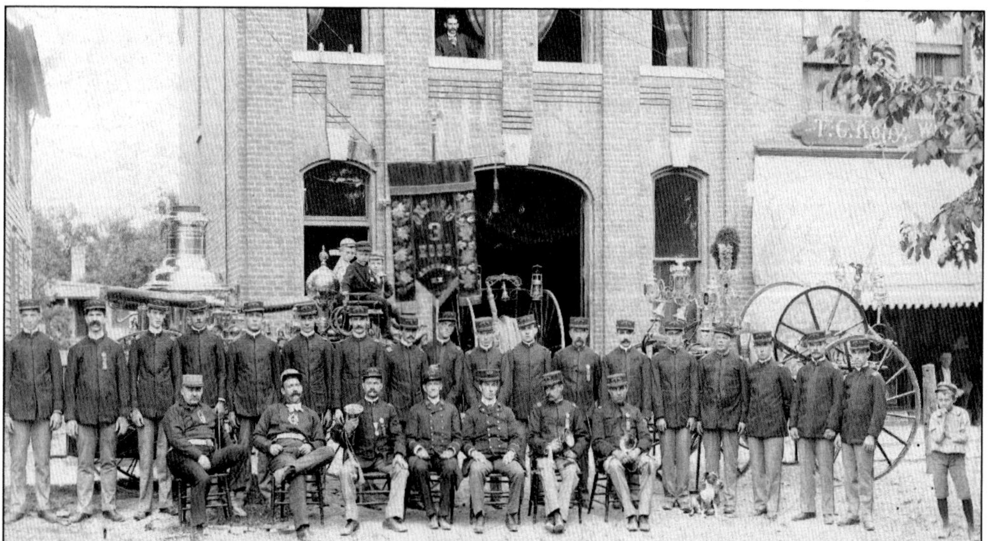

The Ontario County firehouse was built in 1884 and was located on 329 North Main Street in Canandaigua. Behind the company are various apparatuses, including the steamer (left).

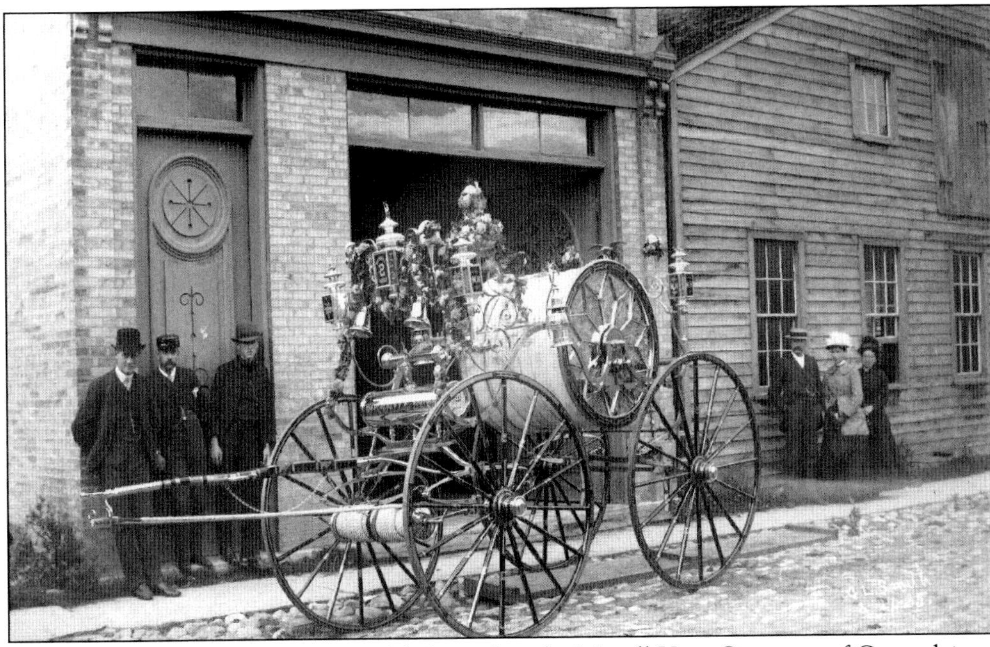

This hose cart was built in 1855 and belonged to the Merrill Hose Company of Canandaigua. It won first place at the Buffalo Fireman's Convention for both drill team carriage and best appearing company. Merrill Hose was located at 20 Phoenix Street in Canandaigua.

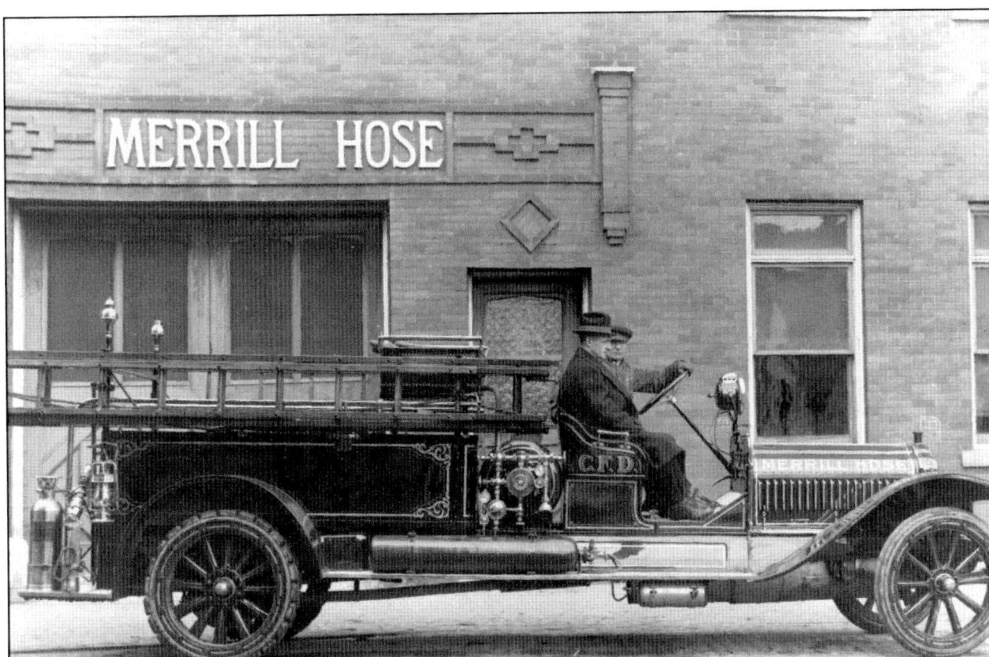

These two unidentified gentlemen look sternly ahead as they advance forward in a 1906 Merrill Hose fire truck.

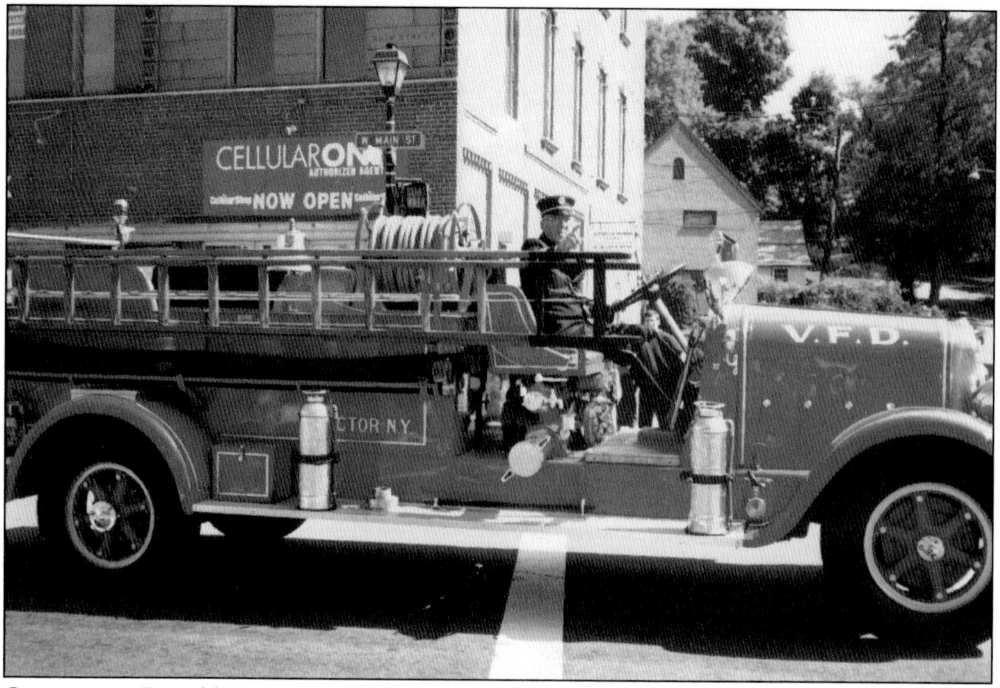

Once again, Donald Green is seen driving the 1931 Buffalo Pumper fire truck through the streets of Victor during a 1998 Memorial Day parade. Green has been driving fire trucks for more than 46 years.

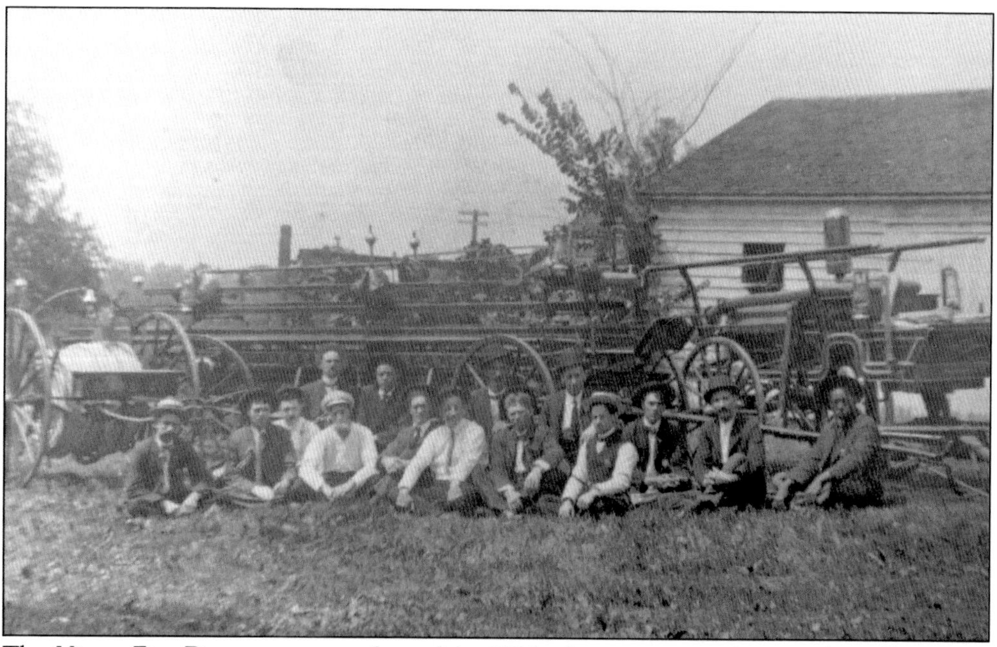

The Victor Fire Department was formed in 1904 after two tragic fires in the village. The first fire destroyed the north side of East Main Street on April 10, 1898, and the second fire destroyed the north side of West Main Street on October 15, 1899.

Seven

AVIATION

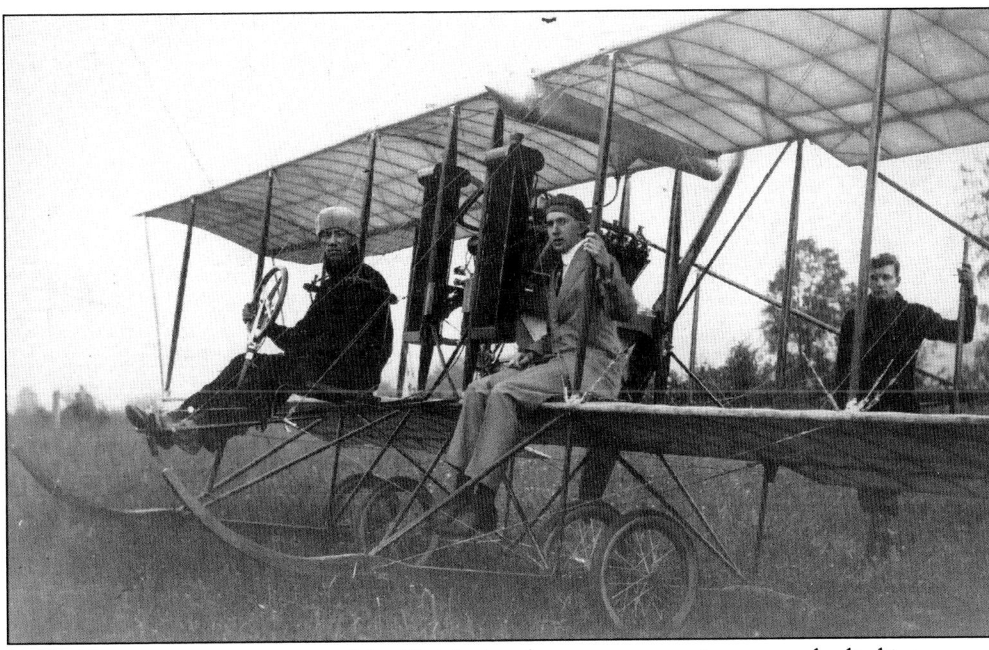

With the ingenious pioneering of the Wright brothers, transportation was embodied into a new form that required something it had not required before: air. This phenomenon did more than turn heads as it created a whole new industry for both businesses and domestic affairs. In the summer of 1911, renowned aviator George Smith of Rutland, Vermont, toured upstate New York with his Curtiss airship. With the help of the New York Central Railroad, Smith and his airship were transported from town to town, allowing people to become both educated of the new technology and to witness the thrill of flying. This early-1900 photograph of a similar airship displays the teamwork that was needed to initiate flight. Local aviator Busnick prepares for his ascent into the morning skies of Geneva.

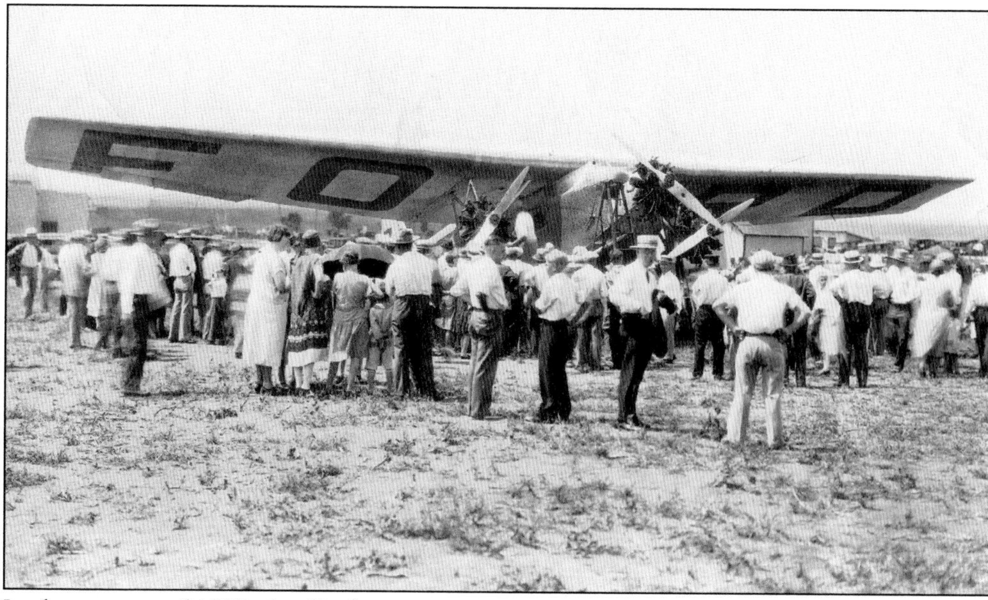

In the summer of 1927, this Ford twin-engine passenger plane, on a goodwill tour, proves to be a spectacle attracting people from the surrounding area of Geneva. The vastness of the near 50-foot wingspan generously provided a canopy for the spectators during a hot August day.

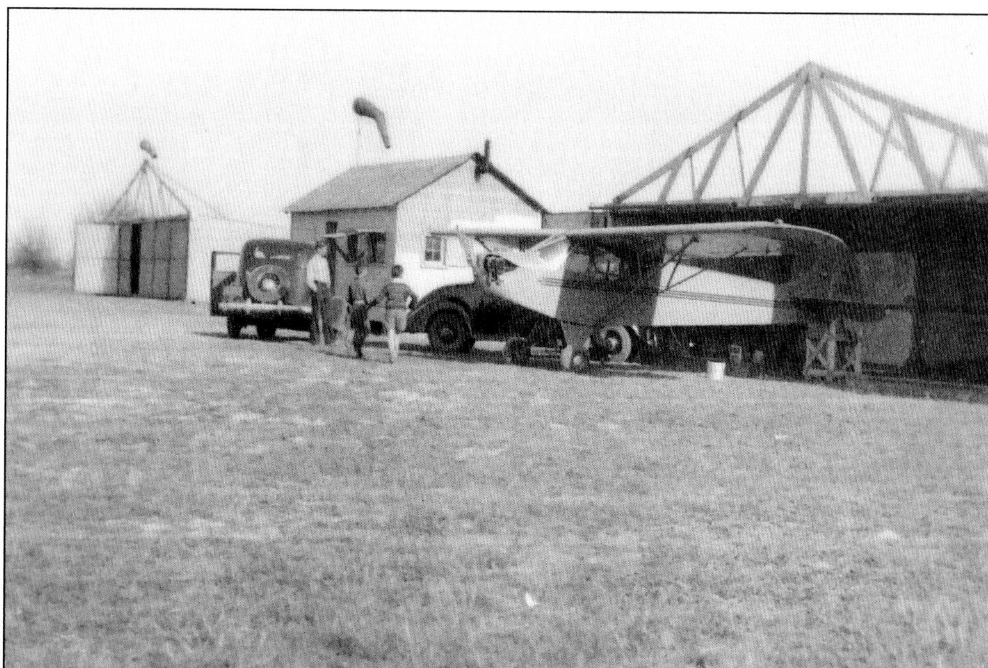

This late-1920s photograph shows recreational aviators removing their aircraft from a hangar at the Geneva flying field, also known as the Finger Lakes Airport. The airport was owned by Spencer Punnett and was located on Canandaigua Road, outside of Geneva.

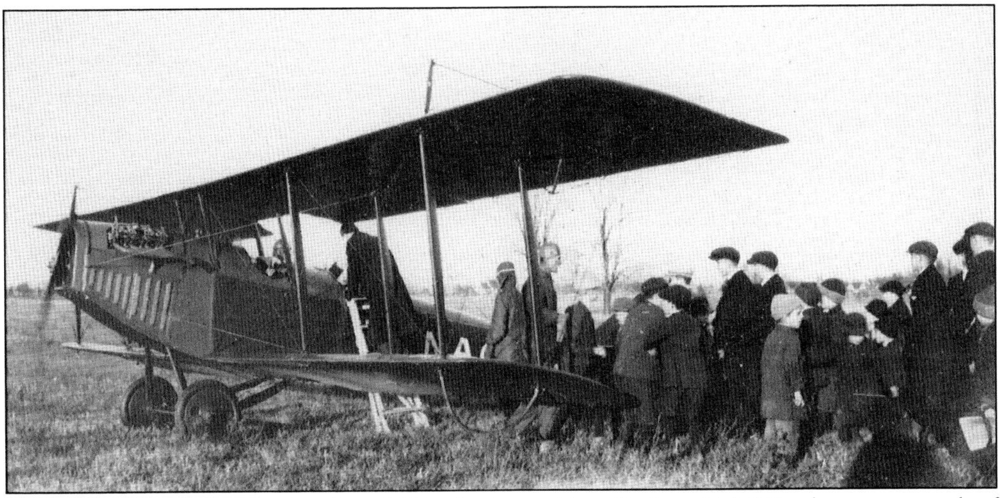

Preparing for departure, this late-1920s biplane, identified as NACO, draws a crowd of well-wishers. Note the ladder used by the pilot to enter the cockpit.

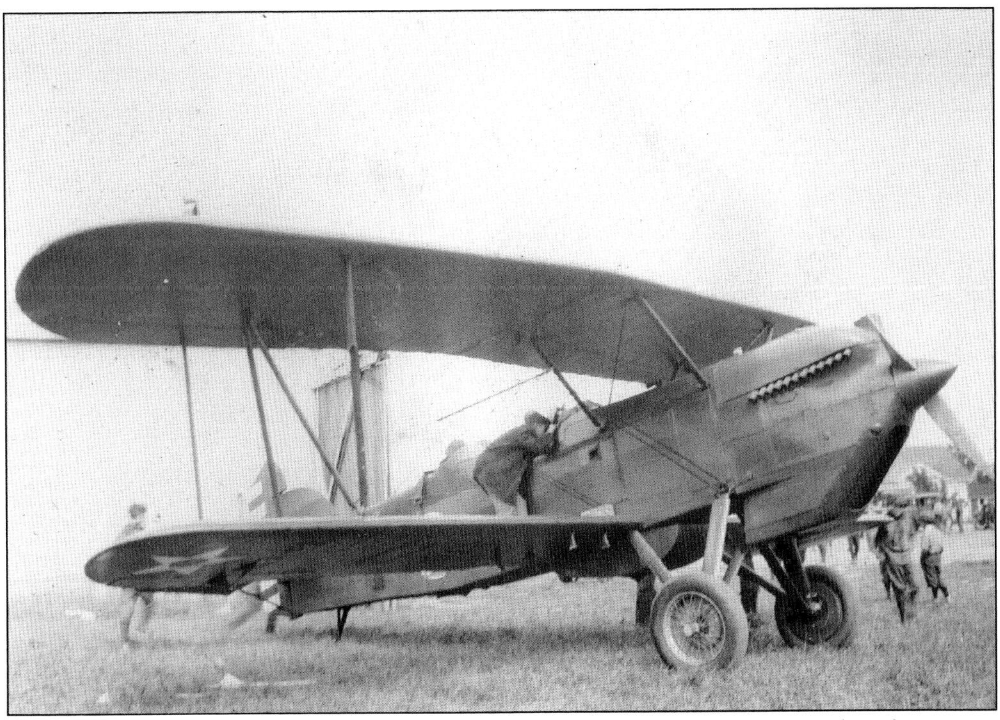

This early military biplane exhibits features that allowed ground troops to identify it as an allied plane. This particular picture was taken by Geneva civilians at an event that displayed military aircraft.

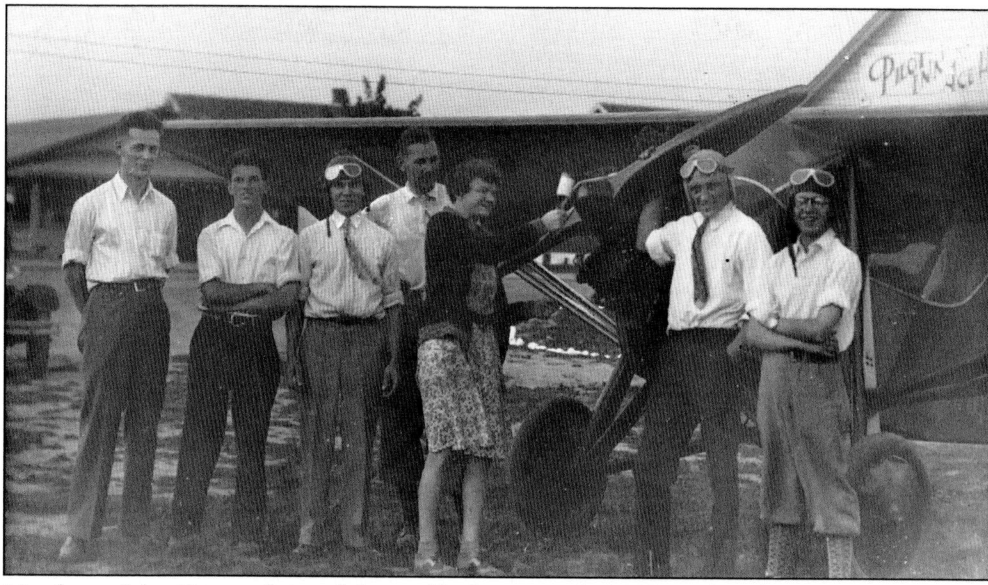

Members of the Geneva flying club stand before an early-1920s airship, known as "Ace High." This first American civil aircraft was produced after World War I. Its wingspan was 28 feet 4 inches, and its length was 19 feet 2 inches. Powered by a 40-horsepower Keane Acemotor, it was capable of reaching speeds of up to 80 mph. Among the flying club's members is Irene Graves, who is shown christening the plane for the club's pilot.

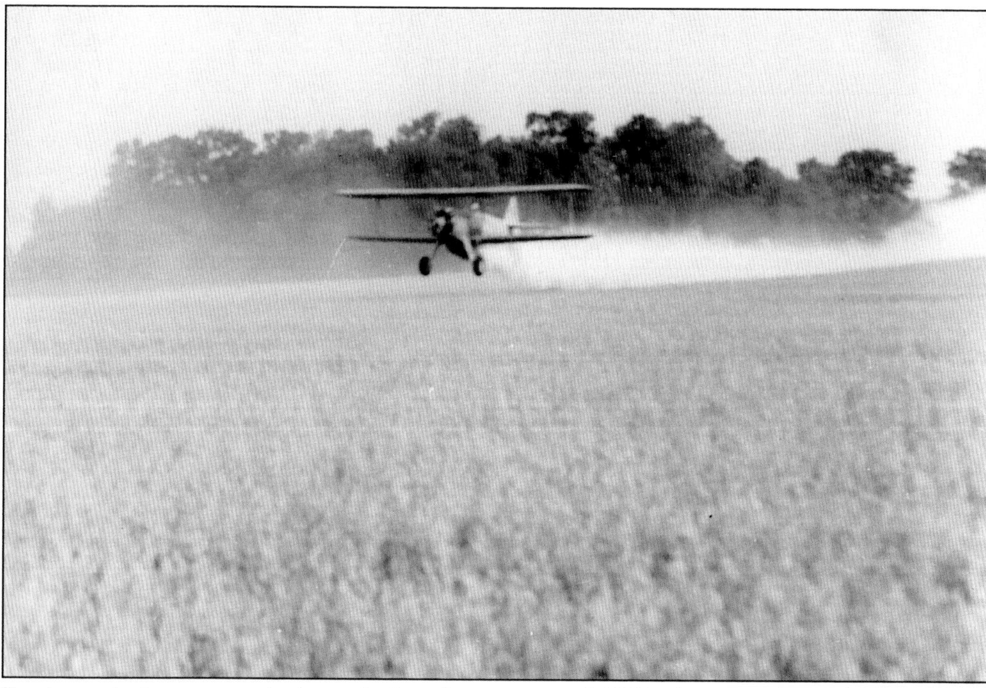

Putting aviation to practical use during the summer of 1954, this crop duster hovers over a regional field to obliterate the damaging armyworms. Ontario County was known for its Flying Farmers, among whom were Everett Blazey and George Purdy. Their hangar was located near the Finger Lakes racetrack in Farmington.

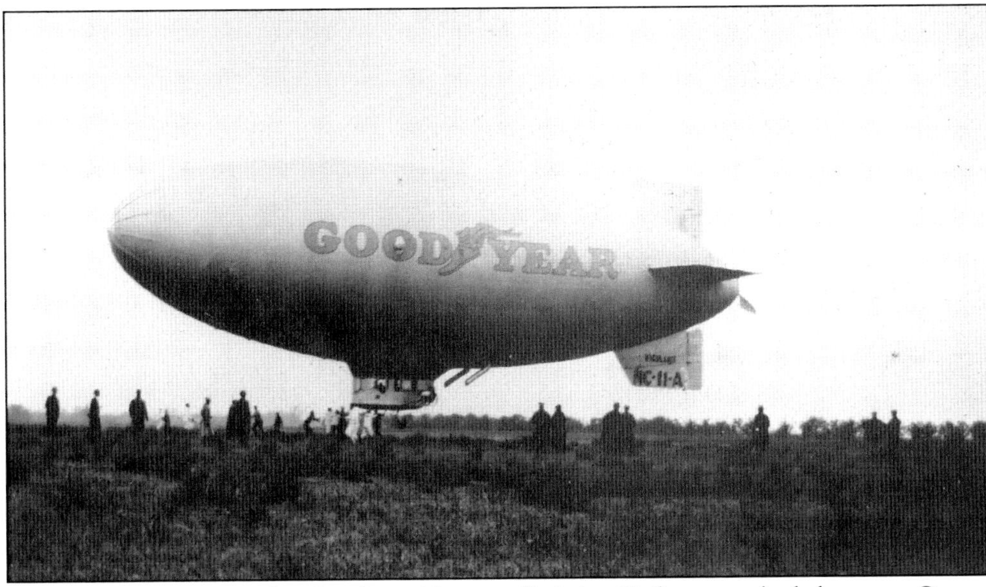

On October 16, 1929, the Goodyear blimp, called the *Vigilant*, touched down on Geneva territory from its home in Akron, Ohio. Pilots Charles Brannigan (an experienced flyer of American ships) and A.T. Sewall (a former naval pilot) took invited passengers on a ride. The cabin of the ship had a carrying capacity of four people, excluding the three spots that were designated for pilots.

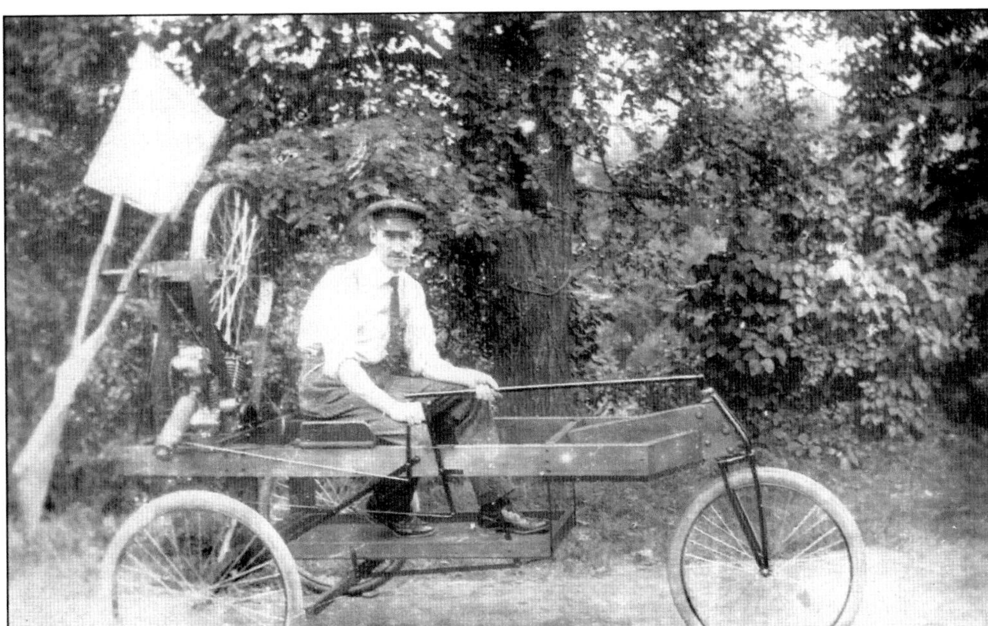

This is a rare glimpse of Glenn Hammond Curtiss, the father of naval aviation. He is shown testing his wind wagon, which is also known as the horse scarer. The results were used to assert a blimp's steering control. During this time, Curtiss's airplane company became part of the Willys Overland automotive company, which was managed by former Canandaigua resident John North Willys.

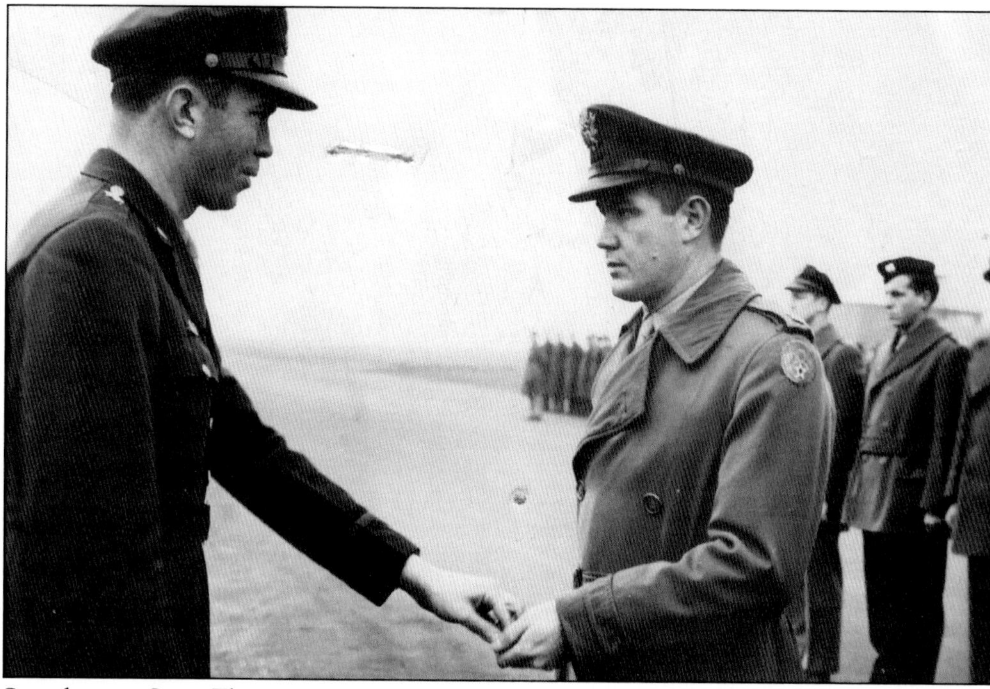

Seen here is Capt. Thomas A. Henry of Shortsville as he receives the Distinguished Flying Cross from Gen. Harold Q. Huglin. Henry was a navigator for the B-17 Flying Fortress component of the 8th Air Force, a bombardment group that led the first American bombing attack on target in Berlin.

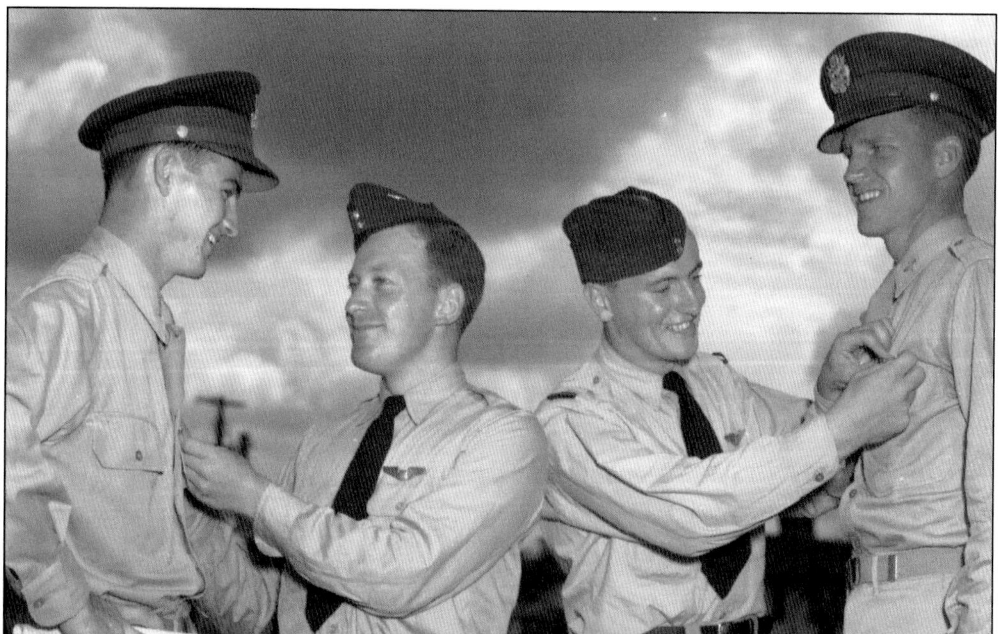

Lt. Francis J. McShea (left) of Manchester is shown receiving his pilot wings from RAF Pilot Officer John G. Giles. On an imperative mission during World War II, McShea was shot down in French territory and was confirmed missing in action.

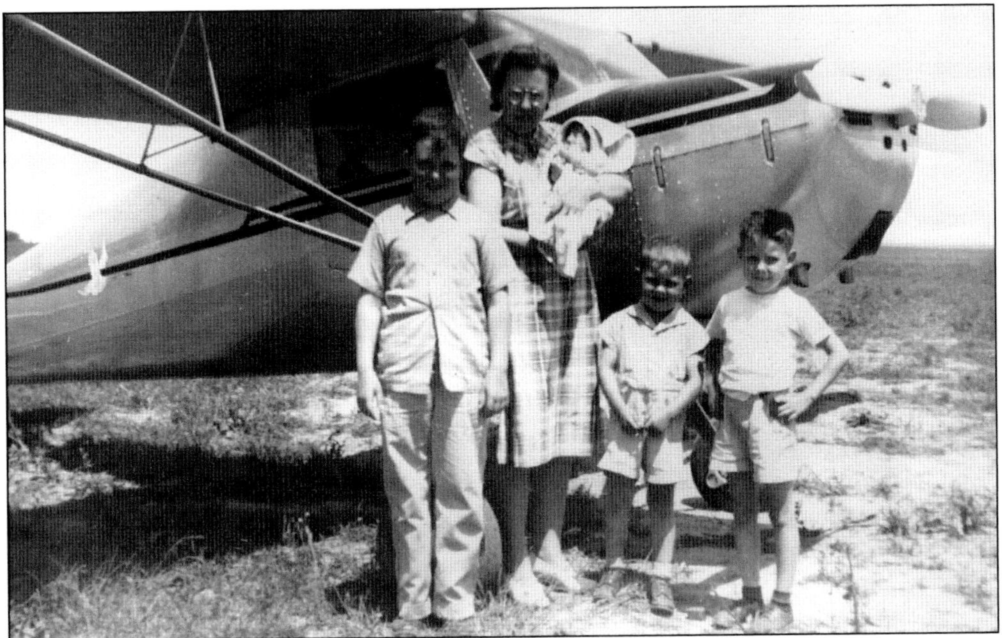

Standing in front of their 1946 Cessna 120 airplane is the Bowerman family. From left to right are David, Jenny (mother), Linda, Larry, and Donald Bowerman. Missing from the photograph is father Robert J. Bowerman. Three generations of the Bowerman family were Flying Farmers, starting with Robert J., his son Larry, and Larry's son Lynn.

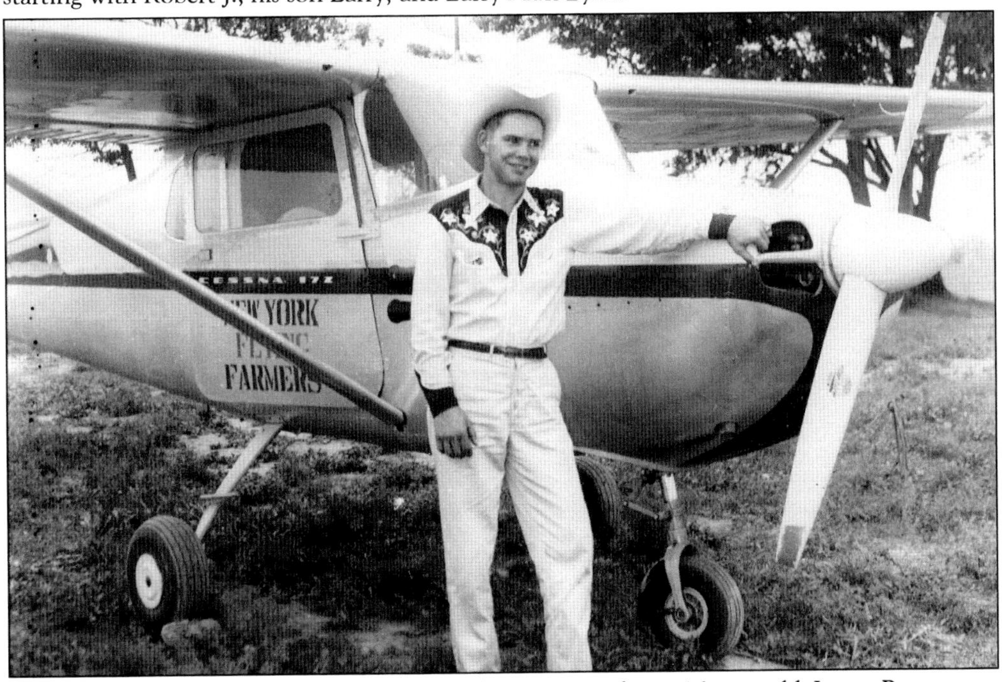

Embracing the nose of his plane in his Sky King outfit is 16-year-old Larry Bowerman. Immediately after a flight instruction lasting only 2 hours and 20 minutes, Larry was in the plane flying solo. He was trained by former World War II pilot Bill Gill, who charged just $7 for instruction.

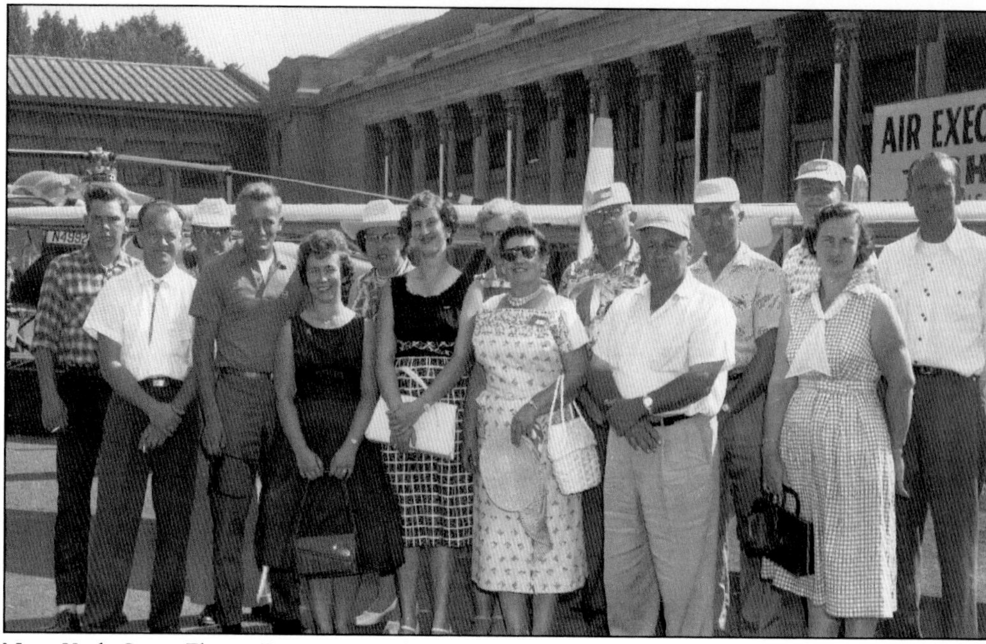

New York State Flying Farmers are shown gathered at the New York State Fairgrounds on September 7, 1960. This particular bunch was referred to as the "core" group and was known to take off from the Canandaigua Hawks in Epic Flight's (CHIEF) landing strip, which was located on the Purdy farm. From left to right are Larry Bowerman, Bob McClure, Robert Bowerman, Glen Maxon, Joyce Maxon, Jenny Bowerman, Shirley Covert, ? Covert, Jesse Barnum, Pete Barnum, Homer Maxon, Asa Culver, Arthur Barnum, Shirley Mead, and Tracey Mead.

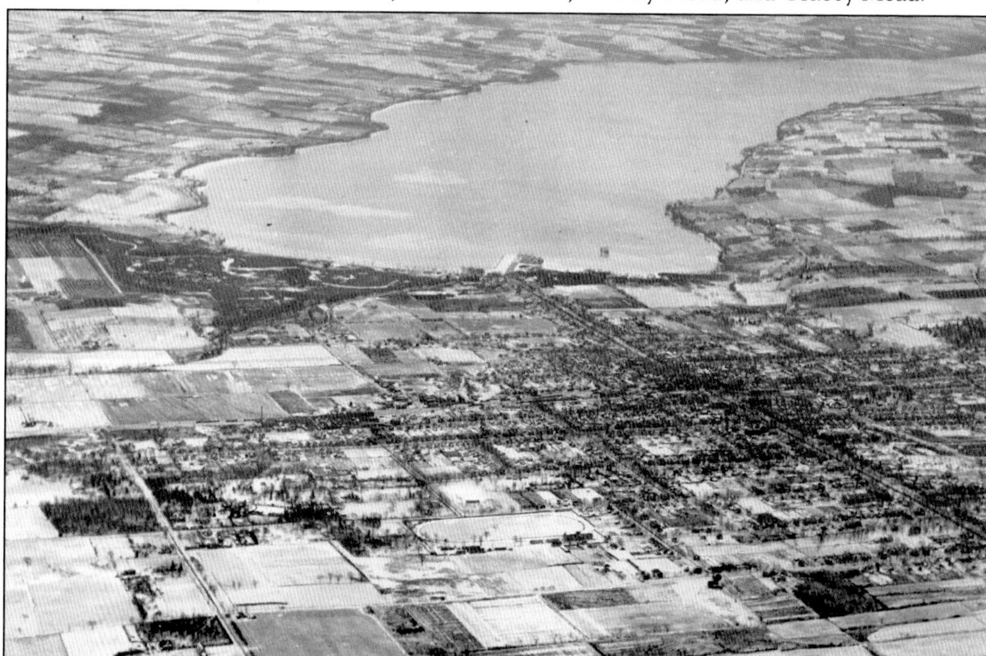

From 5,000 feet above, a perimeter of 10 miles looks like an intricately designed quilt, as is the case in this 19th-century photograph taken from a blimp.

Eight

Delivery Service

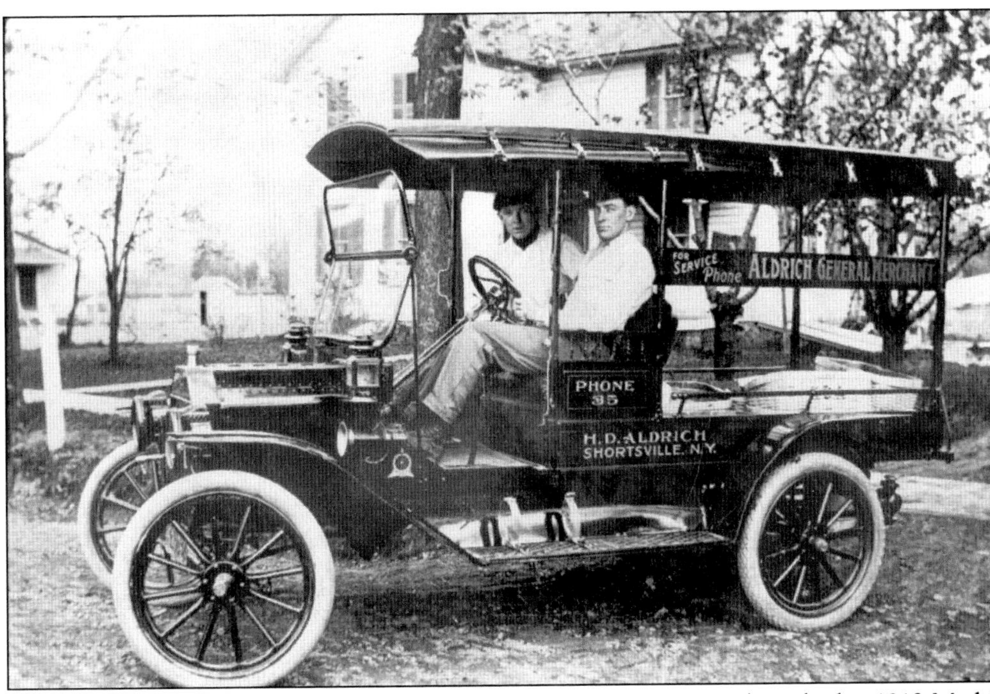

On a delivery run, Mr. Henry (left) and Mr. Aldrich remain composed inside this 1913 Model T express wagon. Aldrich owned the H.D. Aldrich General Store, which was located on Main Street in Shortsville and was established in 1901. The store supplied Shortsville and its neighboring village, Manchester, with such supplies as shoes, sugar, wheat, cracked corn, and other supplies. Aldrich had two delivery wagons.

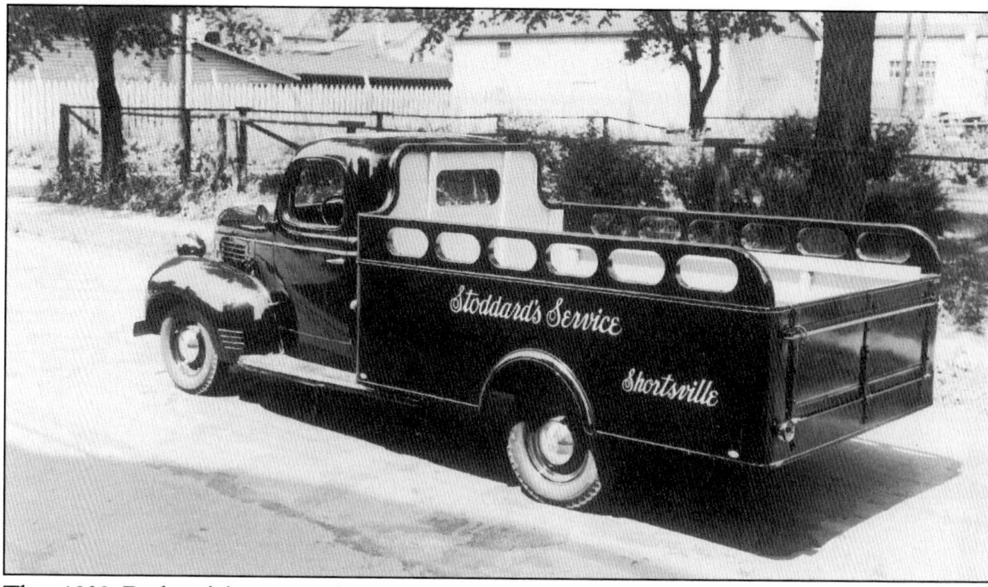

This 1939 Dodge delivery truck was used for Jay M. Stoddard's Shortsville furniture store, which was established in 1881. Stoddard was also an undertaker.

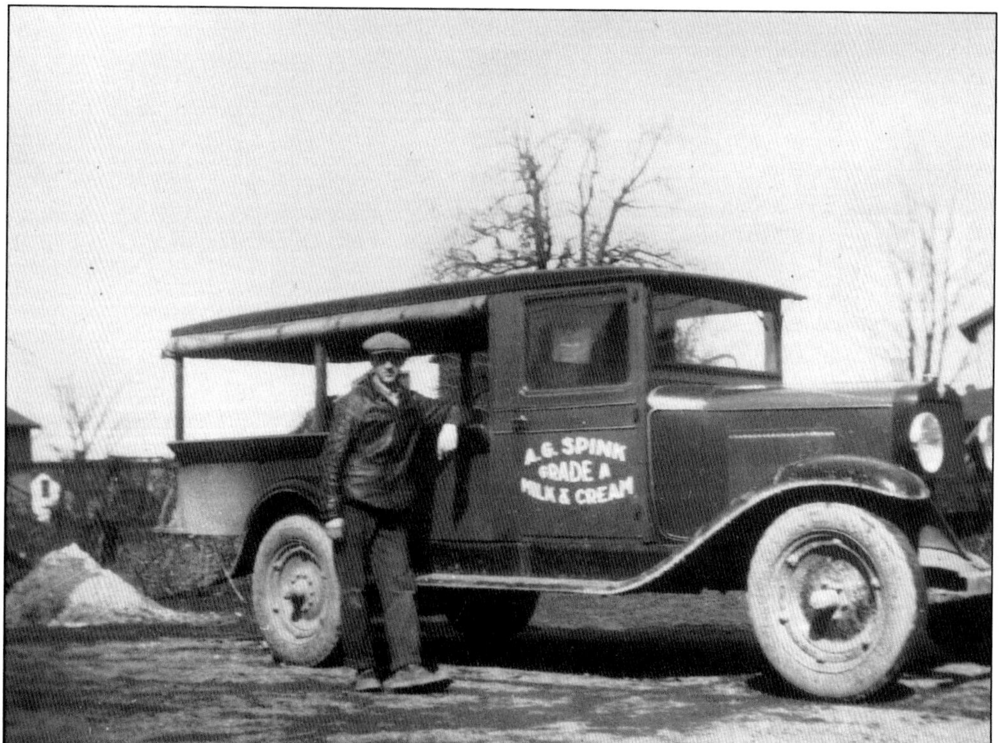

Standing beside his 1931 Chevy truck is Yorkshire, England immigrant Alfred Spink. Spink delivered milk for Phelps from 1924 to the early 1940s, worked from 4:30 a.m. to 12:00 p.m., and was known as a strong fellow despite his short stature. His son said that while serving for his country in World War I he swapped candy with German soldiers.

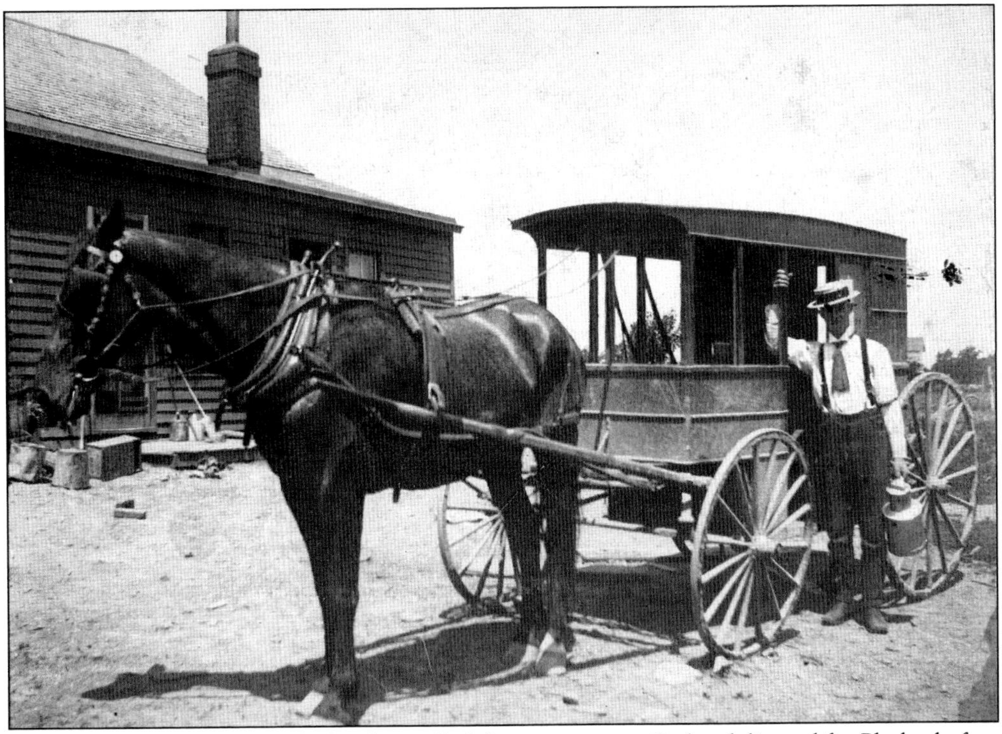

Shown here is Lynn Ottley before his milk delivery carriage. Ottley delivered for Phelps before the advent of pasteurization.

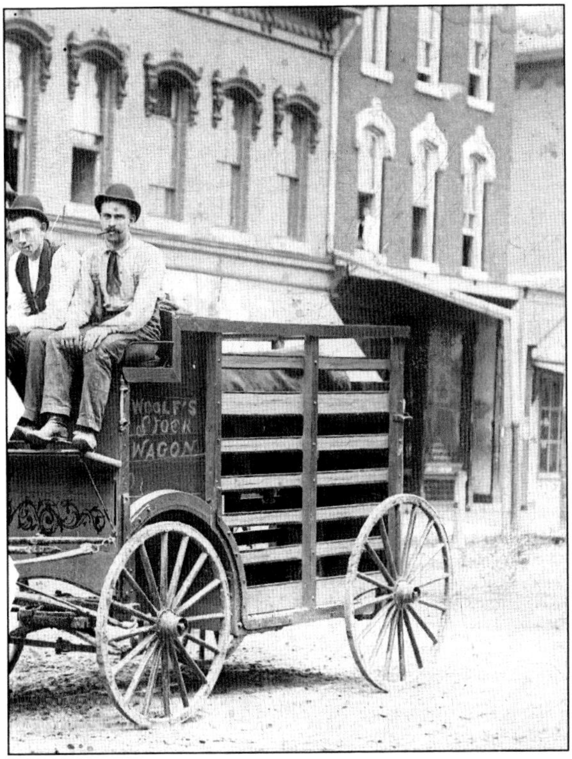

When it was mundane to see a steer pulling a wagon, a steer in this picture is being carried in Woolf's stock wagon. Woolf was a choice meats dealer whose market was on the Carpenter Block in Phelps.

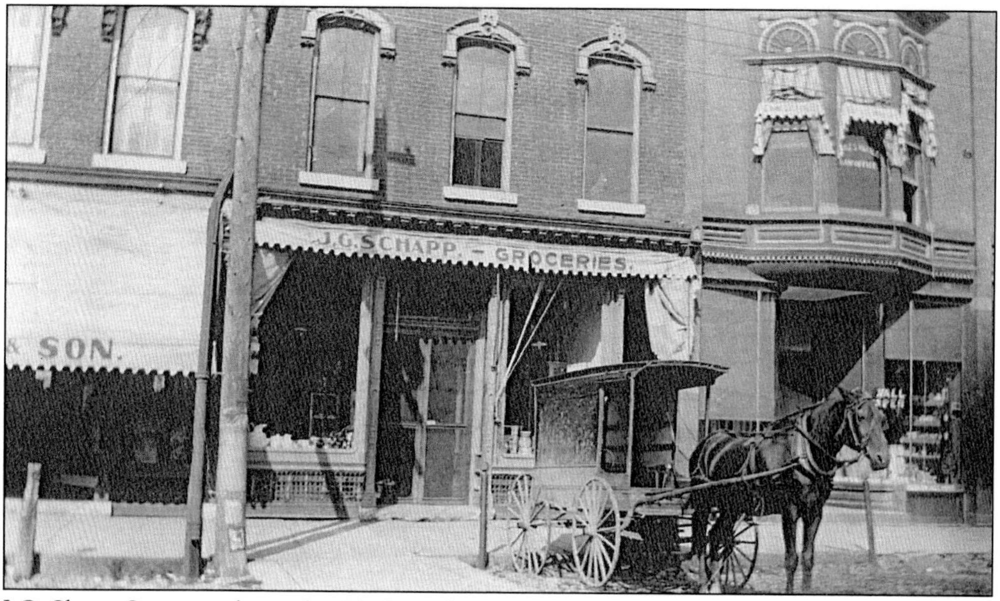

J.G. Shapp Groceries, located in Phelps, offered something for everyone, as it not only supplied the staples but also sold candy. In this image, the horse and delivery wagon wait for an order.

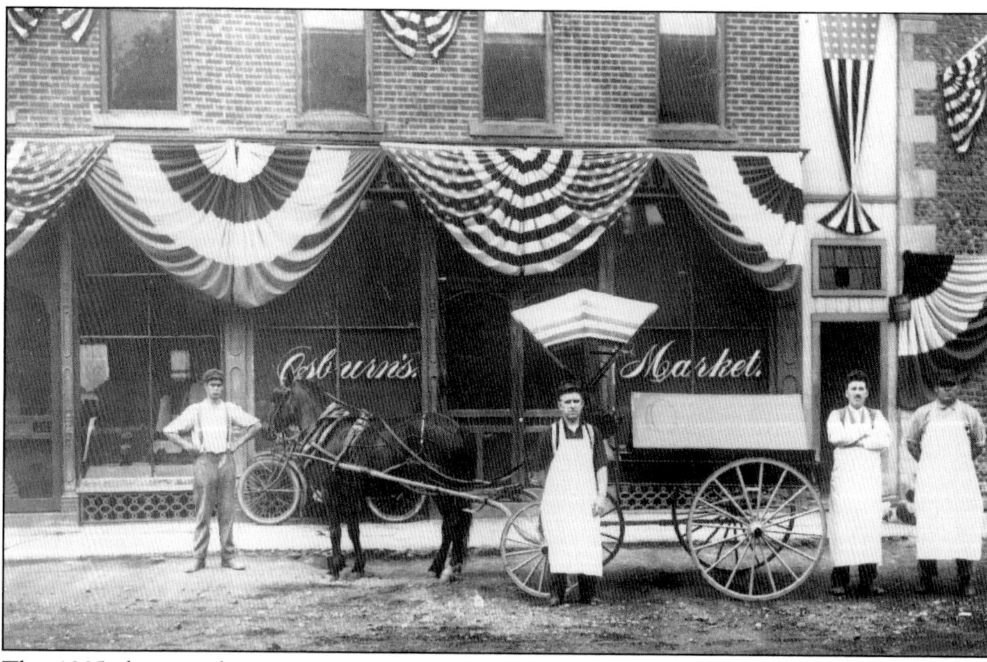

This 1905 photograph captures Osburn's Market with festooning Fourth of July flags. Standing casually in the center is Osburn himself, who had a favorable reputation among the Victor populace. His meat market was known for its excellent sanitary conditions and modern credit system, which simplified bookkeeping and practically eliminated all danger of error in his accounts with customers.

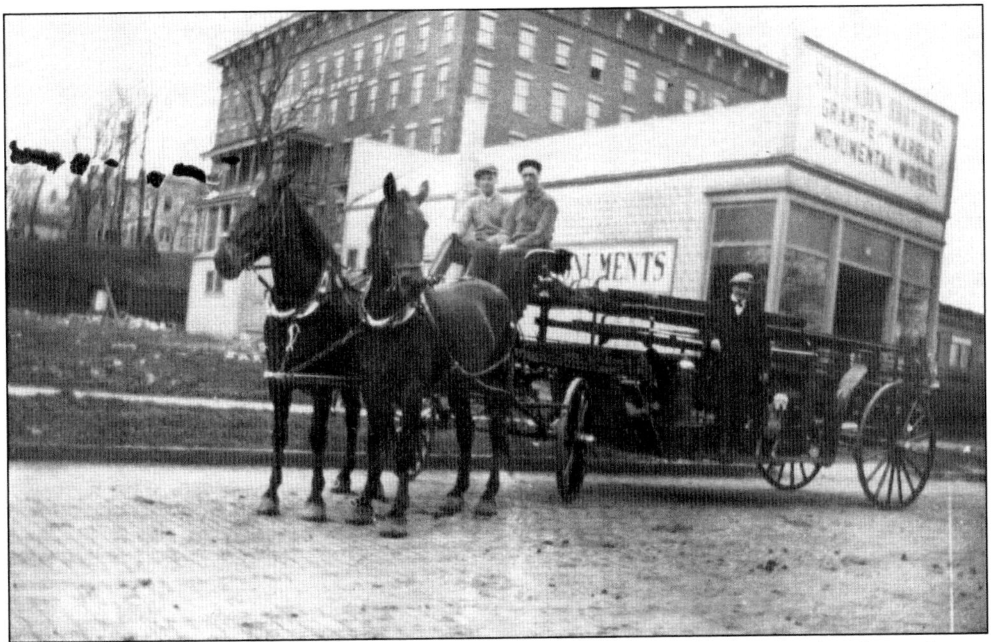

This wagon, driven by William Salladin, delivered cemetery headstones for the Canandaigua Granite Company. Because of the heavy headstones, the wagon was built with steel reinforcements. The Hickey monument was among the many heavy and delicate structures it carried. This picture was taken in 1910.

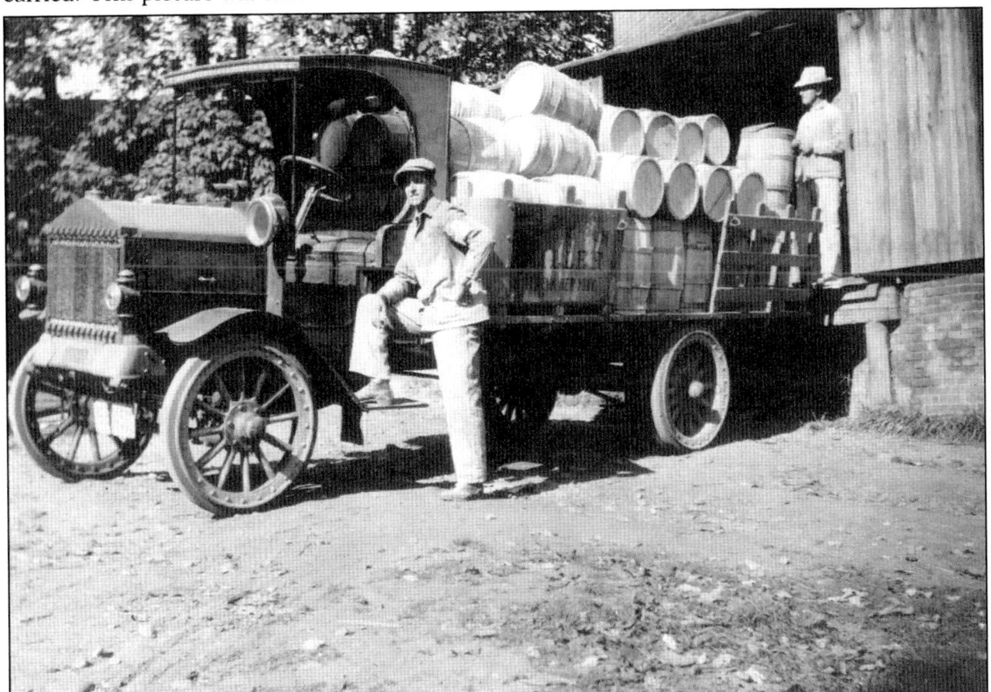

Although sometimes targeted by the Women's Christian Temperance Union (WCTU) as a bootlegging vehicle, this Davidson delivery truck is parked innocently in Geneva as its freight is unloaded.

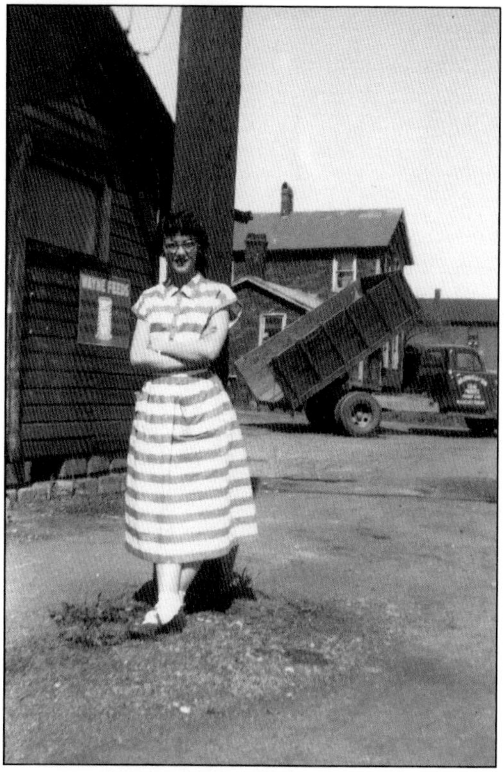

Seen here is Joan Schlecht in front of Crow's Feed Mill and Coal Delivery, which was established in 1930 and was located on the Merrick Circle (in close proximity to the roundhouse). The vehicle behind her is a late-1940s dump truck.

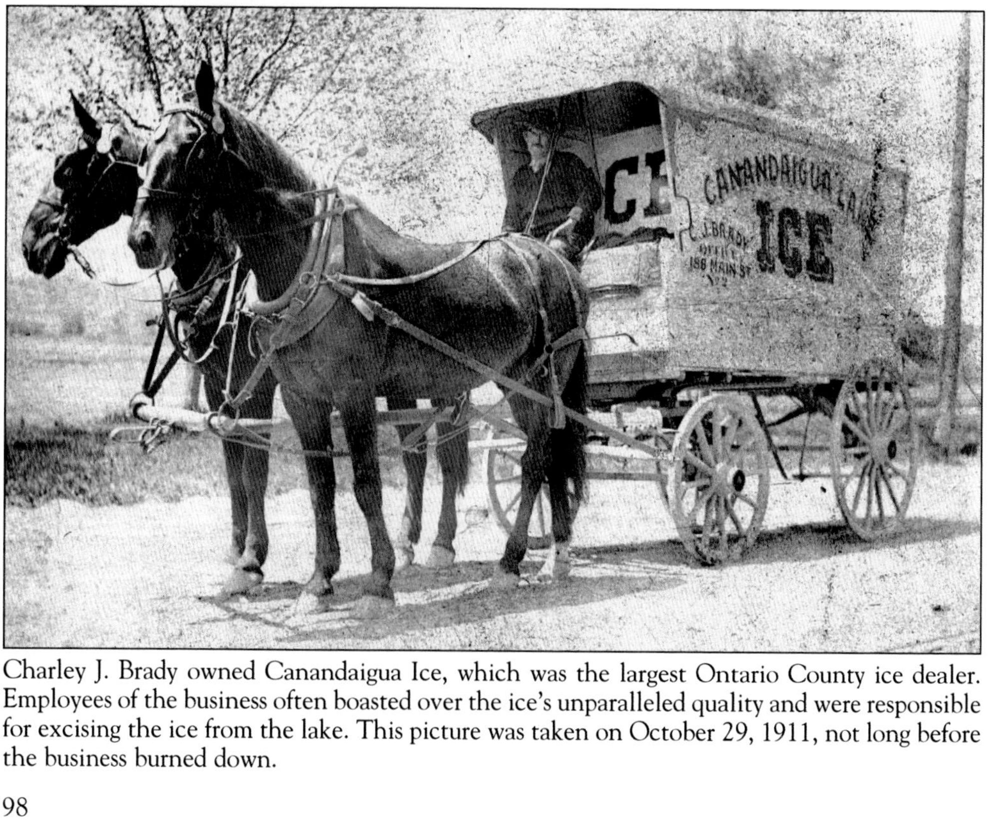

Charley J. Brady owned Canandaigua Ice, which was the largest Ontario County ice dealer. Employees of the business often boasted over the ice's unparalleled quality and were responsible for excising the ice from the lake. This picture was taken on October 29, 1911, not long before the business burned down.

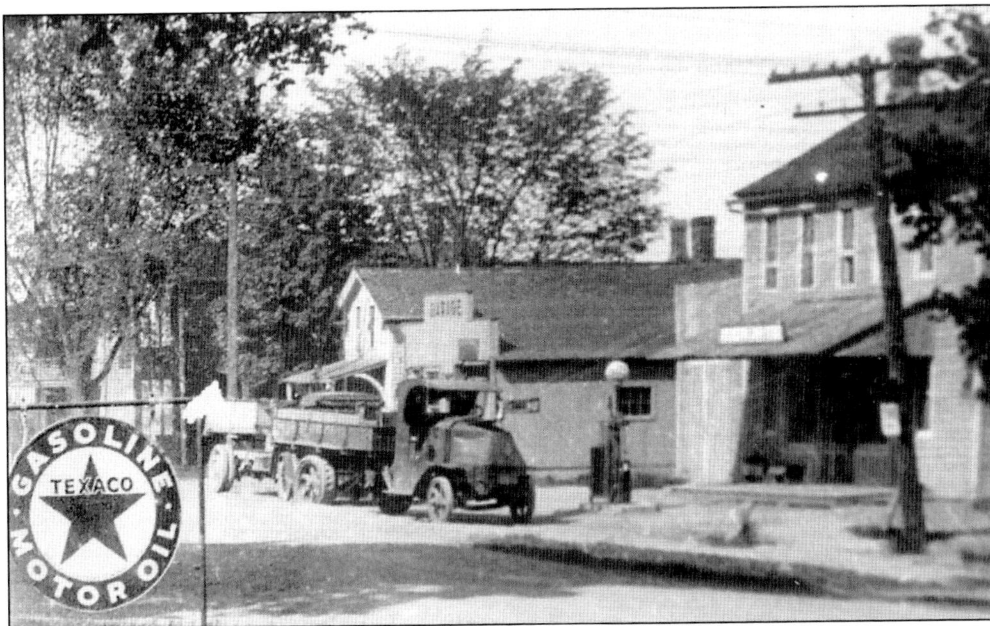

In this 1905 photograph, a Mack truck passes by the Port Gibson Texaco gas station. Today, the building is a general store owned by Elizabeth Combs, whose husband, Richard Combs, is Manchester's historian.

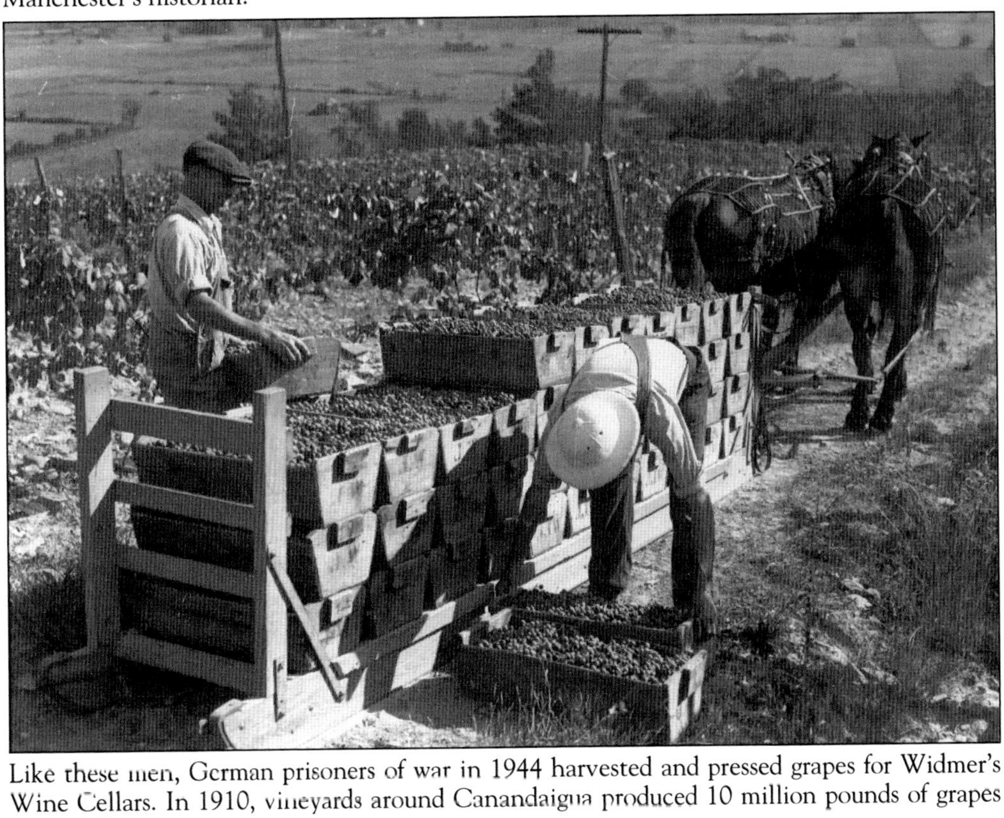

Like these men, German prisoners of war in 1944 harvested and pressed grapes for Widmer's Wine Cellars. In 1910, vineyards around Canandaigua produced 10 million pounds of grapes in 20 different varieties.

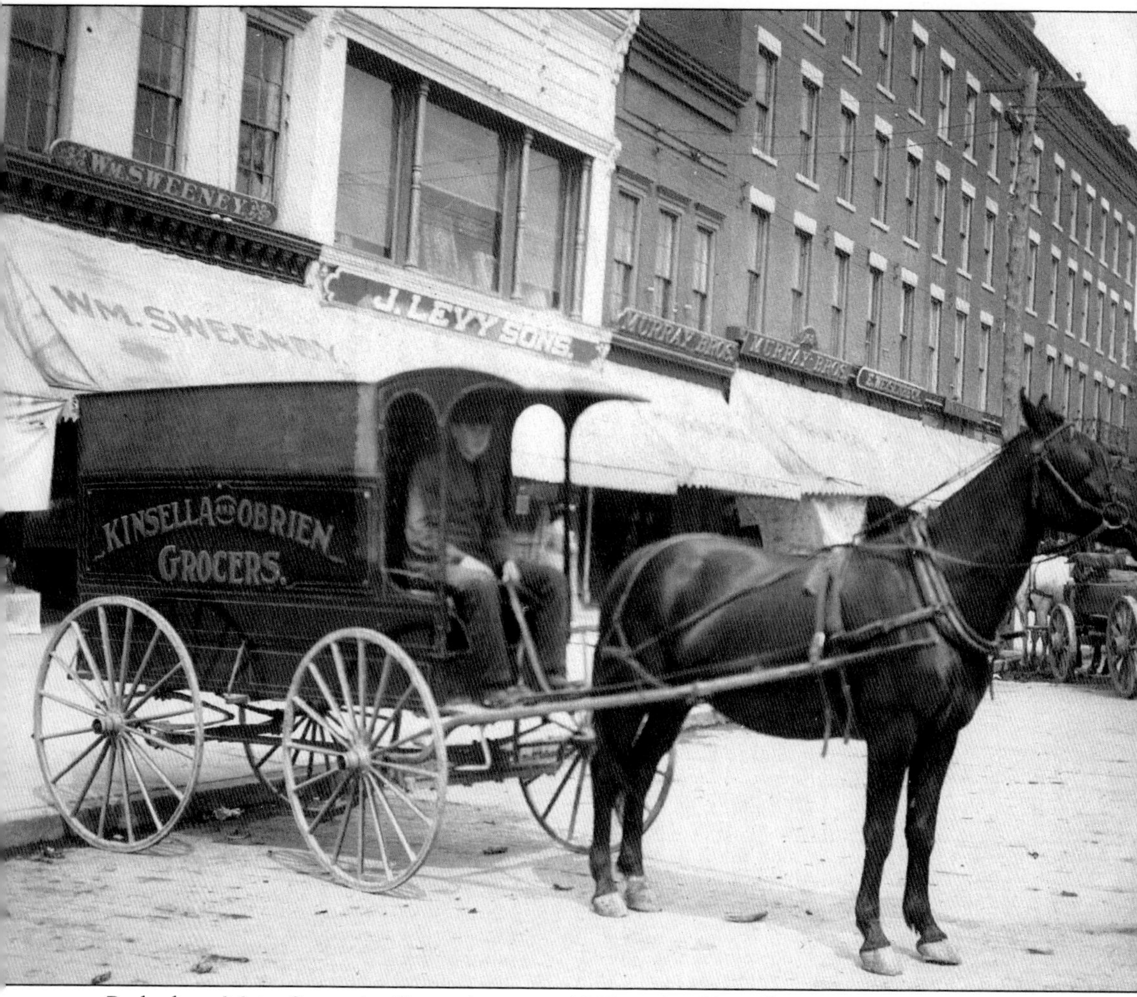

Parked on Main Street in Canandaigua *c.* 1900 is this Kinsella & O'Brien grocery carriage. Because of the business's robust horses, delivery service was conveniently fast.

Nine

MISHAPS

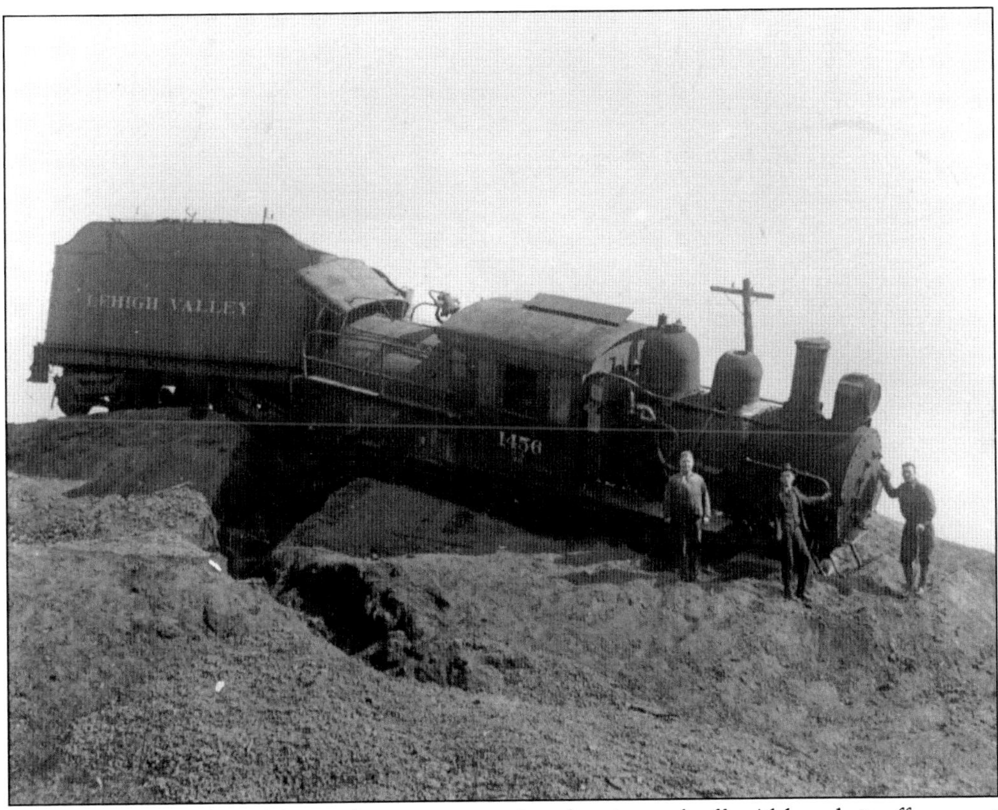

Advancing technology, like modern transportation, has its tradeoffs. Although it offers great convenience, it also offers the risk of malfunctioning, having mechanical flaws, and engineering problems, among other concerns. As seen in this Manchester yard derailment (caused by a washout), some accidents are inevitable and even perhaps irredeemable. The engineer, fireman, and conductor are shown posing unashamedly before a hopeless switcher.

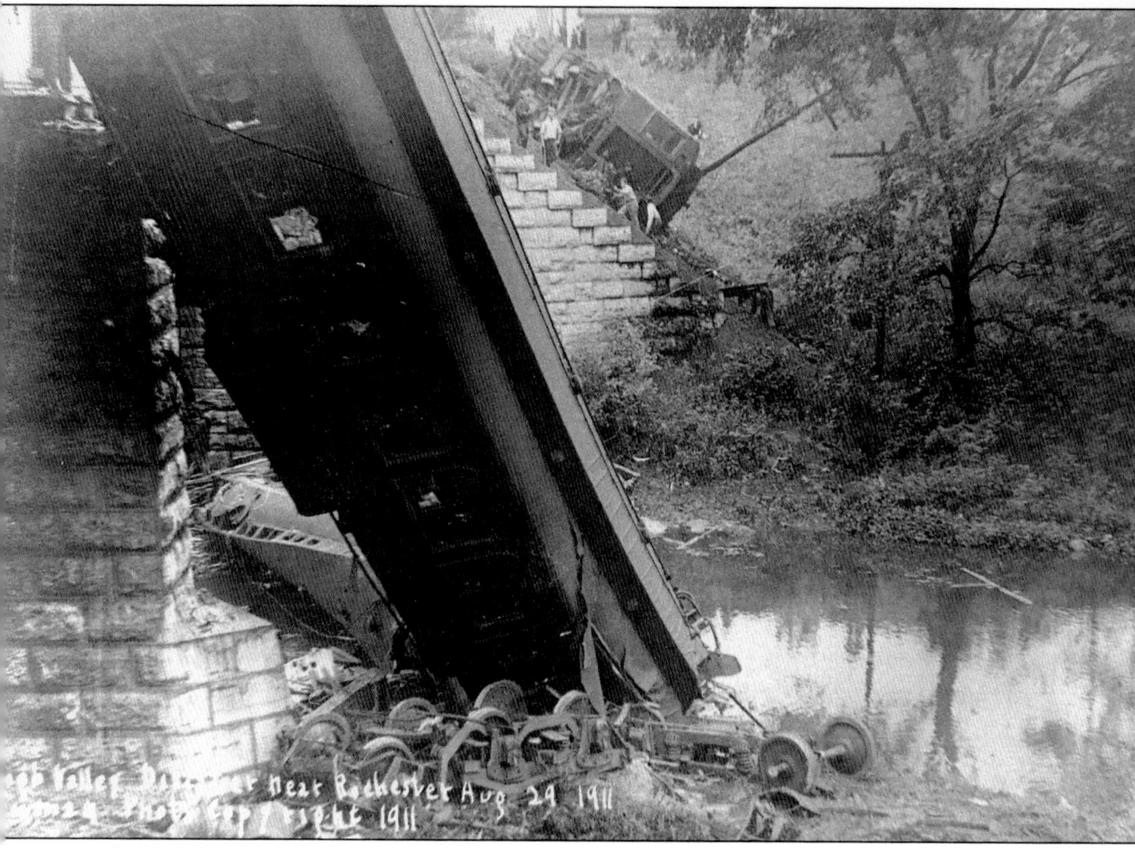

On August 25, 1911, at 12:58, this atrocious accident occurred on the Manchester trestle. It was a Lehigh Valley passenger train carrying mostly Civil War veterans from Philadelphia returning from a Grand Army Republic (GAR) reunion. The train plunged 45 feet below into the outlet, killing 23 instantly, and left 10 who survived only until the following day. Further disaster was prevented by Frank J. Finer of Philadelphia, who pulled the emergency rope that separated the derailed coach from the one that was spared. Immediately after the accident occurred, Finer courageously axed his way through the derailed train and salvaged, among others, a little girl with a broken leg. Finer arrived too late to save the drowned boy at the bottom of the coach.

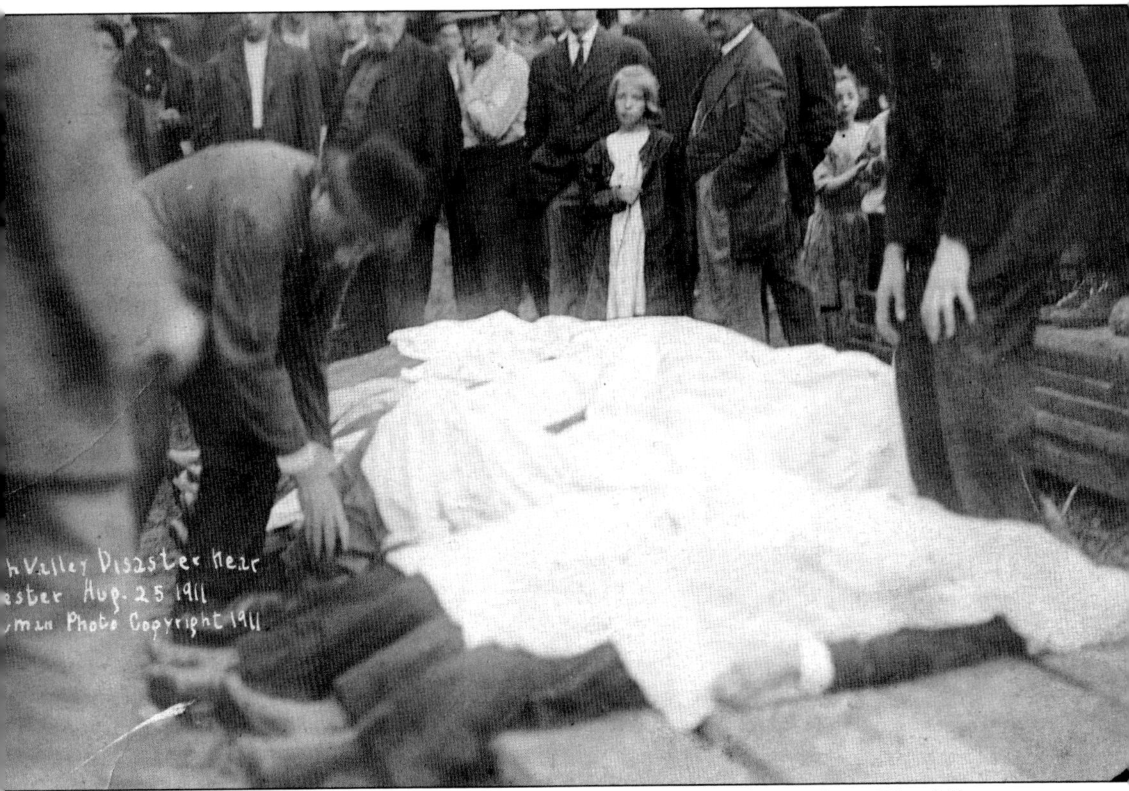

This disturbing sight shows the spectators of the Manchester trestle accident. The following are names of 23 of the 30 people that died in the accident: Henry Becker, D.M. Bellt, Hannah Hassett, Mary E. Hassett, Mrs. Charles B. Headly, Mrs. Bruno Heald, Emily Hill, Joseph Hickey, Charles Hicks, Mrs. Isabelli J. Hicks, A.M. Humsicker, Mrs. G.F. Johnson, Charles Johnson, Mrs. Charles Johnson, Mabel Lawrence, Timothy Madden, Mrs. Timothy Madden, Francis L. Madden, Edgar D. Pangburn, Estella Pownall, Helen Pownall, Henry M. Pownall, W.P. Rundle, Mrs. H.B. Smith, I.S. Uncle, Mrs. I.S. Uncle, Mrs. Rebecca Vanderlip, Barbara Zudeck, Frederica Wrinkler.

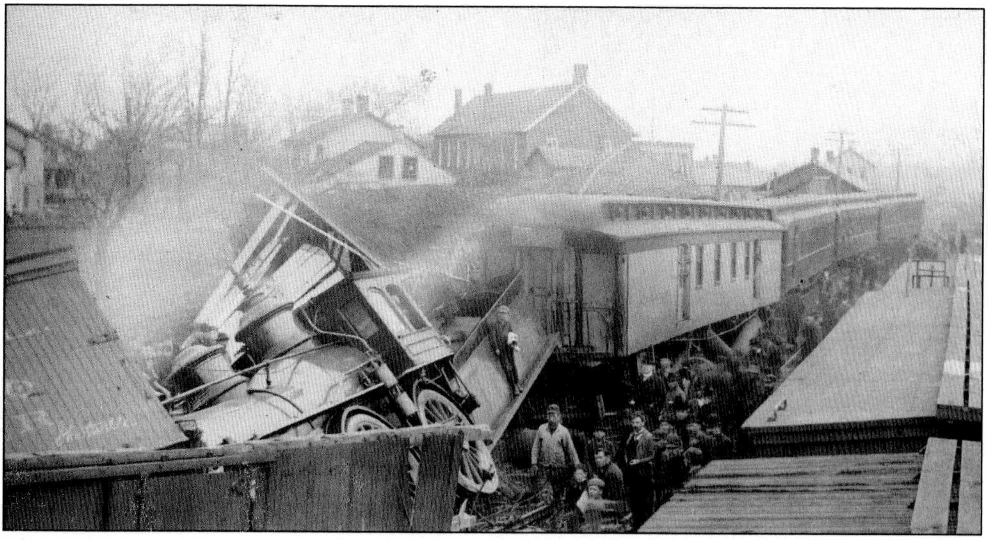

This 1893 train collision at the depot in Shortsville left immense debris that took over a month to clean up. The collision was caused by a westbound flyer running into a switch.

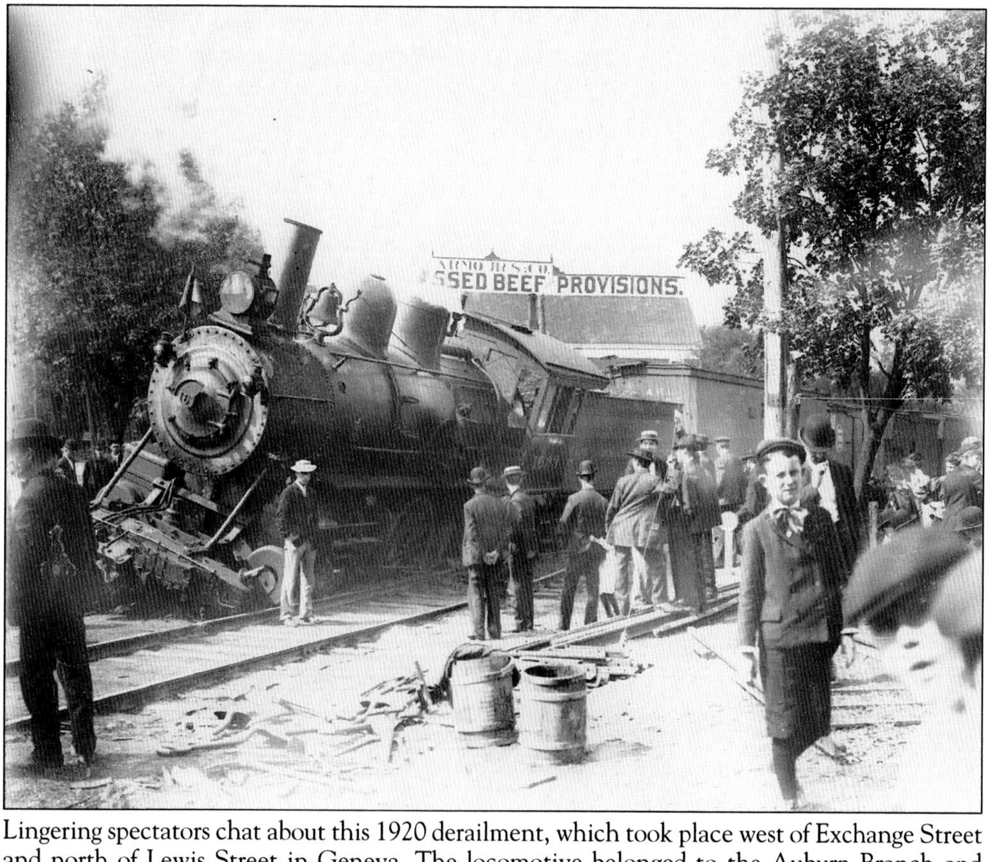

Lingering spectators chat about this 1920 derailment, which took place west of Exchange Street and north of Lewis Street in Geneva. The locomotive belonged to the Auburn Branch and made frequent trips to Geneva warehouses.

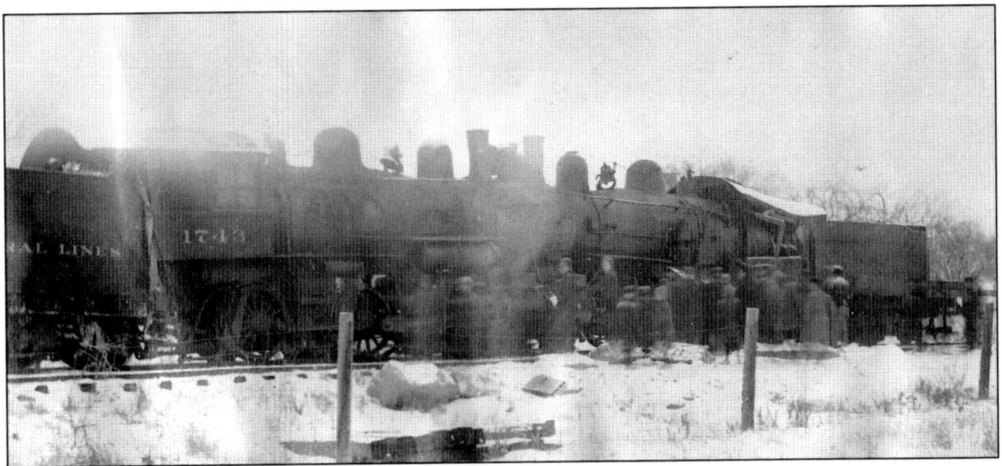

This head-on collision occurred on the Peanut Line in Bloomfield. In the 1890s, not all collisions were accidents. Some were staged to raise money for politicians, important campaigns, and the like.

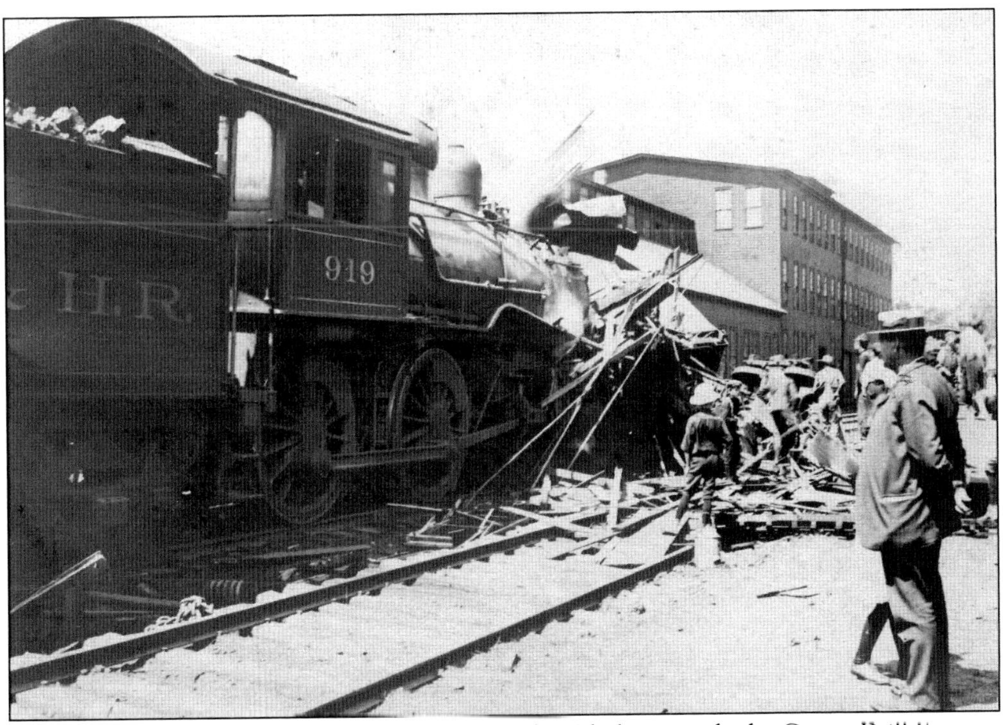

This 1900 train wreck of locomotive 919 occurred in Phelps, outside the Crown Drill Factory.

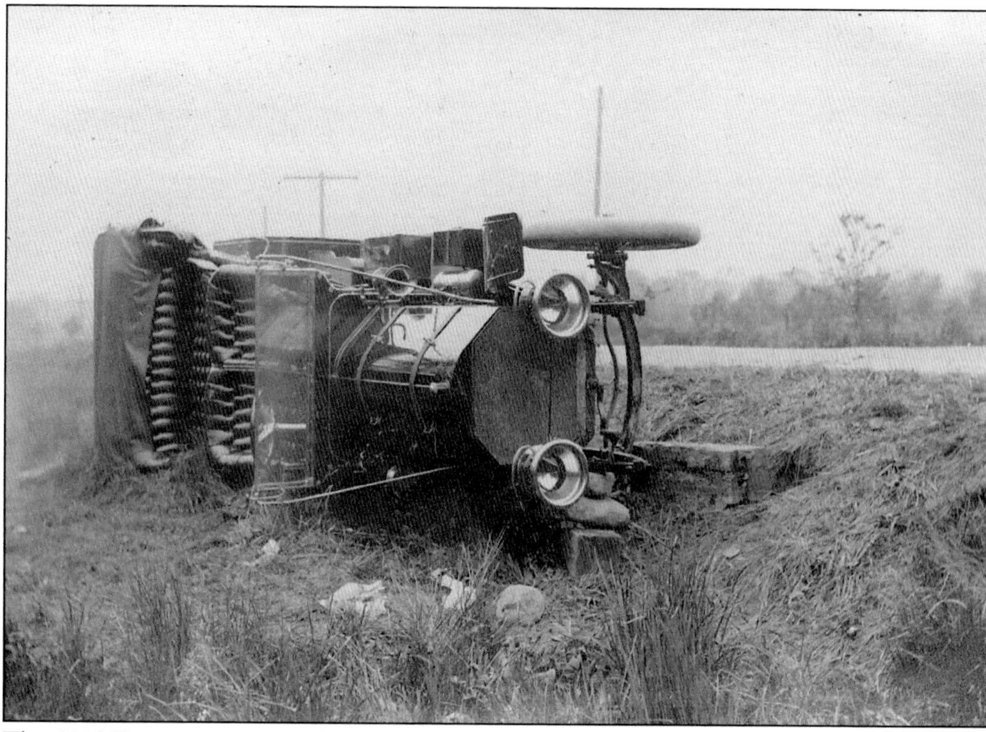

This 1913 Farmington car crash catapulted this vehicle from one shoulder to another. In 1894, the first automobile accident was recorded in New York City.

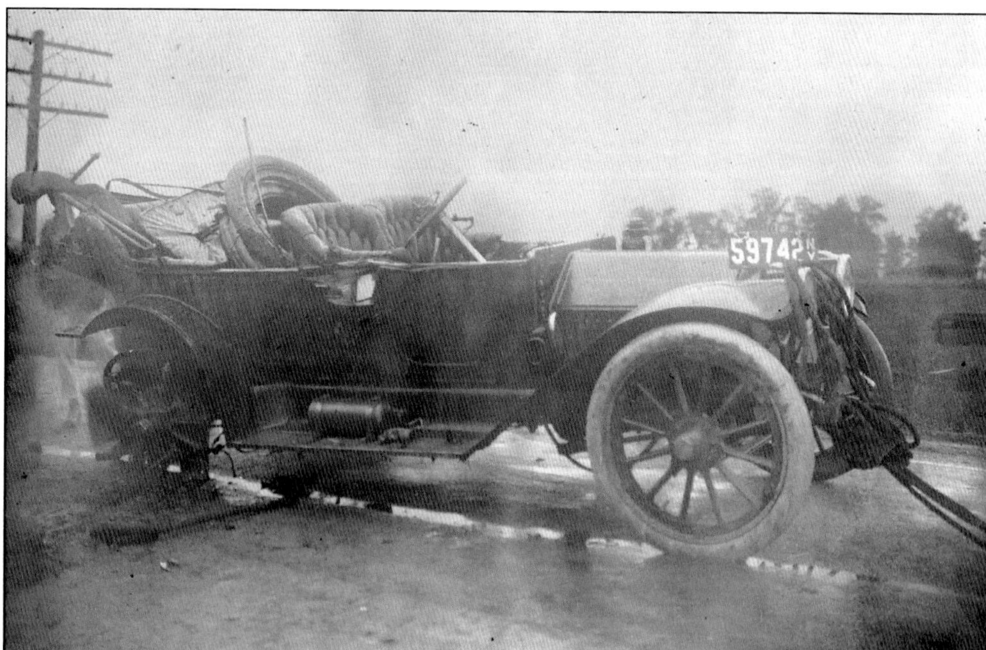

This car was a victim of a 1912 tornado, whose 400-yard width eradicated fruit trees and leveled farms. Although the tornado caused no deaths, estimations reported a damage of about $50,000.

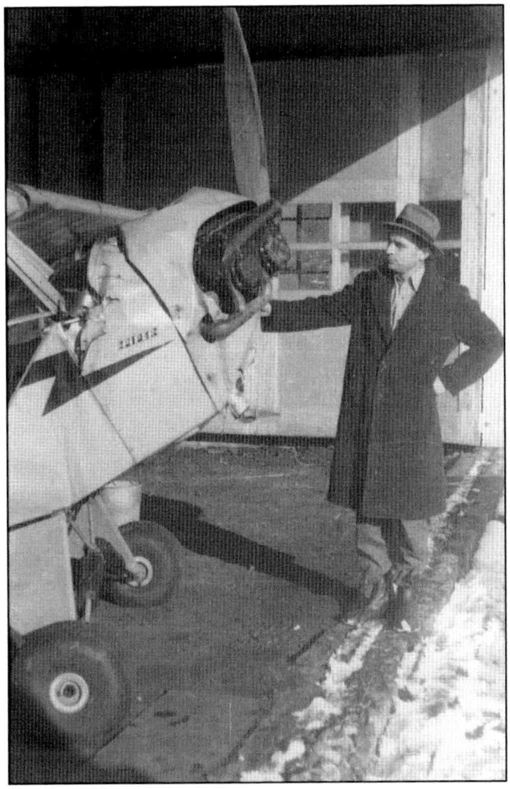

John S. Blazey, a noted Flying Farmer, examines the damage that resulted from abrupt landing. Such damages were not uncommon because landings took place on rough, uneven fields.

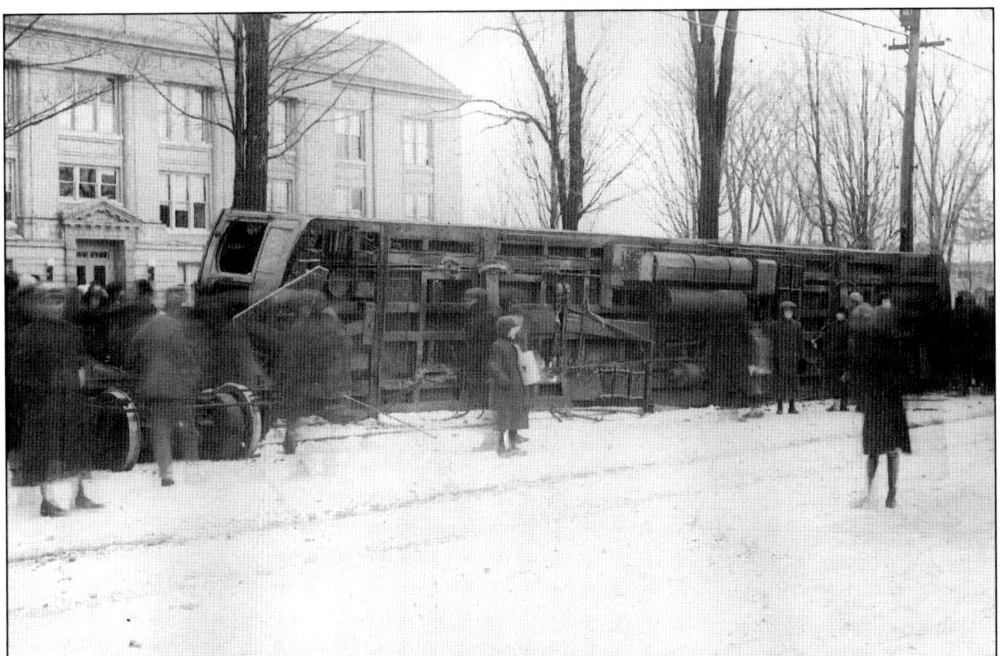

On June 5, 1913, this Rochester & Eastern car derailed on upper Main Street in Canandaigua. The accident was caused by a broken axle. There were 29 passengers on the car, and they were only slightly injured.

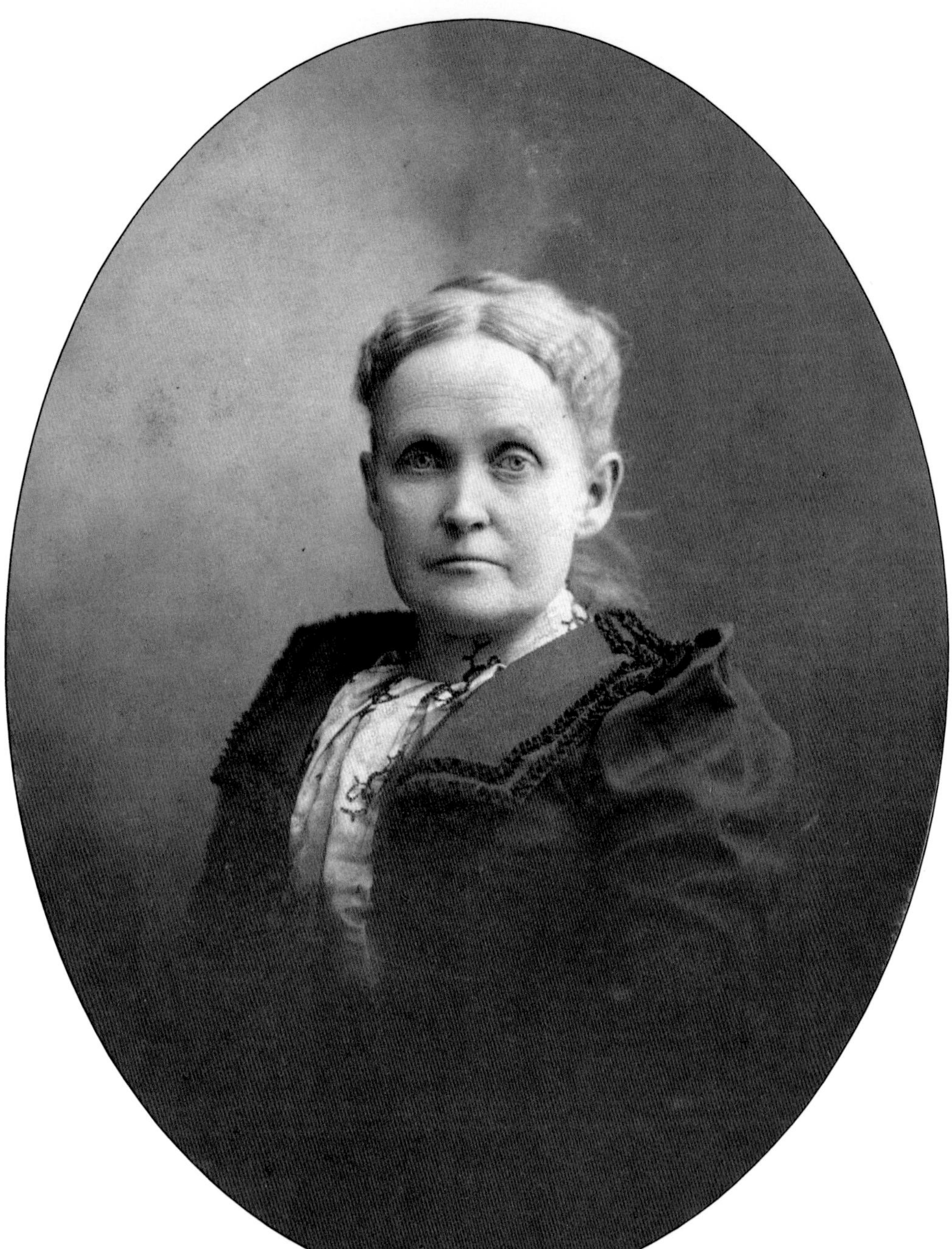

This was the last portrait of Amy Smith before her and some of her family were the victims of a tragedy known as "the saddest day in Farmington history." Coming home from a New Year's Eve party at Joseph Tuttle's house in 1899, the Smith family was hit by the midnight express. Conditions that night were fierce and windy, and the canopy of the buggy in which they were riding was deployed. Amy Smith and four of her five children died. The children were Miranda (23), Albert (22), Glee (14), and Catherine (7). Amy's husband, Porter D. Smith, and Gardner (21) survived the accident. The tragedy later led to safety ordinances.

Ten

Getting Around

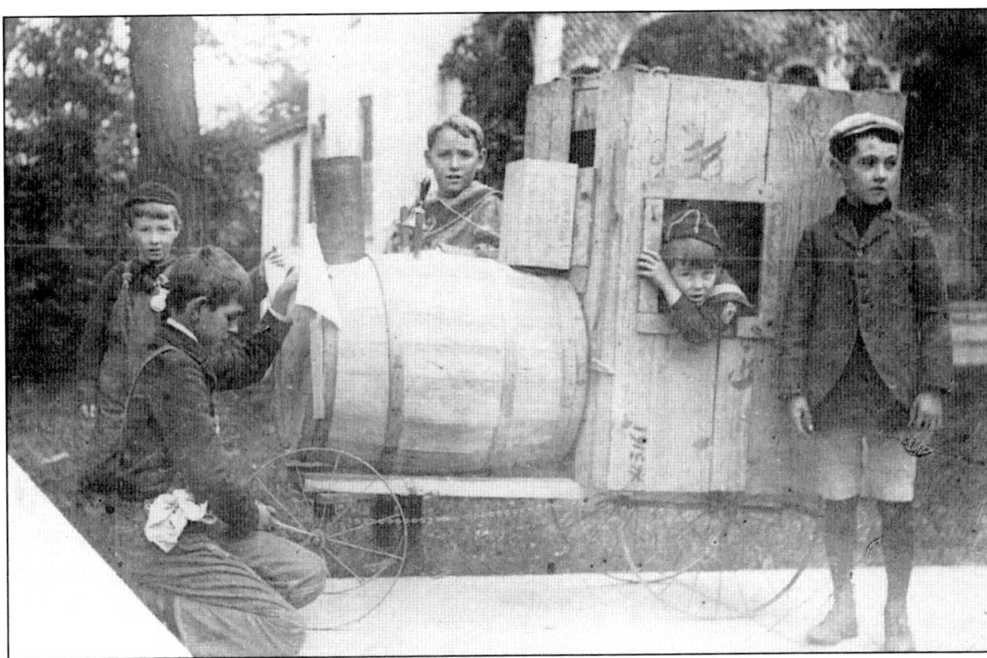

Reminiscent of "Our Gang," these local Geneva boys pose around their creation in an 1895 picture. From left to right are the following: (front row) Louis Lovett and Howard Converse; (back row) Schyler Church, R. Selden Rose, and Norman Lovett. Just as these kids explored their imaginations, innovators developed new ways of getting around.

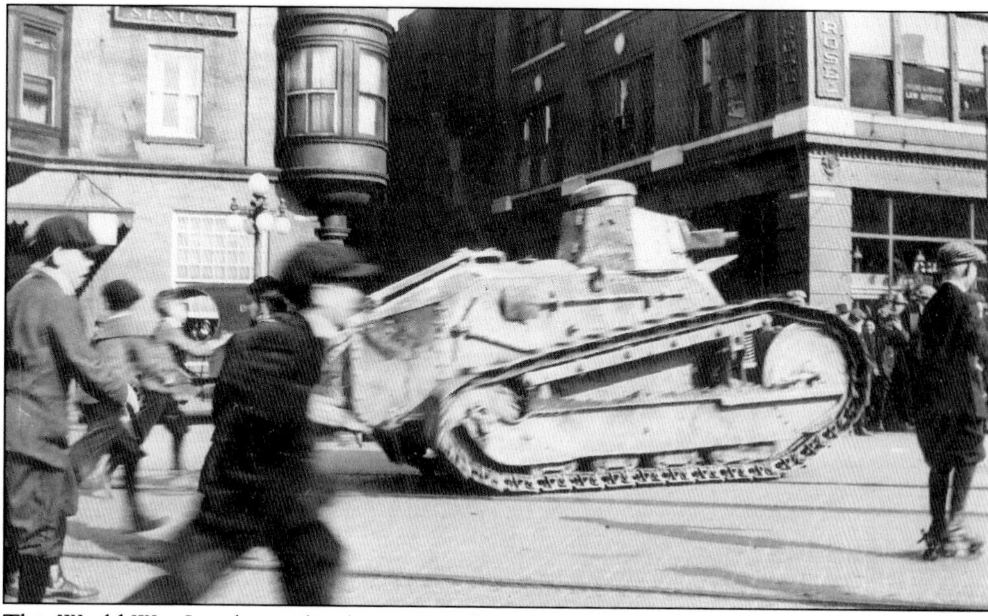

This World War I tank parades the streets of Geneva on Armistice Day to celebrate triumph.

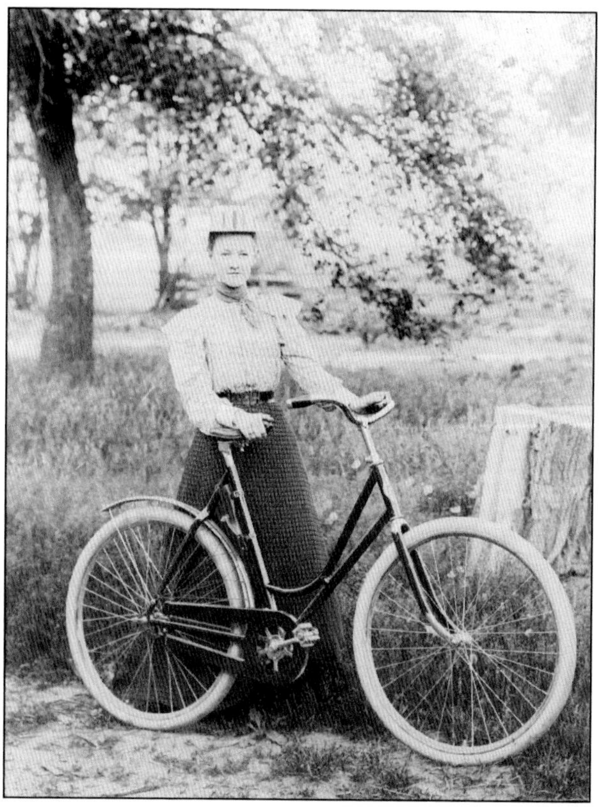

An unidentified Canandaigua woman is shown supporting her bicycle. In 1896, Susan B. Anthony said, "The bicycle has done more for the emancipation of women than anything else." Such praise was given because the bicycle ended the era of the uncomfortable dress of the bustle and corset.

Frances Irene Herendeen is shown celebrating her third birthday on April 2, 1910, by riding her new tricycle.

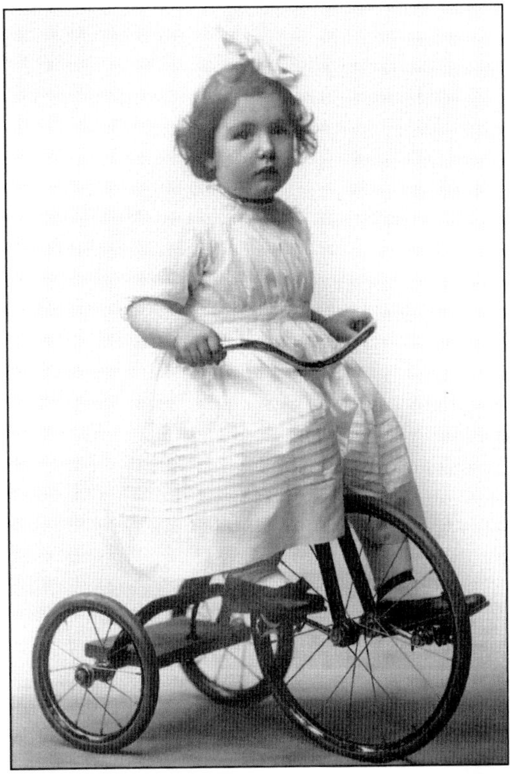

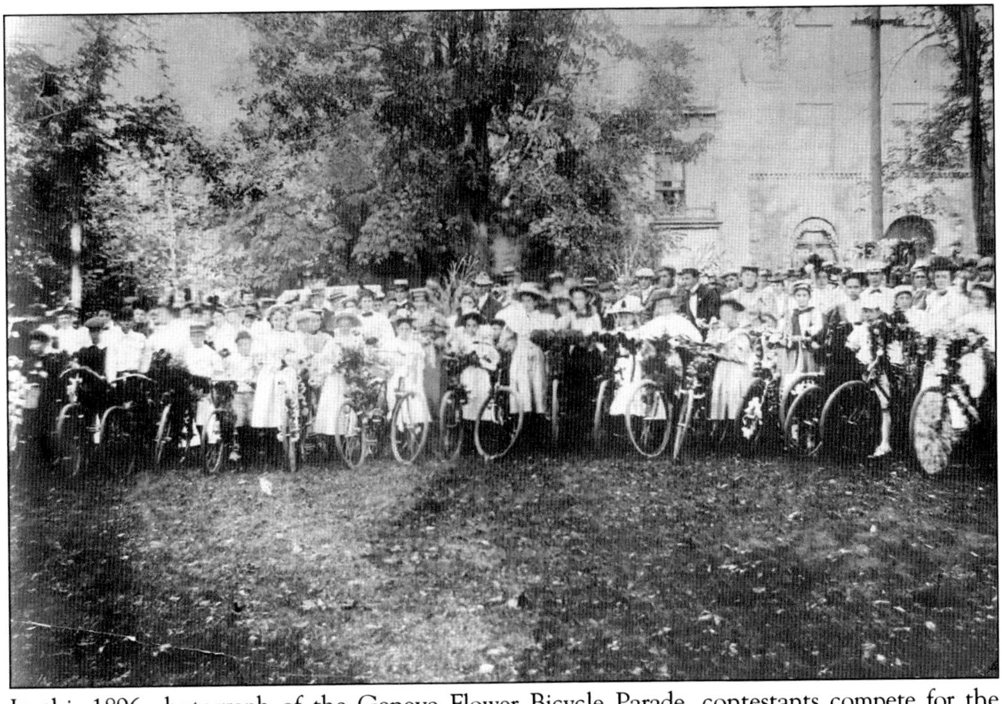

In this 1896 photograph of the Geneva Flower Bicycle Parade, contestants compete for the best-decorated bike. Margaret Cass won the first-place prize. Some of the contestants were Arthur Rose, Henry Palmer, Louis Lovett, Hugh Rose, Teenie Rose, Alice Rose, and Mary C. Rose.

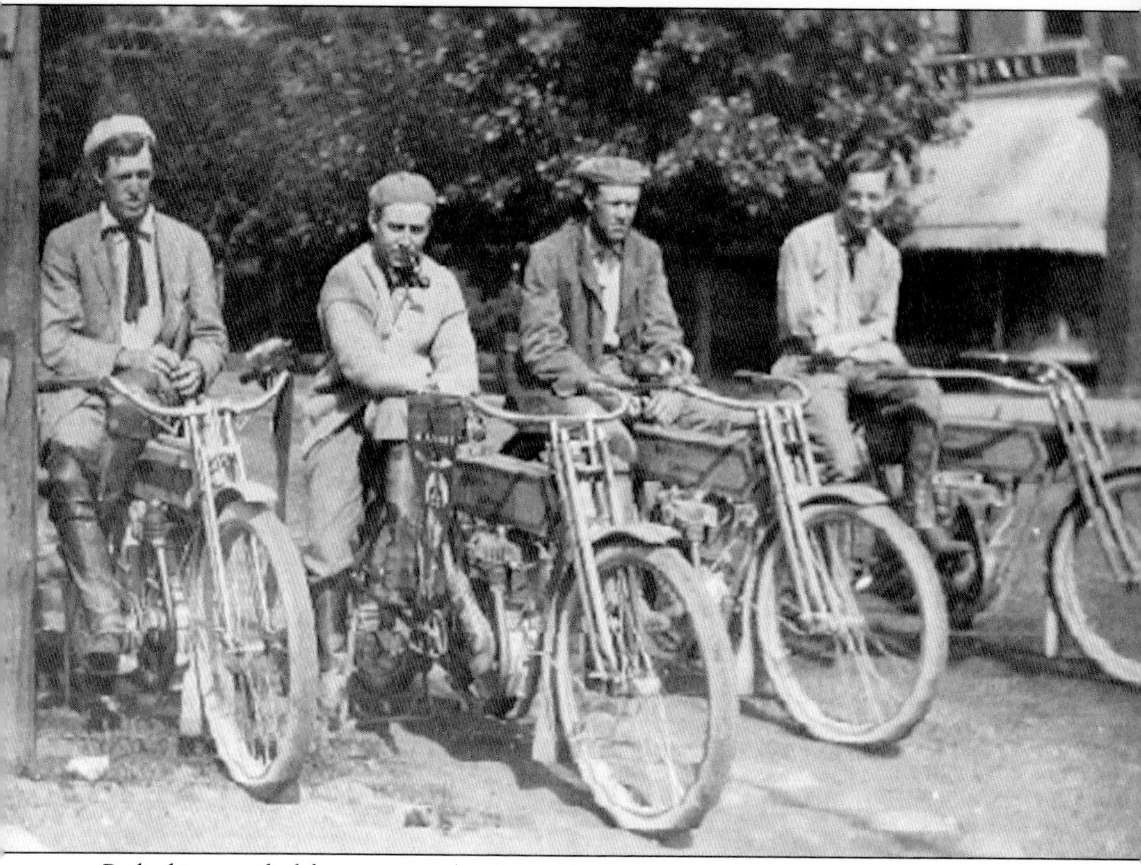

Parked in a unified formation in this September 25, 1911 photograph is the Shortsville Harley Davidson Motorcycle Club. From left to right are Clem Jessup, Myron Horton, Bill Mills, and George Schrader. They once bragged about achieving a 60-mile trip in one day.

In 1935, John S. Blazey (far left) was an International Harvester dealer, selling strictly farm tractors and equipment. However, in 1961, when housing developments began superseding farmland, demand for such products waned. Instead of giving up, Blazey, a man of vision, utilized the opportunity to establish the lawn mower industry. To this day, Blazey's entrepreneurship is well recognized, as many Cub Cadets bear his name.

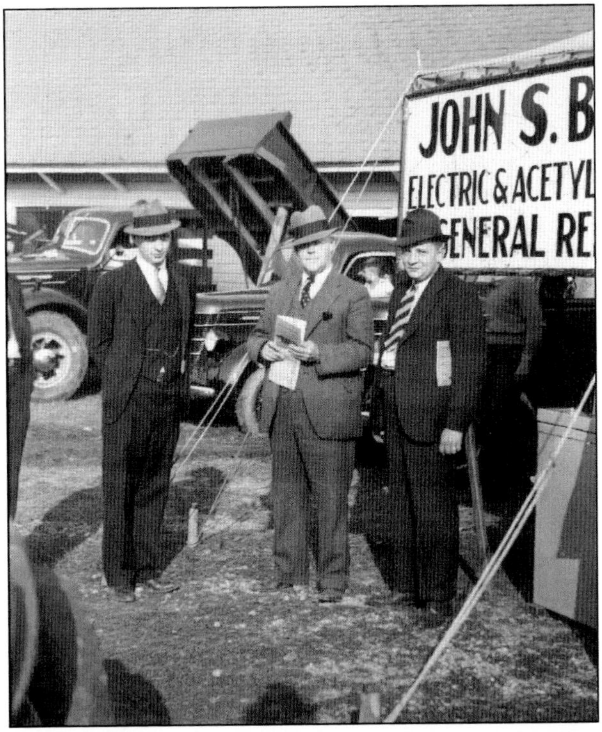

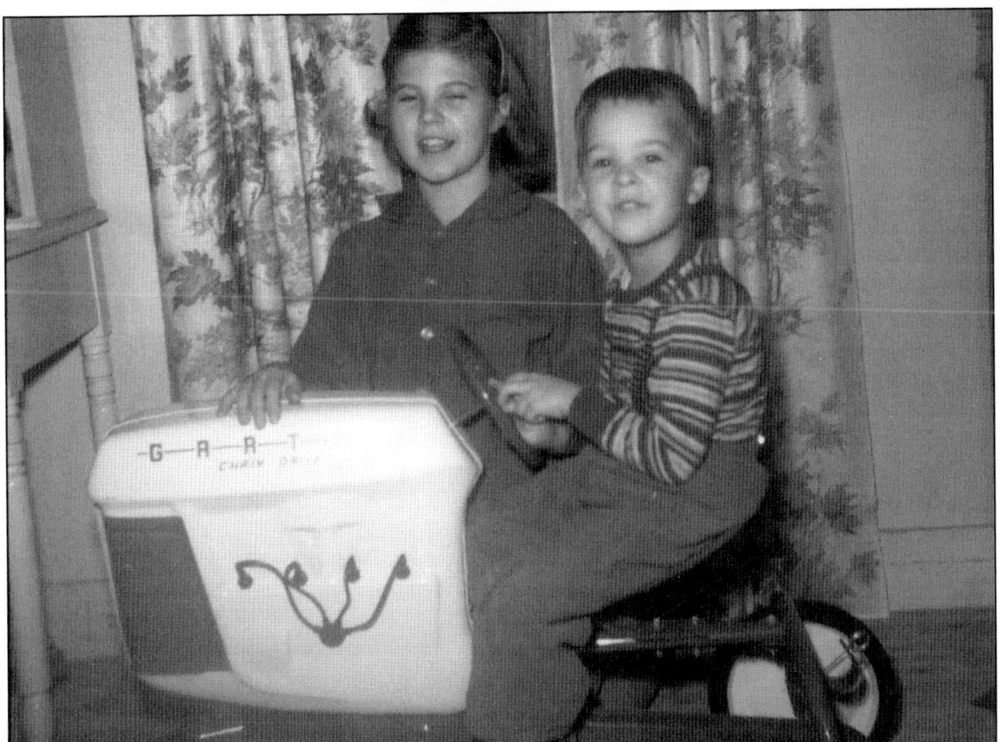

Judy Bloniarz stands next to her brother Mike as he cheerfully sits on his 1963 toy Gart pedal tractor. Today, Mike Bloniarz is on the Ontario County Historical Society Board of Trustees.

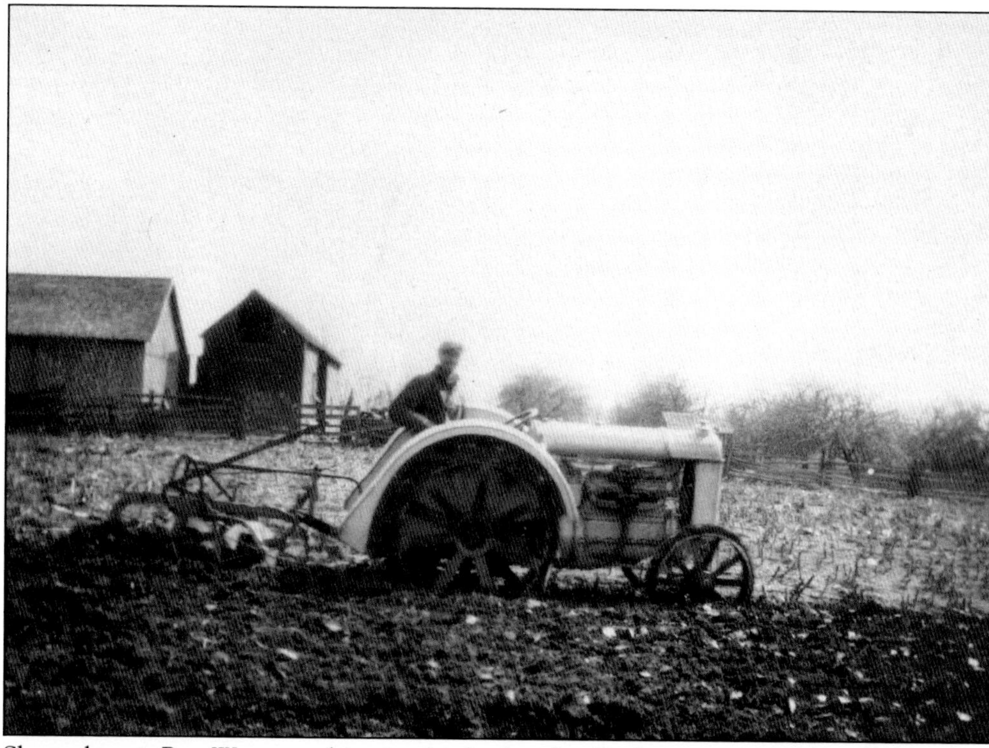

Shown here is Roy Wyman cultivating his land with a Fordson tractor. Today, Guy Lee and Honey Mae Crowell of Manchester own the property. Henry Ford started the Fordson tractor line in 1917.

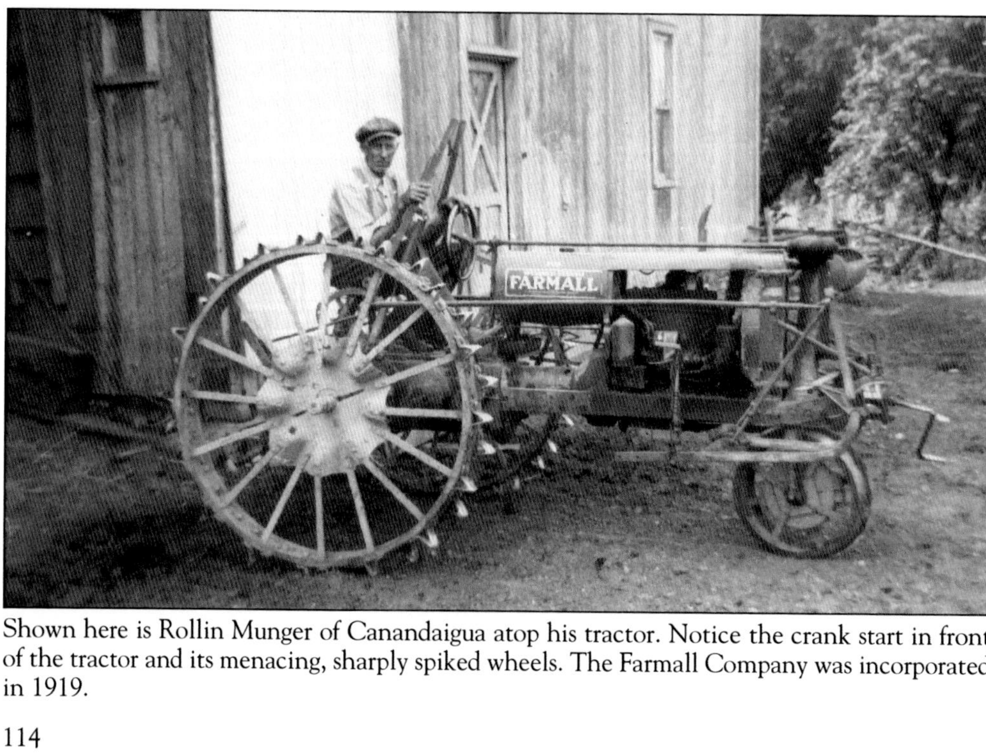

Shown here is Rollin Munger of Canandaigua atop his tractor. Notice the crank start in front of the tractor and its menacing, sharply spiked wheels. The Farmall Company was incorporated in 1919.

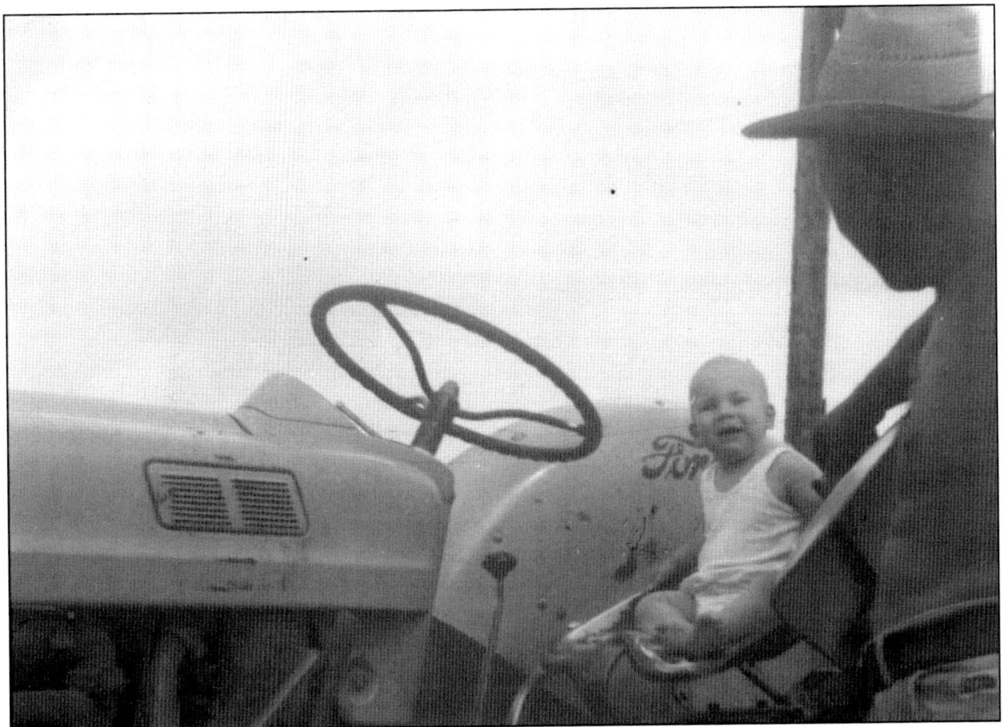

Standing beside his grandson Bob, who is sitting upon the 1954 Ford Jubilee tractor, is Belgium immigrant Henry VanCaeseele. Henry met his wife, Romonie, at the John Deere assembly line in Moline, Illinois. The VanCaeseeles are fourth-generation farmers in Ontario County.

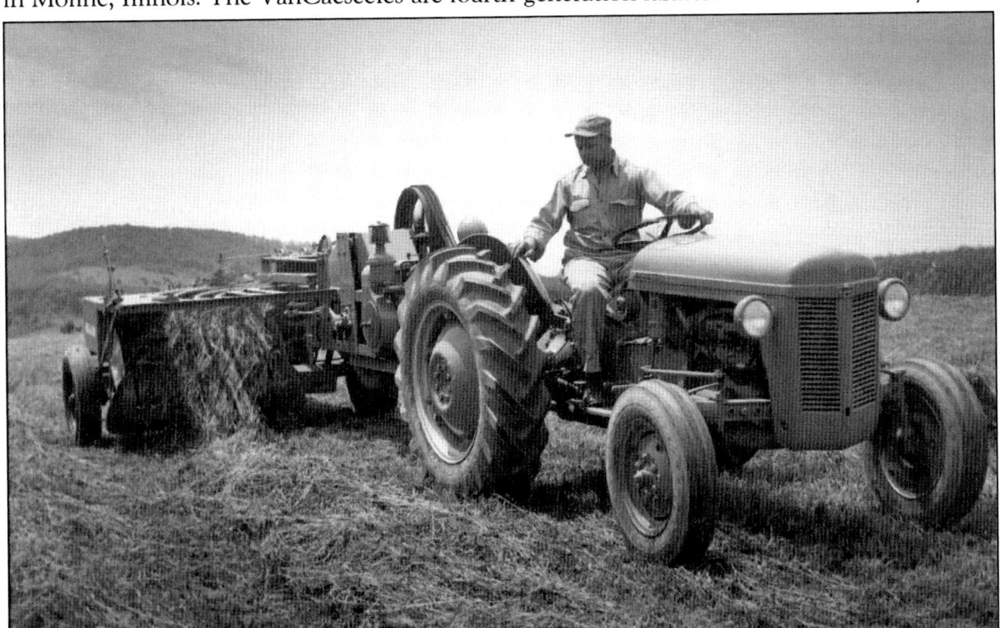

Plowing his fields on a hazy summer day with a Ford Ferguson tractor is Milford N. Herod, who was commonly known as "Milt." Herod's farm was located on Goose Street in Stanley. The Herod family has been recognized as farmers for more than 200 years in Ontario County.

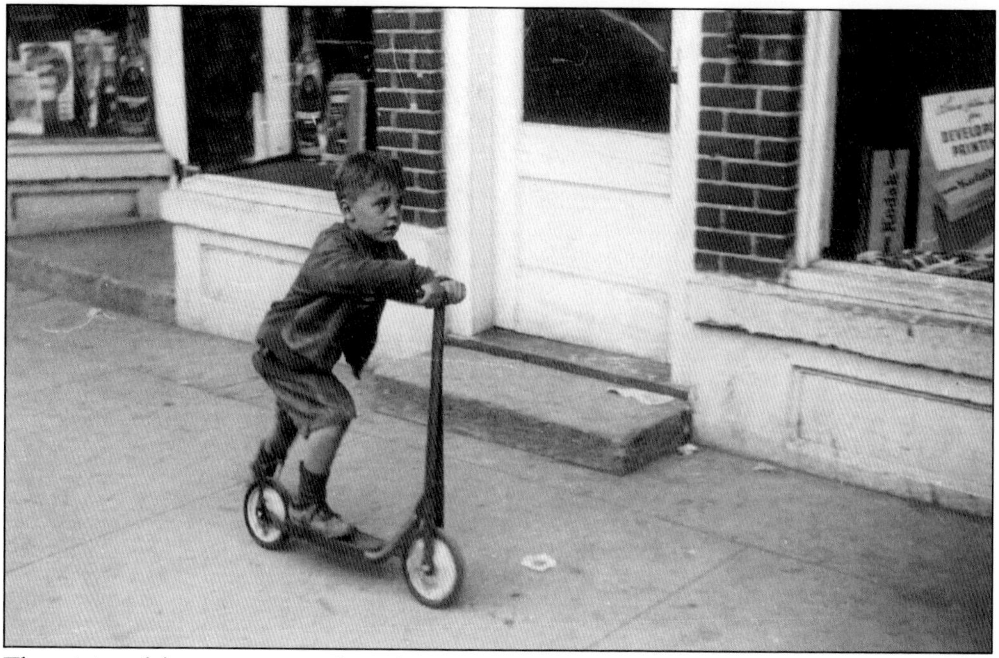

The origins of the scooter were that of a wagon. C. Husemun designed the scooter and received patented rights on November 1, 1921. It gained most of its popularity in the 1940s and 1950s. In this 1944 photograph, five-year-old Paul Potter cruises by the Double E, which, at the time this picture was taken, was called Manions and Ike George's Soda Fountain.

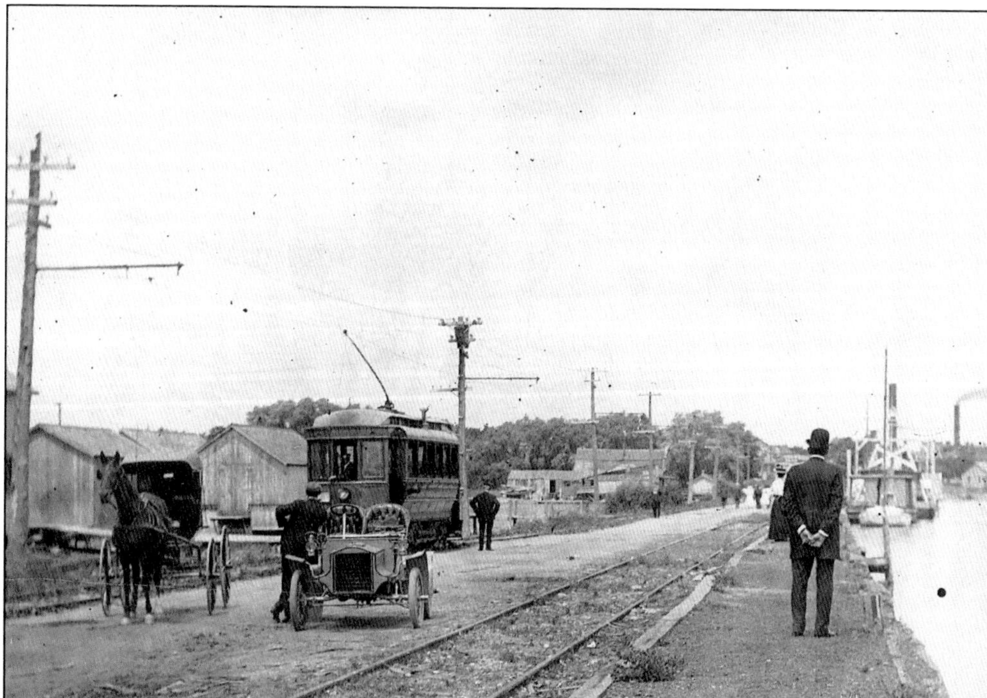

This classic 1910 picture of the Canandaigua pier features each form of travel during the 18th and 19th centuries. All but the imminent arrival of the train is seen.

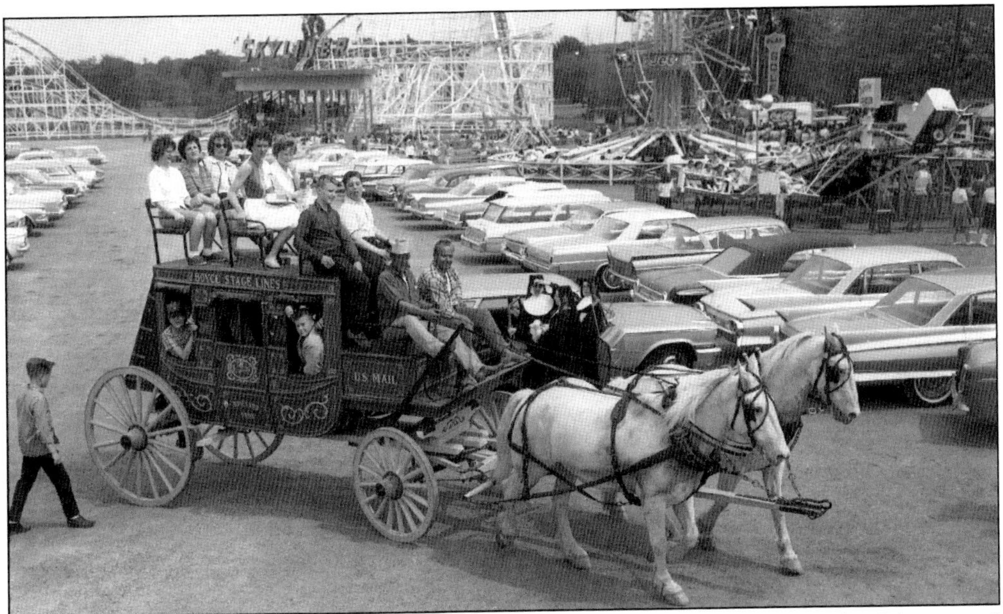

Perhaps the biggest attraction in all of Ontario County from 1925 to 1985 was the "playground of the Finger Lakes," or Roseland Park. Among the most popular attractions in the park were the Skyliner, a thrilling roller coaster; the bumper cars; and the Golden Nugget, a fun house. Although its lofty attractions produced a ubiquitous illusion, Roseland was located at the foot of Canandaigua Lake. The park was owned by Lester Boyce and family. To perpetuate the well-known name throughout Ontario County, a new Roseland Water Park has been built in Canandaigua. After nine months of development, the park was opened to the public on May 26, 2001.

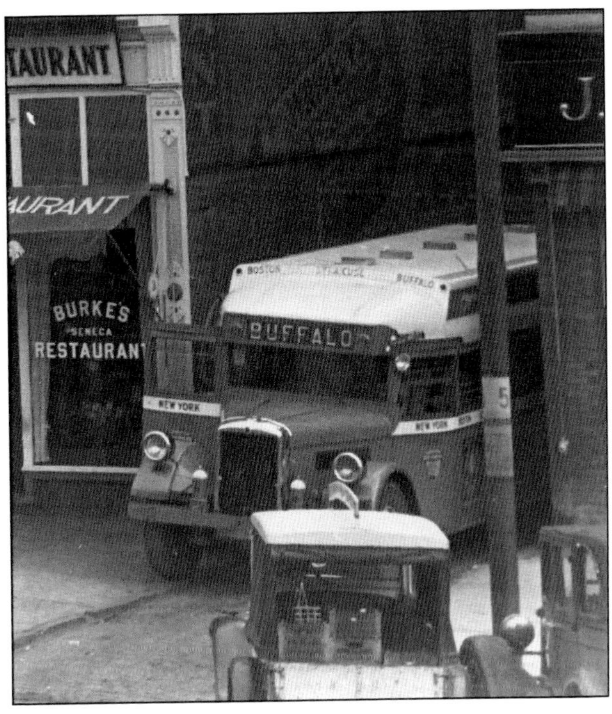

Wasting no time, the emerging bus companies established a depot at the once-favorite restaurant of the many trolley workers. This Canandaigua soup and sandwich restaurant, which was owned by Peter Burke, served up to 200 people daily. On December 28, 1925, the *Geneva Times* validated this with the headline "An Era Ended, Busses Take Over."

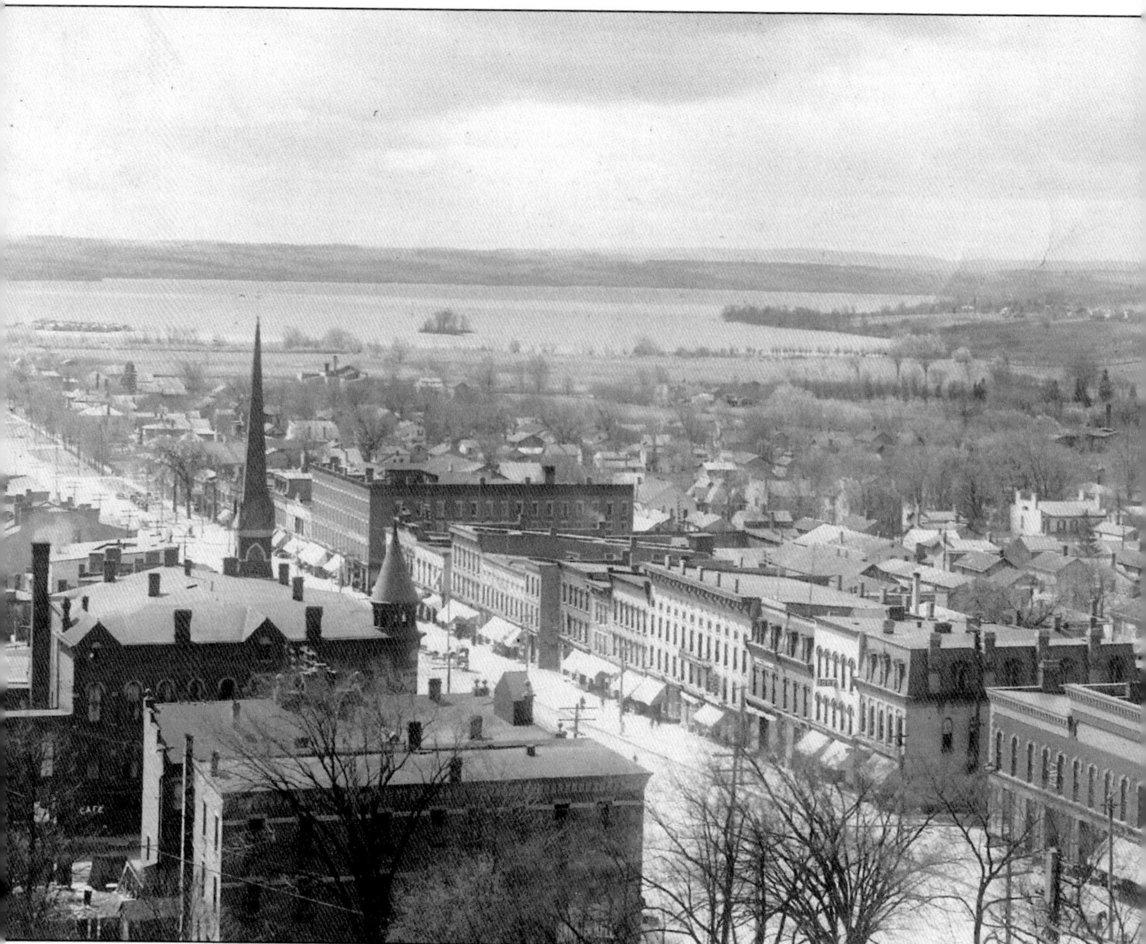

Fredrick Ferris Thompson took this 1880s photograph from the top of the county courthouse in Canandaigua, which was erected in 1857. Like other prominent landmarks, the courthouse became a reference point to travelers and the like. The building still serves this purpose. Squaw Island, obscurely shown in the middle of the picture, acted very much like the courthouse. It also provided a point of reference but did so for sailors and steamboat captains. The present-day courthouse is the office of district attorney Lawrence Tantillo, and Squaw Island's preservation project is spearheaded by Paul Hudson.

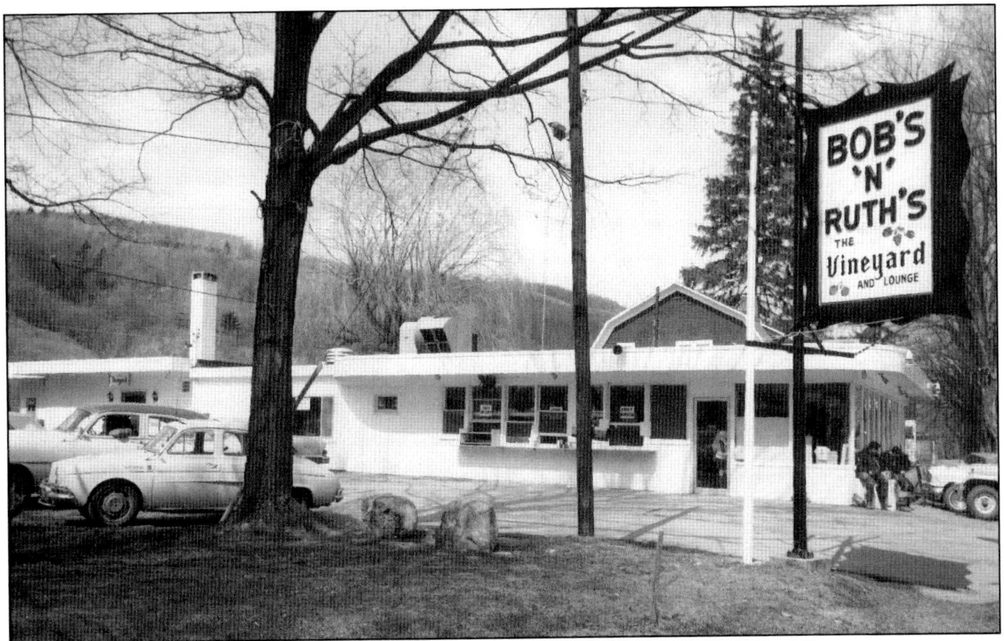

Amid the interwoven hills of Naples, Bob's 'N' Ruth's, established in 1949 and located on the intersection of Routes 21 and 245, still remains a popular place to eat. Because of its trout derbies, grape pies, and antique markets, Naples has acquired the appellation "the Switzerland of Ontario County."

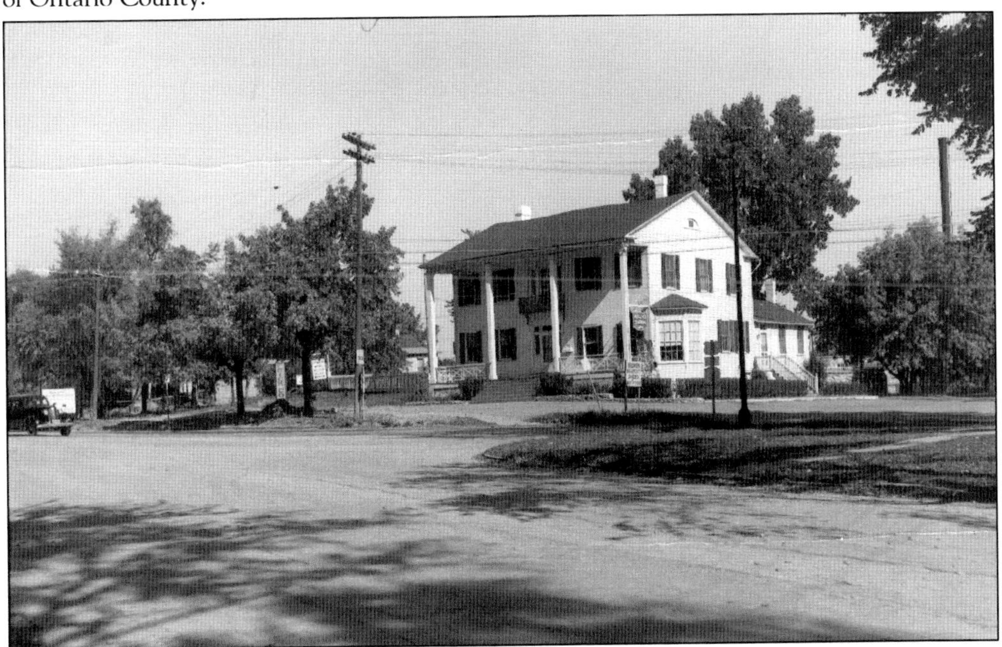

This versatile building has survived three transformations, each meant to accommodate the people's interests of the particular era. First, it was the Lake Breeze Hotel, serving stagecoach and steamboat passengers. It then became a popular gathering spot known as the Colonial Inn. Today, it is McGregor's, a favorite restaurant to many. This picture was taken in the fall of 1949.

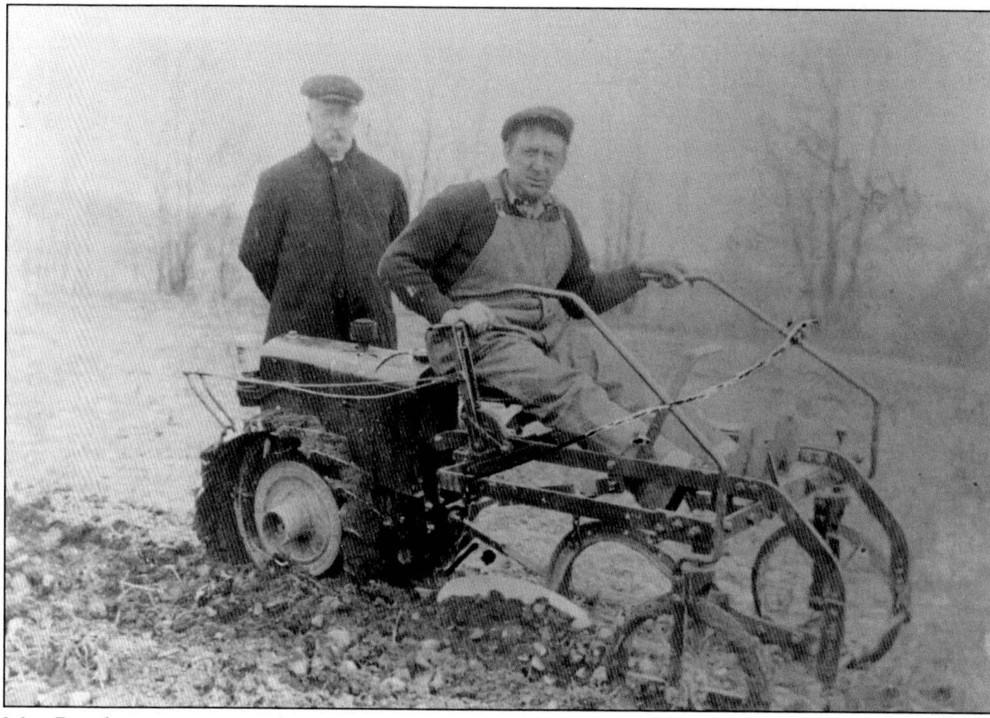

Mr. Repsher maneuvers his primitive tractor before Carlos Pierce Osgood in this 1930 photograph. Osgood was the owner of the Red Jacket Telegraph and Telephone Company.

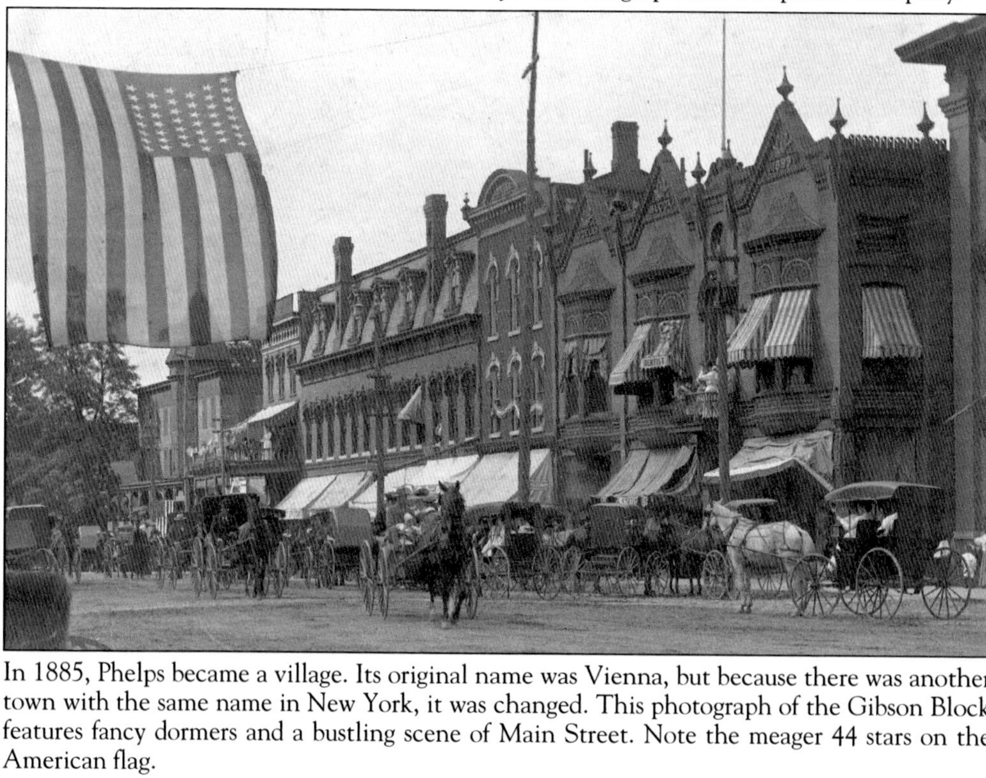

In 1885, Phelps became a village. Its original name was Vienna, but because there was another town with the same name in New York, it was changed. This photograph of the Gibson Block features fancy dormers and a bustling scene of Main Street. Note the meager 44 stars on the American flag.

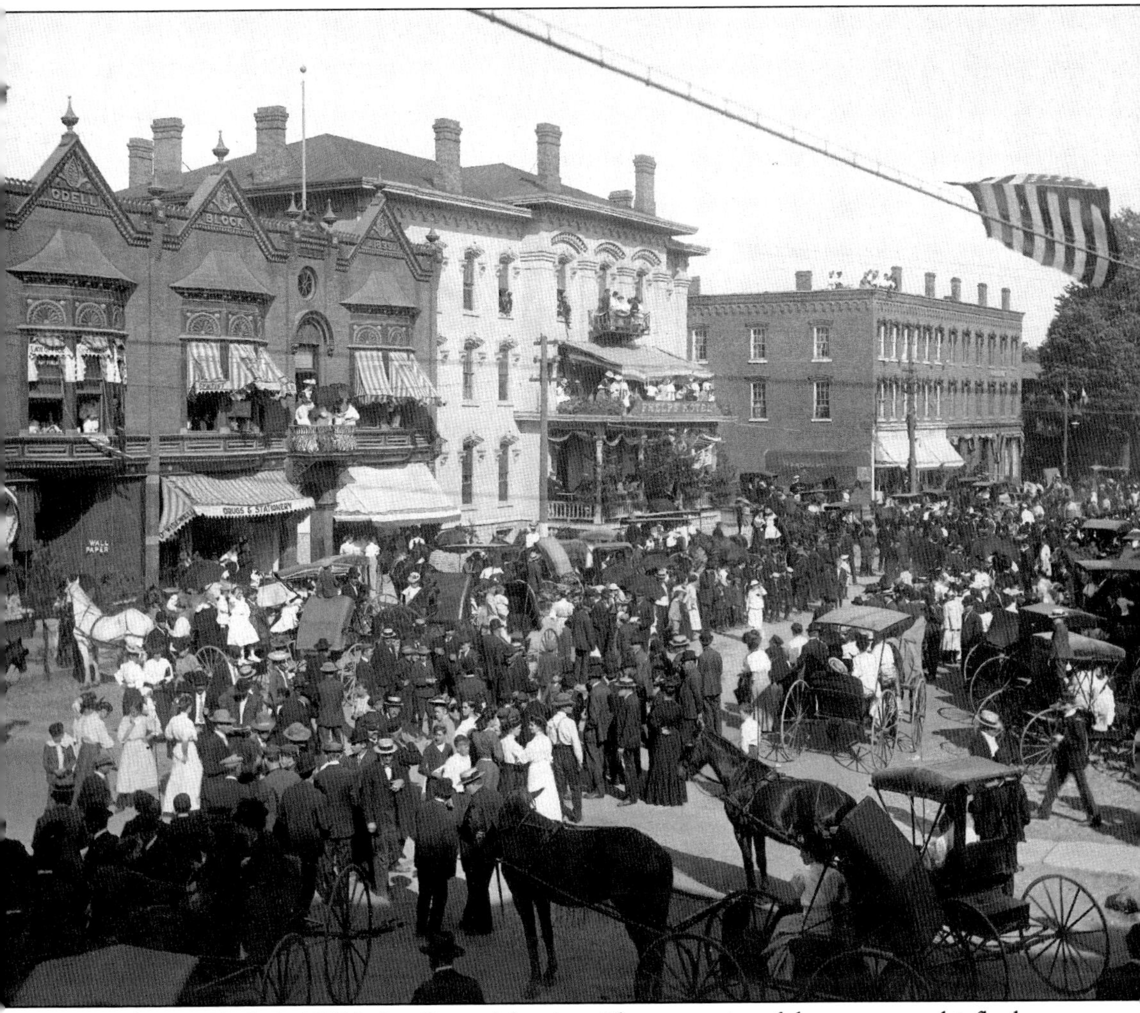

Shown here is Phelps's 1907 Labor Day celebration. The prosperity of the town was chiefly due to the Erie Canal, which promoted farming. The Phelps Hotel can be seen in the middle of the picture. Today, the hotel is managed by Francis and Joanne Sullivan.

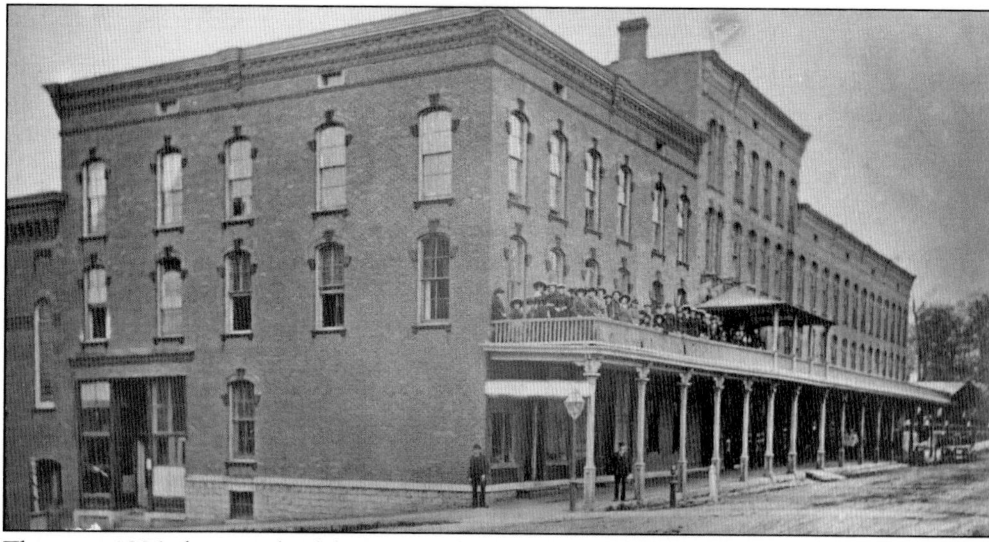

This is an 1886 photograph of the annex, also known as the Foster Block, which was taken by H.E.B. Pardee, a notable photographer in his time. Running parallel to the building is Main Street, perpendicular to which is Crane Street. Connected to the building is one of the oldest active YMCAs in the country. From the 1940s to the late 1980s, the YMCA was managed by the well-liked Mr. Brown, who was commonly called "Brownie." The building has sustained its original structure with the help of the Clifton Springs community and Ellis award winner Drew Morris. The present-day Foster Block is occupied by the following businesses: First Priority Computer Service, Dr. O. Gregory Zazulak at Finger Lakes Eye Care, chiropractor Dr. Stacy R. Davidoff, Brown Bag Deli & Dry Cleaners, Black Sheep Antiques, Auto Desk MBG Systems, and the Rose Petal Gift Shop.

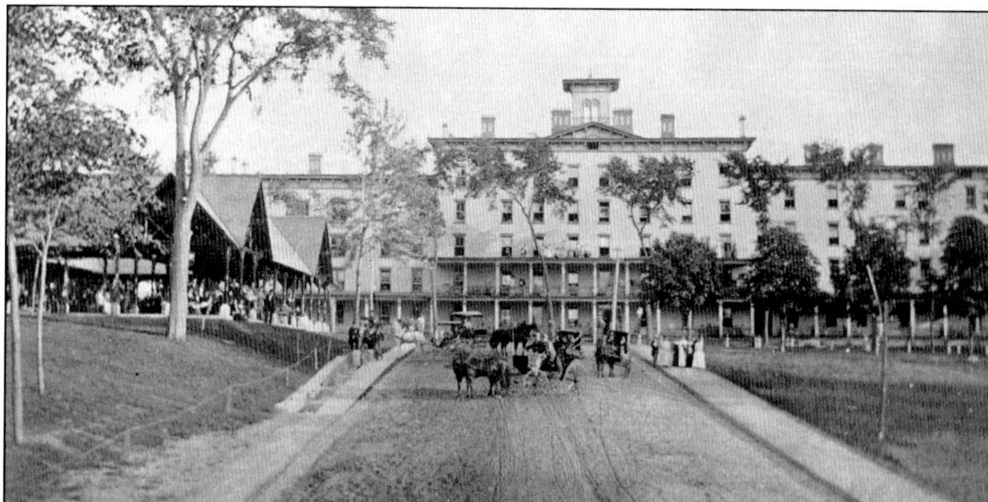

The sanitarium, founded in 1850 by Dr. Henry Foster, was one of the largest facilities of its kind in the United States. The myth of the therapeutic springs attracted many eminent people from all over the county. They visited the sanitarium hoping to alleviate their ailments, among which were rheumatism and consumption. The pavilion in the foreground, built in 1880 by railroad mogul Andrew Pierce, was given to the village sanitarium for helping his wife recuperate from her illness.

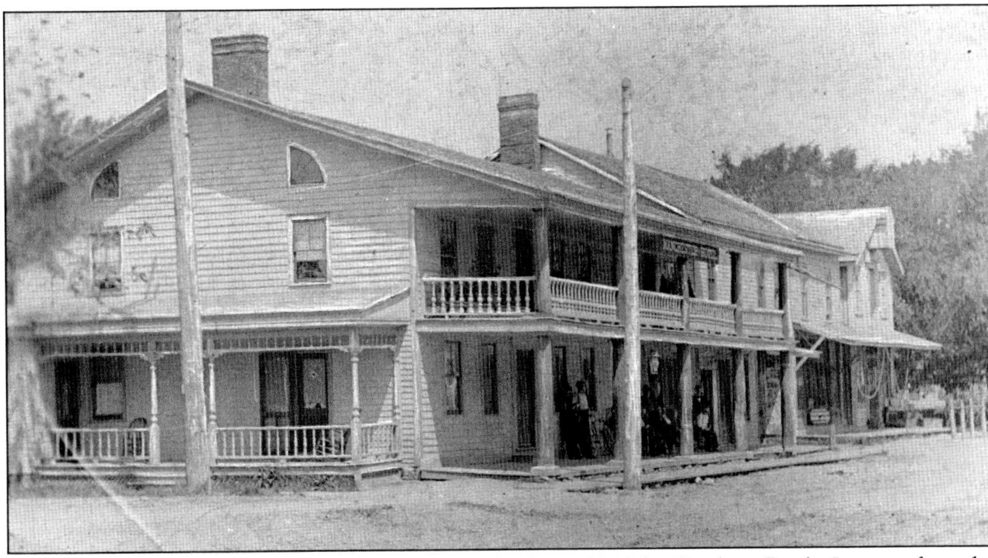

This was Manchester's only hotel, which was built in 1814 by Reuben Buck. It was often the rendezvous for the Masonic lodge members. The members were Elisha Johnson, Theophilus Short, Nathan Barlow, John B. Rumsey, Timothy Allen, Stephen Brewster, Benjamin Brown, J.D. Hoskins, James Devine, Henry Depew, John Crane, S. Clark, J. Miller, H. Howard, Reuben Buck, A.N. Buck, Nathan Pierce, John Averill, Rufus Pierce, Samuel S. Whipple, Peter Brown, James Stewart, Andrew Crocker, Zurial Brown, Benjamin Howland, William Popple, Peter Mitchell, and John Robinson. The hotel stood where today's Petal Pushers Florist is located.

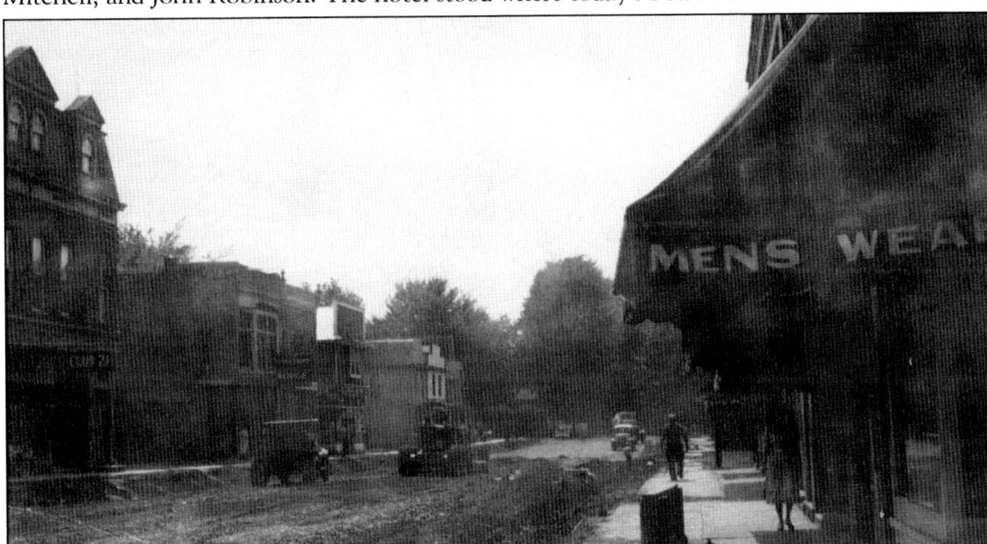

Shown here is the construction of Main Street in Shortsville, a process that included the installation of fire hydrants and paved roads. Businesses on the left side of the picture include Club 21, owned by the Repsher family (now Buffalo Bills, owned by William and Robin Mallwitz); the J.M. Stoddard furniture store (now Sue's Beauty Shop, owned by Sue Schuppenhauer); Ben Slocums's Soda Fountain Shop (now Grandma's Attic); Walt Barry's IGA (now Imp Video, owned by the Mulcock family); and Mary Chamber's Women Shop (now the Leonard "Corky" Insurance Agency). Lynn Gilligan's Men's Wear (now Nino & Judy's hair salon) can be seen on right.

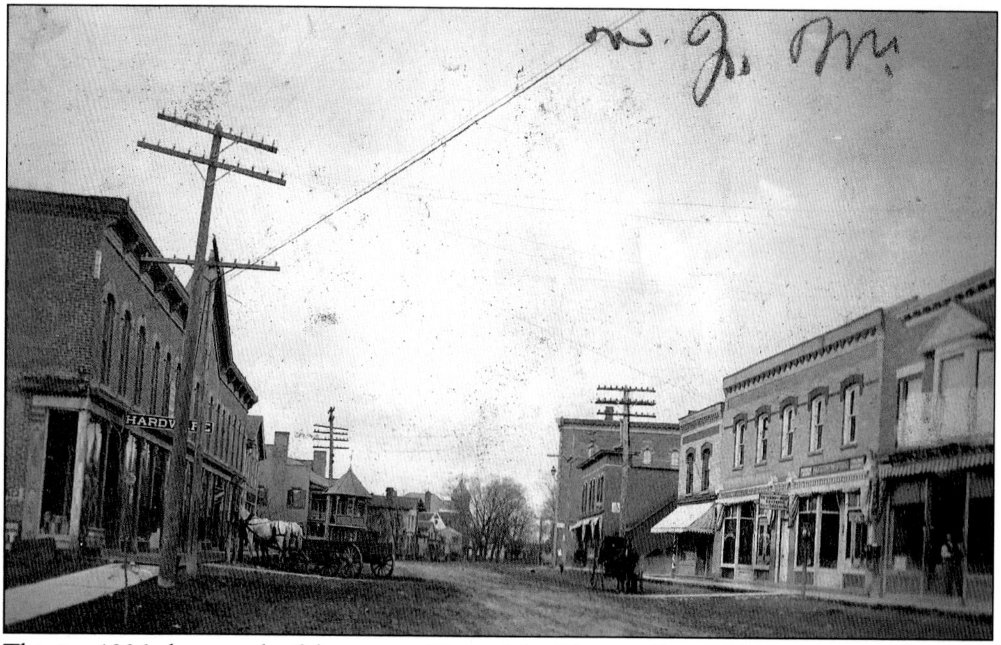

This is a 1906 photograph of downtown Victor (the Western Gate of Ontario County), which was named after Claudius Victor Boughton, a distinguished dispatch runner in the 1812 war. Although it has the semblance of a New England village, Victor has elevated to near city status, as it has a collegelike school campus and many businesses, the most popular of which is East View Mall.

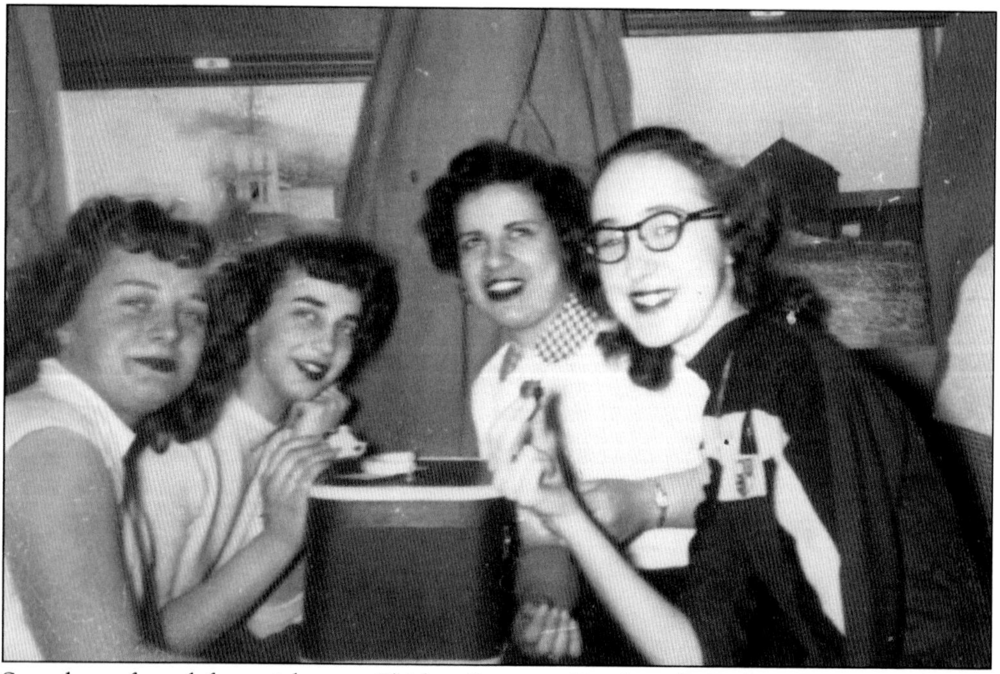

Seen here, from left to right, are Shirley Govenor Vanderwall, Barbara Boisuert Johnson, Pauline Angelina, and Patricia Hogan. These members of Red Jacket's Class of 1951 smile their way to New York City for a class trip.

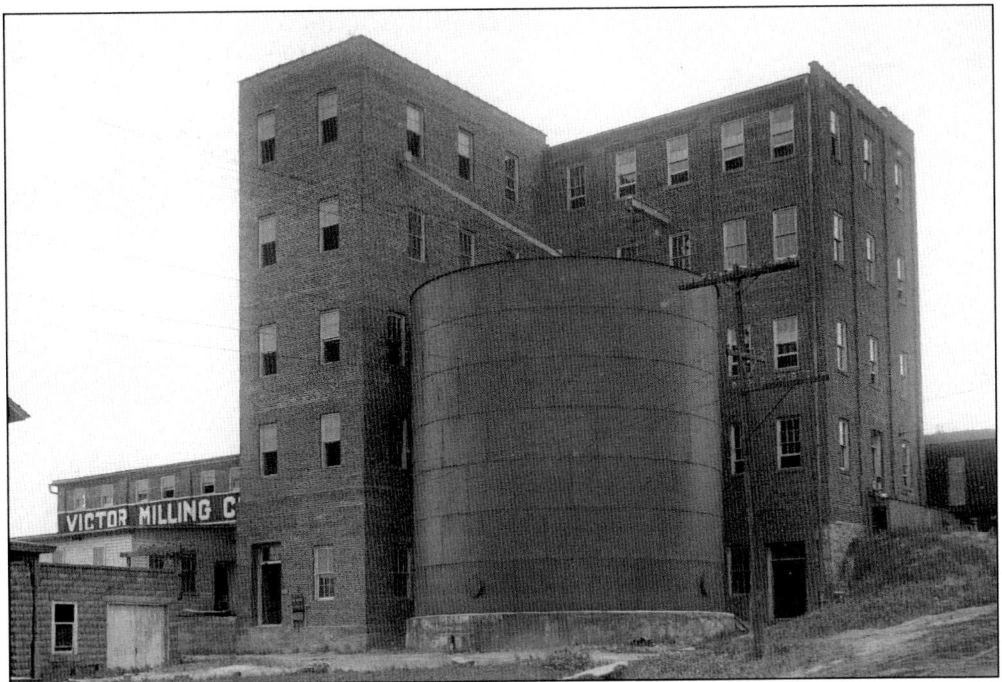

Once the tallest building and a popular railroad stop in Victor, the Victor Milling Company was reduced in size during a 1930s fire. Today, the building is the site of the Mickey Finn's restaurant, which is located on 14 Railroad Street. This picture was taken in 1925.

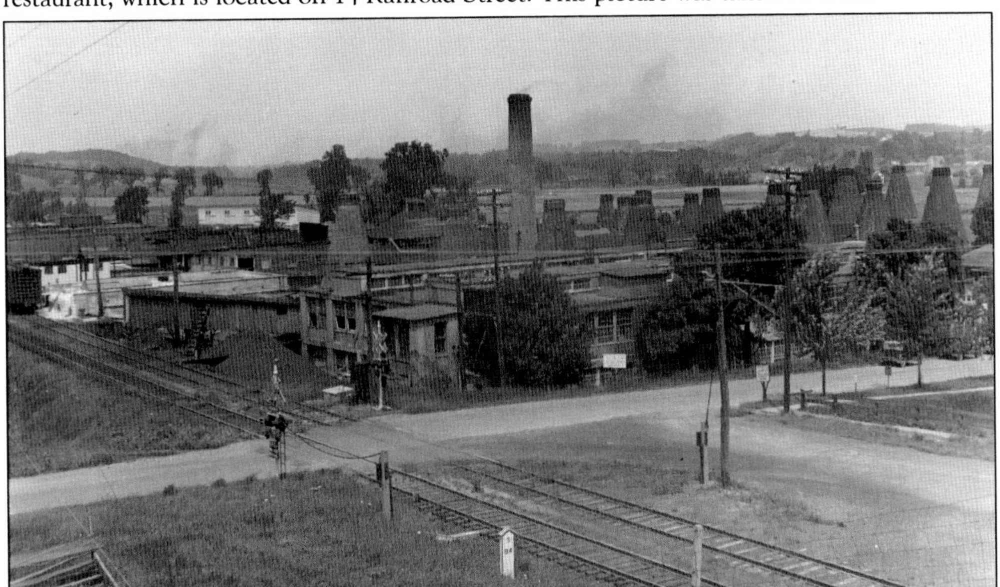

Victor Insulators, located on Maple Avenue in Victor, was known for its breakthrough technology in porcelain insulators and low-expansion glass in 1925. In 1910, the business was managed by John F. Alden, Henry M. Parmele, John S. Lapp, J.W. Cleveland, Frank H. Hamlin, W.A. Higinbotham, Charles H. Palmer, W.E. Moore, and D.D. Sully. Today, Victor Insulators is the home base for the Ontario Central Railroad. William Burt, Maryanne Gilbert, and Don Brown store their locomotives in the Victor Insulator engine house.

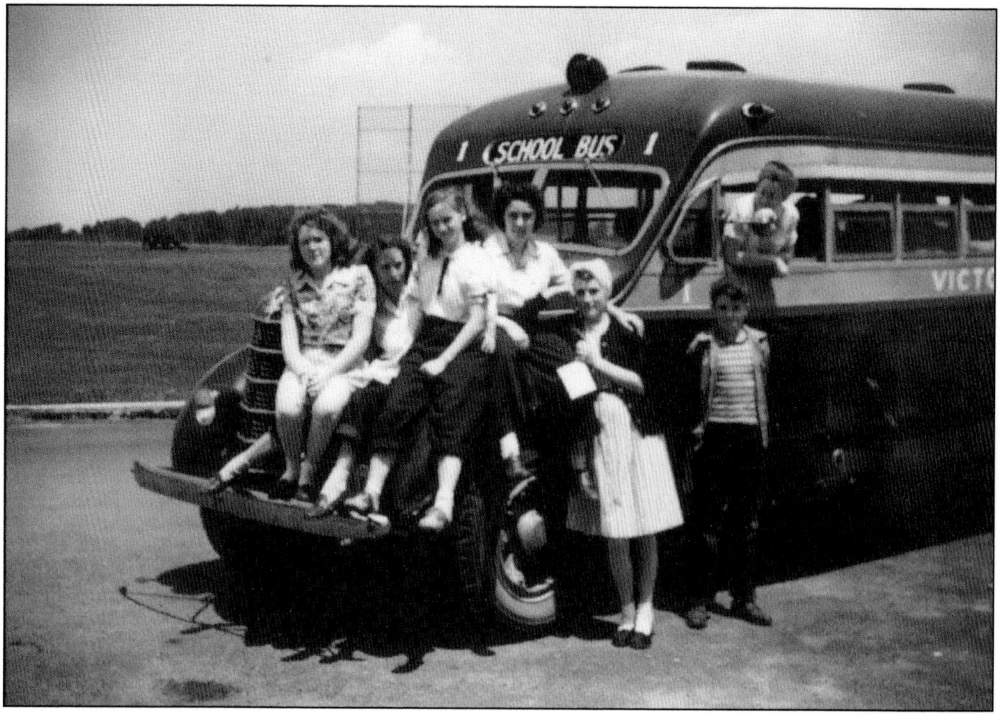

This photograph was taken near the Victor School baseball field in 1948. The bus was blue and gold until 1949, when laws mandated that buses be yellow. It was one of five original Victor School buses.

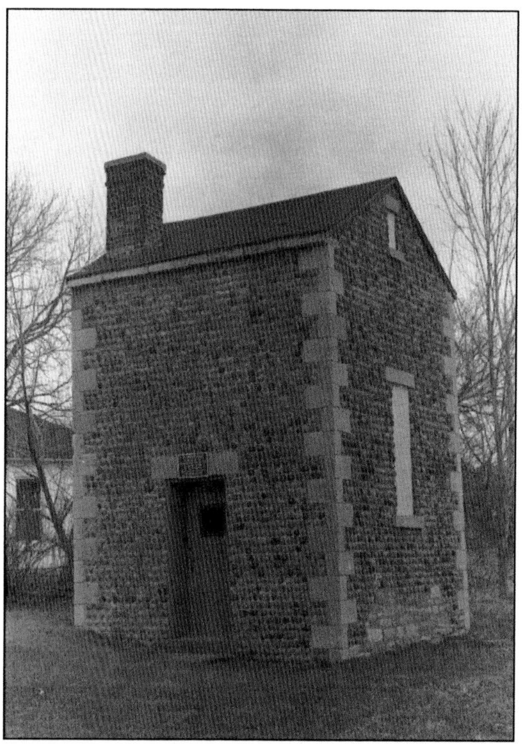

This 1845 Fisher's pump house is one of the oldest railroad structures in New York. It was used to replenish the locomotives' water supply.

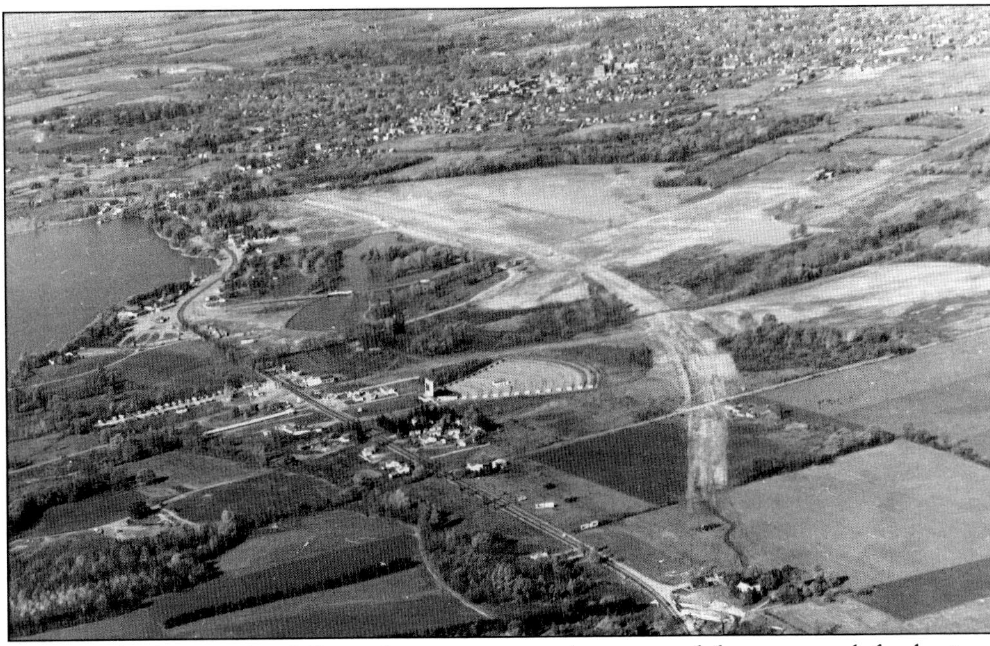

This aerial photograph of Canandaigua captures the onset of farm removal for business demands. In 1956, the 5 and 20 bypass was built to divert traffic to the lakeshore area, a favorite picnic and swimming location. The Canandaigua drive-in, shown in the picture, featured such films as *Splendor in the Grass* and *Star Wars*.

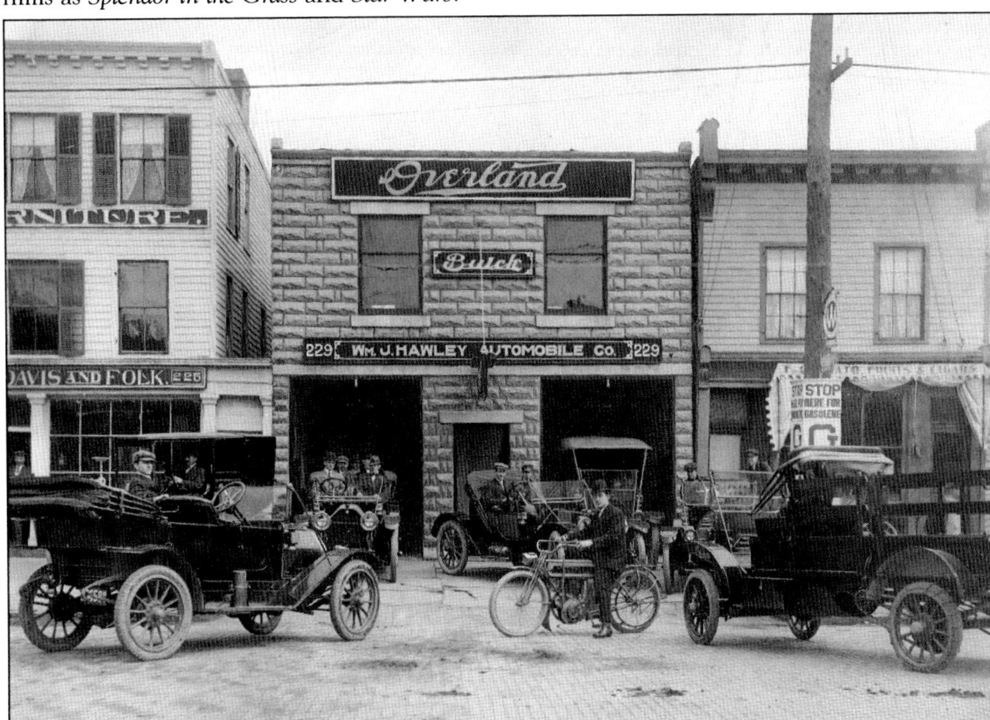

Indicative of the numerous people, Overland received good business. In the early 20th century, the same time this picture was taken, skilled laborers were paid a frugal 65¢ a day.

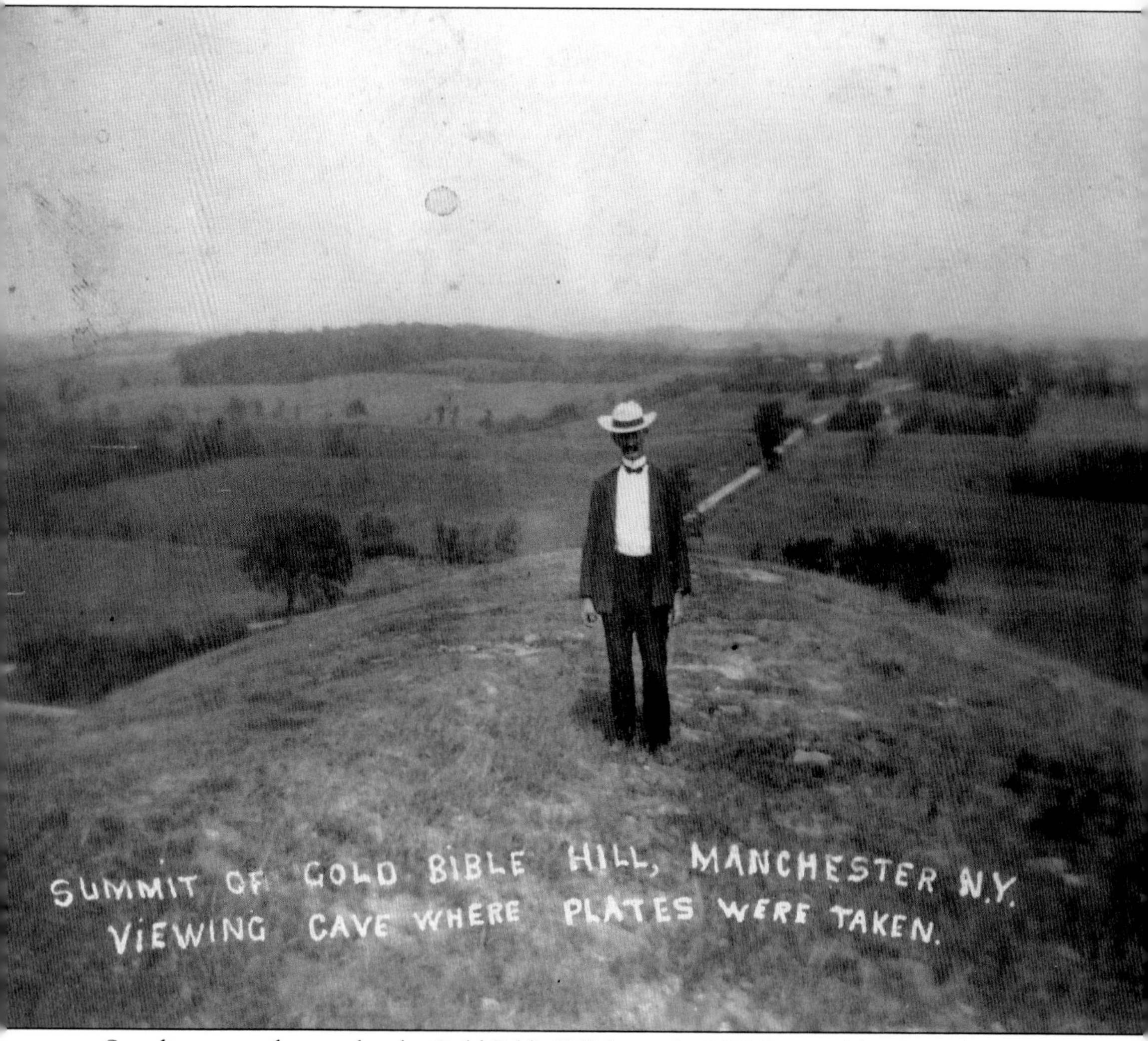

Standing atop what used to be Gold Bible Hill (now the Hill Cumorah) is Patrick Seyman of Manchester. The Hill Cumorah is where the Mormons have their annual pageant. The pageant attracts both a national and international crowd and once featured celebrity Donnie Osmond.